AN ANATOMY OF
SOCIAL WELFARE
SERVICES

MICHAEL JOSEPH BOOKS ON
LIVE ISSUES

Series editors H. L. Beales   O. R. McGregor

AN ANATOMY OF
SOCIAL WELFARE
SERVICES

A SURVEY OF SOCIAL WELFARE STAFF
AND THEIR CLIENTS
IN THE COUNTY OF BUCKINGHAMSHIRE

Margot Jefferys

LONDON
MICHAEL JOSEPH

First published in Great-Britain by
MICHAEL JOSEPH LIMITED
26 Bloomsbury Street
*London, W.C.*1
1965

© 1965 *by Margot Jefferys*

Set and printed in Great-Britain by
Unwin Brothers Limited at the Gresham Press, Woking
in Imprint type, eleven-point leaded, and bound by
James Burn at Esher, Surrey

Author's Preface and Acknowledgements

The enquiry into the operation of the social services upon which this book is based took place in 1960–61. In the previous decade a succession of Working Parties and Committees established by the Governments of the day considered the work and training of distinct groups of social welfare staff and made recommendations for one or other service. The value of their enquiries and recommendations was varied. Limited terms of reference made it impossible for any of them to consider how far the staff of different branches of the social welfare staff duplicated comparable tasks, visited households with similar problems, needed common or distinct types of training, or had established effective ways of working together when this was desirable.

By contrast the enquiry in Bucks attempted an appraisal of work in the entire social welfare field. It sought to overcome the compartmentalism which had limited the value and impact of earlier Government enquiries. It was designed to examine simultaneously and systematically the work of staff in different branches of the social services and the characteristics of those served. It established a set of common definitions and categories for describing the households visited, the problems recorded and the services undertaken by the staff of all the services investigated.

The initiative for this study came from the Clerk of the Bucks County Council, Mr R. E. Millard, and the County Medical Officer of Health, Dr G. W. H. Townsend, C.B.E., who asked the Department of Public Health at the London School of Hygiene and Tropical Medicine to plan and carry out an independent survey of the work of statutory and voluntary social services within the county. An approach was then made to the Nuffield Provincial Hospitals' Trust who generously agreed to support the enquiry with a substantial grant.

Throughout the enquiry I and the research team received unstinted support and encouragement both from Mr McLachlan, the representative of the Nuffield Provincial Hospitals' Trust on the small Steering Committee, from Mr Millard and Dr Townsend and from the Bucks County Council and its other chief executive officers. I am also grateful to those responsible for the work of central government departments in Bucks and to the voluntary social services, which, almost without exception, agreed to assist our enquiries and enlist the co-operation of their staffs.

The success of the enquiry depended in the first instance on the willingness of social welfare staffs to record very detailed information about their work, the individuals and households they served and their own careers and to give the research team their views on many aspects of the services. Our demands placed a considerable burden upon a body of men and women who were already hard pressed. I am grateful, therefore, for the courtesy and kindness with which members of the research team were received and requests for help met.

It is quite impossible to mention by name all those who have contributed in one way or another to this undertaking. I must acknowledge, however, my debt to Professor Walton, head of my department, who encouraged me to accept the challenge of this enquiry and who headed the small Steering Committee which met regularly to hear progress reports and consider proposals. I received generous help, encouragement and constructive criticism from Professor D. V. Donnison, who also served on the Steering Committee, and from Dr Ann Cartwright, Miss E. M. Goldberg, Mrs Winifred Moss, Dr Michael Warren and Mrs Phyllis Willmott. Mrs Kate Allan, Mrs Maureen Brooke, Mrs Julia Faulkner, Mrs Sylvia Jacobs, Mrs Janet Taylor and Miss Rosemary Ward patiently typed and re-typed the various drafts of the report, and I want to place on record my gratitude for their calm efficiency. I was fortunate too in having a team of efficient coders. I also owe much to Miss Margaret Kornitzer who came to my rescue in the final stages and helped to prepare the book for publication.

Finally, I want to thank Joyce Arkley and George Churcher who helped to plan and carry through the enquiry upon which the book is based. I could not have asked for more devoted, hard working colleagues. Needless to say, I alone am responsible for the treatment of the material collected and for the conclusions and recommendations. I am grateful to the Controller of H.M. Stationery Office for permission to reproduce the map from the G.R.O. Census 1961, County of Buckinghamshire, p. xiv, H.M.S.O. 1964.

MARGOT JEFFERYS

May, 1965

Foreword

The individual in need of the help of the social welfare services, in the broadest sense, has available to him or her a bewildering variety of agencies and workers, both paid and voluntary. The choice—or chance—as to the precise source from which the individual receives this help is generally acknowledged to be to some extent haphazard. Furthermore, it may well be that other members of the same family, with the same basic problems, are receiving help from a different source or sources.

All this has been broadly known for many years, but, in spite of numerous major studies of different sectors of the social services, no serious attempt has been made to ascertain the impact on individuals or groups of the proliferation and overlapping of the existing services. The survey of Buckinghamshire social welfare services was accordingly undertaken in an attempt to obtain for the first time a representative picture of the whole field of the social services at work in one county.

The project was jointly sponsored by the Buckinghamshire County Council, the London School of Hygiene and Tropical Medicine, and the Nuffield Provincial Hospitals' Trust; the two former bodies provided staff and facilities, and the Trust made a generous grant without which the project would not have been possible. This may perhaps be regarded as an interesting example of co-operation between a university, a research foundation and a local authority providing many of the services which were examined.

As the representatives on the steering committee of the project of the County Council and the School of Hygiene, we are very pleased to write this short foreword to Mrs. Jeffery's book, which represents the distilled essence of the findings of the very detailed survey which she and her team carried out. If, as we hope, this

A*

account makes a real contribution to an improvement in the integration and co-ordination of the many different social agencies, the bodies whom we represent will feel that their sponsoring of the project has been well worth while.

R. E. MILLARD
Clerk of the Buckinghamshire County Council
W. S. WALTON
Professor of Public Health in the University of London

Contents

PART 5

Non-statutory Organisations in Social Welfare

PART 6

APPENDICES

IMPORTANT NOTE

*In order to keep down the cost of the
report, many tables have had to be
omitted. Anyone wishing for further
information from the survey should
write to the author, c/o Social Studies
Department,   Bedford   College,
Regents Park, London, N.W.1.*

List of Tables

CHAPTER I

Introducing the Survey

The primary object of the survey whose results are given here was to provide a picture of the work of the staff of social welfare services in an English county and of those served by them. It was hoped that if the staff of all the services were willing to use the same definitions and categories to describe those they helped and the services performed, a more sharply focused picture would emerge of the contribution which each branch of the social services was making to the collective welfare of different sections of the community.

This more clearly focused picture was in its turn intended to provide a sounder basis for considering how to improve the services to the public and to increase the satisfactions which those who serve derive from their work. In particular, the survey was designed to throw light on two major issues of social policy—the extent of the need to provide some form of training in social work for the staff of different branches of the social welfare services, and the desirability of re-deploying staff between the branches with a view to making better use of the limited man and womanpower available.

The survey was limited to the social services of a single county —Buckinghamshire. There is no such thing as a representative or typical county, and it cannot be claimed that the results of the study or the conclusions drawn from them necessarily hold good elsewhere. Nevertheless, the population of Bucks in its age, household and social class composition was very like those of neighbouring counties, Berks, Herts and Oxon, and its social welfare services faced similar problems. Many of the findings and conclusions are likely to be of interest and use, therefore, to those concerned with one or other aspect of the planning and operation of statutory and voluntary social welfare services at a national or local level or with the training of staff for these services.

The scope of the enquiry

The first problem facing the research team was to determine how widely the enquiry should range. There is no general agreement as to which statutory social services and which voluntary associations can properly be described as social welfare services and which cannot. In the broadest sense, for example, those who teach in local authority schools, maintain law and order, man the library service or children's playgrounds and many others are performing social welfare services.

The interests of the enquiry's sponsors, however, was a narrower one than that. They were interested primarily in the work of staff who had to help or deal with those who had personal problems arising from social, economic, psychological or physical inadequacies or handicaps. Circumscribing the field of interest in this way was still not sufficient, however, to determine which staff should be included in the enquiry, and other criteria were added.

It was agreed, for example, to study only the work done for individuals, families and households in face to face contacts in the privacy of private homes or of workers' consulting rooms in public buildings. Thus social group work, although increasingly important as a form of help to the socially, physically and mentally handicapped, was not studied. It was further decided to consider only those whose work was primarily with those who were normally resident in private dwellings and not in residential institutions for the long term care of the aged, the severely handicapped or the child deprived of a normal home life.

The detailed enquiry was also limited to the *staff* of the statutory and voluntary services, that is, to those who were paid for their services. At the same time, if the contribution made by voluntary workers had not been taken into account the survey would have presented a seriously distorted picture of the county's social welfare provision. Consequently, a number of special enquiries of a less detailed kind was undertaken, covering the social welfare work of voluntary societies, of the clergy and their parishioners and of personnel management in industry.[1]

Yet another issue was whether or not to examine the work of professional groups of men and women who are not commonly thought of as social workers but who are intimately concerned with the welfare of the sick, the disabled or the socially deviant

---

[1] Shortage of space prevents the presentation in this book of the study made of the social welfare work of clergy and welfare officers employed in industry.

in the community. In the event, it seemed essential in an enquiry such as this to find out how far general practitioners and district nurses gave advice and help on other than strictly medical or nursing matters, and how far they were aware of the community services which could help patients whose illnesses or handicaps might lead to social or economic difficulties. Again, although the primary duty of the police is to maintain law and order and to apprehend or warn those who defy the law, their work inevitably brings them into contact with socially deviant individuals and disturbed families and provides them with either the necessity or the opportunity to help or advise. On the advice of the Chief Constable of Buckinghamshire, however, the work of the men of the county police force was not investigated: but women members of the force were asked to provide information on that part of their work which was concerned with the protection of women, girls and young children from physical or moral danger.

The eventual scope of the survey is indicated by the chapter headings of this book, and by Table 34 in Appendix A. A catalogue of departments and categories of staff in itself gives some indication of the complex framework of the social welfare services.

Bucks County Council has a combined health and welfare department and the survey covered the work of its district nurse-midwives, health visitors, medical social workers, welfare and mental welfare officers, home help organisers, home teachers of the blind, and occupational therapists. Information was obtained too from social workers attached to child guidance clinics, special welfare workers, school attendance officers, youth employment officers and youth leaders who were all employees of the county's education department. The work of child care officers came under examination as well as that of police women and probation officers. The housing authorities in the county, that is the borough, urban and rural district councils, were asked to provide information on housing welfare work as was the London County Council in respect of the estates it had developed in south Bucks to re-house Londoners.

Almoners and psychiatric social workers based on the hospitals which served Bucks were included in the enquiry. So were some employees of central government departments, including National Assistance Board officers who visited the homes of applicants for assistance, those undertaking disablement resettlement officers' work at the local employment exchanges of the Ministry of Labour and the staff of the Ministry of Pensions and National Insurance War Pensioners' welfare service who were responsible for the work in Bucks.

The paid staff of a number of voluntary organisations in the fields of social welfare participated fully in the enquiry, and many voluntary organisations and clergy of various denominations provided as much information as they could on the help which they gave to those in financial or social difficulties. A majority of the firms employing 50 or more workers at establishments within the county also responded to a request for information on their 'welfare' policy.

With limited time and resources it was not possible to undertake a thorough investigation of the work of general practitioners and its relevance to social welfare policies. However, a limited study was carried out with a sample of one in five of the general practitioners on the Buckinghamshire Executive Council list.

The information collected

In the initial stages of the enquiry, routine records and statistics relating to the population of Bucks and the work of departments employing social welfare workers were examined and the broad outline of the picture which they presented is given in Chapter II. The quantity and quality of the records of different departments varied greatly, however, and the absence of commonly agreed terms to describe the recipients of services or the services themselves made it impossible to make meaningful comparisons between the work of different departments.

Consequently, social welfare staff were asked to make special records of work over a limited period.[1] In order to ensure comparability, they were supplied with standard record forms and a booklet which indicated the significance of each item of information for the research and gave definitions for the terms used.

Most social welfare staff were asked to complete a record sheet for every individual seen during a specific week in the twelve months from October 1960 to September 1961, or for a consecutive sequence of 25 cases if fewer than 25 were seen in the week chosen

[1] See Appendix A for a description of method and questions asked.

for the recording. Exceptions to this rule were made for police women who were told to ignore individuals seen in connection with traffic offences, lost property or aliens' registration, and for housing welfare workers who were not asked for information about those who made simple enquiries or about tenants who enquired about repairs. A different procedure was adopted for recording the work of general practitioners.[1]

To avoid seasonal bias and to spread the burden of extra recording, the study took place over a twelve month period. The study year itself was deliberately chosen to permit comparisons of social welfare service recipients with the population of Bucks as recorded at the April 1961 Census enumeration, that is, at the mid-point of the enquiry. A list was compiled of all the staff in the relevant services, and each person on it was allocated a recording week during the study year. Shortly before this recording week was due to begin, the individual was visited by a member of the research team and the enquiry explained in considerable detail. The pre-recording week visits were also used to obtain standard information from the staff about their social and educational background, their training and their attitudes to their work.

Information obtained about individuals served

The information recorded by the staff for each individual seen was of five main kinds. First, a record was made of the age, sex, marital status, occupation, income[2] and schooling of all members of the household to which the recipient of the service belonged. In the analysis this information was summarised in order to classify the recipient and his household by such characteristics as size, age and family composition of the household and the occupational status of the chief economic supporter.

Secondly, there were data which related to the housing of the household.[3] They included information on the number of rooms, on the housing amenities, on sharing, on type of tenure and length of residence, and subjective assessments made by the

[1] See Chapter IX and Appendix C.
[2] The data on household income were so often incomplete that they were not used in the analysis.
[3] As far as possible the same definitions were used as in the 1961 Census.

recorder of the structure and state of decoration of the dwelling and the standard of cleanliness maintained by the household.[1]

Reporting ill-health and social problems

The third type of information concerned the health of household members and the social, psychological or economic difficulties which they might face or cause others.

Staff were asked to indicate whether each individual in the recipient's household was known to be suffering from a chronic or recurring illness or disability severe enough to limit economic or social functioning. In cases of mental illness or subnormality positive answers were only to be given if the worker knew either that the individual had had hospital treatment or a firm diagnosis by a medically qualified practitioner.

The reporting of social, economic or psychological problems raised more serious difficulties. There are no objective criteria securing universal or even near universal agreement which can be used to distinguish those who have or cause 'social' problems, and it was not feasible in an enquiry of this kind to attempt to establish them. Most social welfare departments classify the problems of those they help; but the terms each service employs to describe problems have been devised for its own internal administrative purposes and cannot be used to compare the problems it encounters with those dealt with by other services.

Fundamentally, there were two different ways in which to approach the recording of 'social problems', and both were tested in a small pilot enquiry in Hertfordshire which preceded the Bucks survey. In the first, staff were asked to describe in their own words the problems which the individual recipient of their service or members of his household presented. These descriptions were subsequently considered and classified into categories by the research workers. In the second, the worker was presented with a set of different general categories of problem and asked to indicate whether or not they were present in any particular case.

The main advantage of the first method was that the staff felt free to describe the situation as they saw it, without imposing on

---

[1] Where individual cases have been used to illustrate a point, details have been changed to prevent its identification.

their observations a classificatory system which might seem to them to distort the reality. On the other hand, this method of recording was extremely time consuming and in the pilot survey began to be carried out more and more perfunctorily. It also complicated and prolonged the classifying and coding which had to be undertaken by the research team on receipt of the records. In addition, it was found that staff tended to record only those aspects of the problem which particularly concerned them and failed to mention other problems which they subsequently agreed were important in the individual case. These disadvantages were so serious that, despite its shortcomings, the second method of obtaining information was used. Staff were encouraged, however, to supplement the simple checking of listed items with their own observations or interpretation of the data, and many took advantage of the opportunity to do so.

There were 21 categories of problems which workers were asked to consider in connection with each case,[1] and these are listed in Table 1.

Table 1

CATEGORIES OF SOCIAL PROBLEM DISTINGUISHED
IN THE SURVEY

Inadequate means	Criminal activities (adult)
Housing accommodation	Juvenile delinquency
Rent arrears	School truancy or refusal
Finding work suitable for skills	Child neglect or cruelty
Keeping jobs suited to skill	Childhood behaviour problems
Practical problems of adjustment to illness or disability	Sexual behaviour in adults
Adjustment to retirement from work	Personality problems or inadequacy
Loneliness	Marital relationships
Bereavement	Parent-child relationships
Mismanagement of means	Other family relationships
	Adoption problems

With reluctance it was decided that it was not possible to establish a rigorous set of criteria to determine whether an

[1] The list was drawn up after examining the problems which had been identified by the staff of different services in the pilot survey and earlier attempts to classify the kind of difficulties which social welfare staff encountered. (cf. in particular. J. A. Scott, 'Problem Families'. 1957.)

individual or household could be said to have or cause one or more of these social problems. The workers' decisions were, therefore, subjective and unverified, based only on a general description of situations and behaviour which would generally be considered problem ones. Consequently, the estimate of the numbers seen by social welfare staff in a normal working week who displayed each type of problem is based on the sum of these unverified subjective judgements. The unsatisfactory nature of these judgements as a basis for measuring prevalence was confirmed by the findings of the survey itself which demonstrated that, in many instances, where two workers visited the same household, they reported different numbers and types of problem.

Nevertheless, the exercise was not a useless one. Social welfare staff were encouraged to consider systematically whether or not their patients or clients presented problems and the criteria upon which their judgements should be based. Moreover, comparisons of the relative frequency with which staff from different branches of the welfare services believed they encountered particular types of problem are provocative and can be used to stimulate inter-service discussion of the problems of defining, identifying and treating the particular social situations or relationships which can be considered abnormal.

In itself, however, an estimate of the prevalence of particular categories of problem has only limited value. It is also important to know what factors have contributed to the creation of the problems. For example, inadequate means could be due to a chief economic supporter's neglect of his dependents or to the smallness of the pension to which a severely disabled elderly person is entitled. Appropriate action in the two instances would be very different. For each case, therefore, the worker was asked to assess how long the problem had persisted and was likely to persist, how severe or mild it was and what had caused it.[1]

Reporting services and relationships of the staff to the clients

The fourth kind of information recorded concerned the relationship between the recipient of the service and the social welfare worker. Here the aim was to find out how long the

[1] Shortage of time and money prevented the team from making any detailed analysis of these data.

recipient had been known to the worker's department or organisation, and both the reasons for the establishment of the relationship and the channel through which it had been achieved. In addition, the staff were asked who had taken the initiative in arranging the interview which occurred during the recording period, their own purpose in arranging it if the initiative had come from them, and the services which they believed they had given the client at or following the interview.

The problems of defining 'purpose' and 'service' were very comparable to those of defining 'social problem'. Most welfare departments and organisations had standard ways of recording the outcome of interviews by their staff but each had its own terms and not all of these were meaningful for the purposes of a survey which was essentially comparative.

Alternative ways of defining and recording purpose and service were tested in the pilot study, and a list of the potential component elements of the service given by social welfare staff was ultimately drawn up. These elements were categorised as shown in Table 2. Another list was devised to indicate the purpose for which the interview had been arranged. Since the purpose of many visits

Table 2

CATEGORIES OF SERVICE GIVEN BY STAFF TO CLIENTS AT
OR FOLLOWING THE RECORDING PERIOD INTERVIEWS

Actual service or advice given or referral undertaken

Financial assistance	Help with employment
Material goods or medical equipment provided	Help with adoption, fostering or child care
Domestic help	Legal aid, action or advice
Housing difficulties tackled	Occupational therapy
Training or educational help or advice	Advice or help on family relationships
Nursing or medical advice and care	Help with emotional problems
Hospital, institutional or convalescent care arranged or advised	Practical instruction in child rearing, domestic tasks, the management of illness

was to render a particular service to a patient, applicant or client, many of the items on it were the same as on the list of services.

Reporting relationships with other social welfare services

Fifthly, the contacts which the worker had had with the staff of other social welfare services in connection with each of the cases seen were recorded. If a contact had been established the staff were asked to note with whom it had been and who had been responsible for taking the initiative. They were also asked whether social welfare staff with whom they had made no personal contact were also known to be visiting their clients' households.

Completeness and quality of the recording by staff

Although the survey team had always obtained the consent of the person responsible for the service in the county before approaching an individual member of the staff, the decision to participate or not in the survey rested with the latter. The great majority of the 398 persons who were interviewed agreed to record and many expressed great interest in the survey. Some undertook the recording, which entailed a good deal of extra work, with reluctance; but only 35 or less than 9 per cent failed to record altogether. A further five sent in their records too late for inclusion in the analysis. Ten others had had no cases coming within the scope of the study during the recording period.[1]

There was great variation in the quality of the records and more than half the staff had to be visited a second time by a member of the research team to check on apparent inaccuracies or to complete schedules. In addition, most members of the staff did not provide information about as many individuals as they had led the team to suppose they saw in a normal working week. This could have been due to one or both of two reasons. Visits or interviews may have been deliberately reduced during the recording week in order to cope with the extra work involved in recording; alternatively, records may have been returned for only a portion of those who were seen during the week.

It is not possible to assess the extent and kind of bias which was thus introduced. Some of the staff may have elected to visit or see those whose problems were comparatively simple to record; others may have unconsciously selected the more com-

---

[1] These were four policewomen, four youth leaders, one almoner from a hospital in another county and one social caseworker from the national headquarters of a voluntary organisation.

plicated cases in order to show how frequently they dealt with difficult problems.

Again, failure to record at all and under-reporting both reduced the reliability of the results, and this must be recognised.[1] Nevertheless, the results can be taken as a first attempt to describe in quantitative terms some characteristics of the recipients of social welfare services in an English county and some aspects of the services which they received.

Information obtained about social welfare staff

The information obtained about the social welfare staff was more complete and more reliable than that obtained about their clients. With one exception, all the staff agreed to answer questions put to them by a member of the research team, although one or two preferred not to answer some of the questions.[2]

The questions were intended to provide a detailed picture of the characteristics of the men and women who staff the social welfare services. First, considerable care was taken to obtain an accurate account of social origins, educational attainments and occupational histories, in short, of the paths by which the staff had come to posts in the social welfare services. Questions were also asked about past and present involvement in different forms of voluntary social welfare work and about religious observance.

Secondly, attention was directed towards training. Those who had had a recognised training for the work they were then doing were asked how satisfactory they now considered it to be and whether they felt the need for continued training. Those who had not had a recognised training were asked whether they felt that they would have benefited from one.

A third group of questions was designed to elicit views about present work, its satisfactions and rewards, its drawbacks and disadvantages, and the extent to which it provided a satisfying

[1] The additional work involved in the detailed recording for this survey accounted, in the view of the research team, for most of the deficiencies in the data concerning clients. If the survey were repeated elsewhere, consideration should be given to simplifying the recording as far as possible, and possibly to obtaining data on those already seen and not on those to be seen.

[2] See Appendix B for a description of methods and questions used to obtain information about social welfare workers.

career. These questions were general and intended to bring out spontaneous answers.

Finally, when the staff returned the forms relating to the individuals they had seen during the recording period, they were asked to complete a summarised diary sheet showing the approximate division of their time between different kinds of activities during a normal working week.

The result is a mass of material which so far has been subjected only to a comparatively superficial analysis. Much of it would repay a more detailed examination than the research team was able to give it. However, it is hoped that this preliminary analysis will contribute useful data and ideas to the contemporary discussion on the future of the social welfare services.

CHAPTER II

The County and its People

In 1961, Buckinghamshire had a population of 486,000. It is a long, narrow county to the north west of London. Its neighbours are the counties of Berkshire to the south, Oxfordshire to the west, Northamptonshire to the north, and Bedfordshire, Hertfordshire and Middlesex to the east.[1] From east to west it is seldom more than 20 miles broad; but from the north it stretches almost 60 miles south to the playing fields of Eton on the banks of the Thames.

Its proximity to the Greater London conurbation has brought it increasingly within the metropolitan commuting belt. Improved public and private transport has increased the popularity of the area for the city worker and many of the residents in the south of the county travel daily to work in greater London. Much of the county's industry too is situated in the south, in and around Slough and High Wycombe, which are both centres of varied light goods manufacture. The greater part of the 25 per cent increase in population which occurred between 1951 and 1961 took place in and around these towns and in the mainly residential areas of Amersham, Chesham, Beaconsfield and Marlow. Further north, in the centre of the county, there were also substantial population increases associated with the growth of Aylesbury as an administrative centre for County services, and as an expanded town with developing opportunities in light goods industries and in printing. Aylesbury still retained its character, however, as a market town for the surrounding prosperous agricultural area.

In the north of the county the population in the inter-censal period barely increased except in Bletchley, an expanded town with special provisions for attracting industry and re-housing families from local authority areas in Greater London. The decade 1951–1961, however, may be the last to record such small increases in population in the north. The building of the M.1 Motorway

---

[1] Middlesex as an administrative county totally disappeared in 1965, on the formation of the Greater London Council, into the complex of new London boroughs.

has opened up relatively inaccessible rural areas to commuters working in such industrial centres as Bedford, Luton and Northampton, and is even making it possible for motorists to live in the area and work in London or the Midlands. Improved road transport facilities may also encourage an expansion of industry in rural areas which have hitherto relied predominantly on farming, quarrying and brickmaking to provide employment opportunities for local residents.

The substantial increase in the county's population during the decade 1951–61 was due partly to a high rate of natural increase (that is, excess of births over deaths) but mainly to immigration from other parts of Britain. The newcomers, especially to the expanding industrial centres, were mainly young married couples with incomplete families who also contributed to the high birth rate. In the early 1950's, the birth rate in Bucks was very similar to or a little below that of England and Wales. After 1954, how-ever, the Bucks rate was substantially higher than that for the country as a whole and increased faster.[1] During the same period, crude death rates were fairly stable both nationally and in Bucks.[2] The effect of rapid population growth is usually to increase both the absolute and the relative numbers of young people in the community, and this was the case in Bucks. In 1951, there were just over 50,000 children in schools maintained by the county education authority. By 1961, the number had risen to nearly 76,000, an increase of over 50 per cent in a decade or about 5 per cent per annum. The proportion of children aged 0 to 14 in the population in Bucks in 1951 had been 21·7 per cent compared with 22·1 per cent in England and Wales as a whole. By 1961, however, while the child population of England and Wales had increased to 23 per cent that of Bucks had risen to 24·5 per cent.

At the same time, the proportion of the population aged 65 or more, which had risen in England and Wales from 11·0 per cent to 11·9 per cent, fell in Bucks from 11·0 per cent to 10·5 per cent, and Bucks had a smaller proportion of 1 and 2 person households with someone of pensionable age in them than the national

[1] In 1953, for example, the birth rate for England/Wales was 15·5 per 1,000 population and for Bucks, 14·9. By 1961, the rate had risen nationally to 17·4, while in Bucks it had risen to 18·6.

[2] Death rates in England and Wales ranged annually from 11·0 to 12·0 per 1,000, and in Bucks from 9·0 to 9·9.

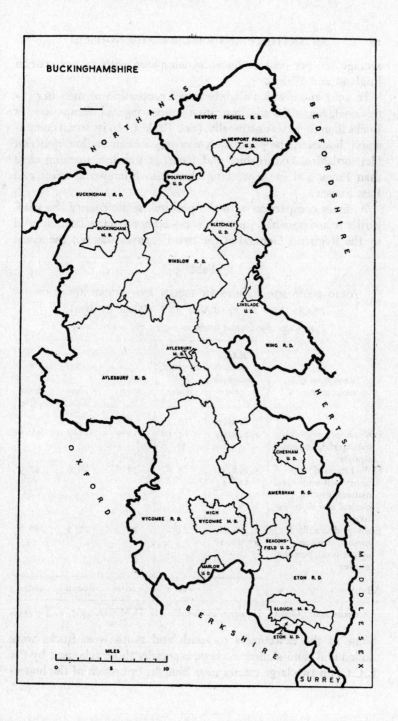

BUCKINGHAMSHIRE

NORTHANTS

BEDFORDSHIRE

NEWPORT PAGNELL R. D.

NEWPORT PAGNELL U. D.

WOLVERTON U. D.

BUCKINGHAM R. D.

BUCKINGHAM M. B.

BLETCHLEY U. D.

WINSLOW R. D.

LINSLADE U. D.

WING R. D.

AYLESBURY M. B.

AYLESBURY R. D.

HERTS.

OXFORD

CHESHAM U. D.

AMERSHAM R. D.

WYCOMBE R. D.

HIGH WYCOMBE M. B.

BEACONS-FIELD U. D.

MARLOW U. D.

ETON R. D.

MIDDLESEX

BERKSHIRE

SLOUGH M. B.

ETON U. D.

SURREY

MILES

0   5   10

average (19 per cent in Bucks as compared with 22 per cent in England and Wales).

In 1961 there was a slightly larger proportion of men in professional, scientific, administrative and managerial occupations in Bucks than there was nationally. (See Table 3.) In its social composition, however, the population was very similar to that of Berks, Hertfordshire, Oxfordshire and Kent. It was less working class than Essex and more working class than Surrey and West and East Sussex.

A direct comparison with the position in the county ten years earlier is not possible, since the socio-economic classification used by the Registrar General at the two Censuses was not the same.

Table 3

SOCIO-ECONOMIC GROUPS IN URBAN AND RURAL AREAS OF BUCKS AND IN ENGLAND AND WALES IN 1961

Percentage distribution among occupied and retired males

| Description of social status | R.G.'s socio- economic group | England and Wales | BUCKS. | | |
			All areas	Urban	Rural
	numbers	%	%	%	%
Professional, scientific, managerial, administrative	1, 2, 3, 4, 13	14·1	17·7	13·7	21·5
Skilled manual, supervisory, self-employed manual, routine clerical and distributive	5, 6, 8, 9, 12, 14	54·8	53·0	58·4	47·9
Semi- and unskilled manual workers, agricultural, personal service	7, 10, 11, 15, 16, 17	31·2	29·3	27·9	30·6
All		100·1	100·0	100·0	100·0

Census 1961. G.R.O. Housing Tables. Pt. III. H.M.S.O. 1965, p. 317–319.

Some of the newcomers to south and south west Bucks were skilled and semi-skilled workers, especially those rehoused by the L.C.C. on two large estates near Slough; but much of the housebuilding in these areas between 1945 and 1961 was done by private builders, it is fair to assume, mainly for middle class families whose chief economic supporters either commuted to work in London or were employed in a technical, scientific or managerial capacity in the county's own expanding industries.

In the north of the county, on the other hand, the largest proportion of post-war housebuilding was undertaken by local authorities. Most of these houses were intended to rehouse local inhabitants living in poor or overcrowded conditions and not to provide for newcomers. In Bletchley, however, the considerable housing development of the fifties mainly provided accommodation for skilled manual workers and their families from London.

The Census data indicated considerable differences between the socio-economic groupings of the urban and rural population in the county. There were considerably more middle class men in the rural districts, except in the north, than in the urban districts. The towns as a whole were conspicuous in the high proportion of men in the skilled manual, supervisory and routine clerical socio-economic groupings. Only Beaconsfield and Marlow among the urban districts departed substantially from this picture. Both these towns were in commuter belt country and resembled socially the rural districts by which they were surrounded.

Bucks in 1961 had not attracted many of the coloured immigrants from the West Indies and the subcontinent of India. Only 4,689 (less than 1 per cent) of the residents were born in these countries and some of them may have been of European origin. Over half of them were living in Slough and High Wycombe. In other areas, however, there were almost comparable numbers of men and women of European origin. For example, nearly 3,000 were born in Poland, 2,000 in Italy, and about the same number in Germany. Many of these had come to the county first during the war, either as allies in the free forces or as prisoners, and had opted to remain or come back when the war ended.

The need for social welfare services

In the absence of generally agreed definitions or precise concepts of need, the requirements of a county like Bucks in 1961 for social welfare services cannot be reliably estimated, and can only be described in the most general terms.

B

Nevertheless, the characteristics of the population and the changes which occurred in it in the 1950's help to provide general clues as to the county's requirements for different kinds of social welfare assistance, the extent to which these were expanding or contracting, and the context in which the social welfare services worked.

With the addition of over 100,000 persons to the population in a decade the first problem was to prevent a lowering of the standards already achieved in the social services.

As far as housing went, there was some easing of the situation in the county between 1951 and 1961. There was sufficient new building to house newcomers and the local authorities made some headway in reducing overcrowding and replacing houses which were unfit for human habitation. As a consequence, the increase in the number of dwellings was greater than the increase in either population or the number of private households. There was consequently less sharing of basic domestic amenities and fewer people living in overcrowded conditions. By 1961, nearly 4 out of every 5 households had exclusive use of all domestic amenities, that is of tapped cold and hot water, a fixed bath and a water closet.

Nevertheless, much still remained to be done. Fourteen per cent of all households occupied dwellings without fixed baths and 5 per cent had no water closets. In the rural north of the county the situation was worse. In the five local authority rural districts north of Aylesbury more than a quarter of the households had no bath and 14 per cent no water closet, and in one rural district (Newport Pagnell) there was no cold water supply to 6 per cent of the dwellings; 1,943 houses of the 4,426 houses which had been condemned in 1955 were still occupied and others had become unfit.

Housing was the responsibility of the borough, urban and rural district councils, and collectively they provided accommodation for over a quarter (26 per cent) of the households in the county in 1961. It was the county council which had to ensure that additional ante-natal, midwifery and infant welfare services as well as new schools were available to meet the demands created not merely by the post-war years but by the influx of newcomers to the county.

Other things being equal a simple increase in numbers was likely to produce some increase in the numbers requiring special help from the social welfare services, as well as greater demands on the health and educational services. Families who move from one part of the country to another are often amongst the most enterprising and self-reliant; but moving from a familiar environment to a strange one is in itself stressful; and, at least for a short time, newcomers may both make heavier demands on some of the personal services than longer settled inhabitants and show more evidence of behaviour which is disturbing to the wider community.[1] That newcomers seemed to require more help and show more signs of disturbance certainly seemed to be the case in the areas in and around Slough in the south and Bletchley in the north, where new local authority estates had been built to re-house Londoners. Some general practitioners and social welfare staff also believed it to be true of those living in the smaller new private housing estates in the south and south-west of the county.

Population expansion and especially the increase in the proportion of young people in the community, therefore, provided part of the context within which the social welfare services of Bucks worked in the early sixties. In this their experience was not unique, for many counties especially in southern England and the midlands had similar increases in population at the same time.

In many other respects, too, factors affecting the social welfare needs of Bucks were comparable with those of other counties in the south and midlands. For example, throughout the post war years, unemployment in the county was negligible. Vacancies at all the employment exchanges consistently exceeded the numbers seeking employment. As a consequence, finding suitable work for disabled people was relatively easy and there was little poverty arising directly from the lack of employment opportunities.

At the same time, problems associated with caring for the elderly and the chronic sick and disabled were growing con-

---

[1] The evidence for this statement comes from a number of studies including those of Young M. and Willmott, P., Mogey, J., Keuper, L., Hodges, M. W., Taylor, S. and Chave, S. and Jefferys, M., all of which relate to housing developments intended primarily for the families of manual workers. There is no evidence relating to new private estates of houses sold mainly to non-manual workers.

tinuously. It is true that the proportion of the population aged 65 and over in Bucks fell between 1951 and 1961; but the total numbers grew from 42,000 to 51,000 and the increase from 14,500 in 1951 to nearly 20,000 in 1961 in the number over 75 was even steeper. At the time of the Census, 26·2 per cent of those over 65 were living alone. There were approximately three women to every two men of this age, and over 64 per cent of the women were single, widowed or divorced. Many of both sexes, as this study showed, faced problems of bereavement and loneliness as well as financial difficulties, ebbing physical strength and chronic disabling ailments.

Indeed, many of the difficulties which called for social welfare help were found predominantly among the elderly. Seven out of ten of the National Assistance Board's recipients of regular allowances, and over seven out of ten of the registered blind in the county, for example, were of pensionable age.

Increasing concern was felt also for other than the elderly and severely physically handicapped. The fifties saw a dramatic change in the community's sense of responsibility towards the mentally ill and subnormal and their relatives. It was in all probability this change in outlook, rather than any increase in actual numbers, which accounted for the recorded increase in the numbers of mentally disordered assisted.

At the same time, a growing belief that some forms of mental disturbance, personality disorder and deviant behaviour frequently resulted from disturbed family relationships brought about conscious efforts to prevent family breakdown and the institutional care of children and to improve the quality of emotional relationships within the family group.

Part of the concern with family relationships and particularly with parental control was undoubtedly occasioned by increases in Bucks, comparable to those which were occurring nationally, in delinquency among young people and in illegitimate births. Between 1955 and 1961 convictions of juveniles for indictable offences rose by 125 per cent while the total number of the age group rose by less than 30 per cent; there was a comparable increase in the conviction rate amongst young people aged 17 to 20. During the fifties, illegitimate births in Bucks increased proportionately rather more than legitimate births; but the rate in 1960 (4·7 per cent), was lower than that for England and Wales as a whole (5·4 per cent). Since many unmarried mothers prefer to have their babies in areas where they are not known, however, and many find their way to the anonymity and comparatively lavish provision of the London area, the figures do not necessarily indicate a lower incidence of illegitimate births to women and girls normally resident in the county.

In Bucks, as elsewhere, at the beginning of the sixties increasing faith began to be placed in community in contrast to institutional care. The former seemed to be made the panacea for almost every kind of situation which social welfare services were meeting. Emphasis was everywhere given to the negative features of institutional life, whether this involved children deprived of their own families, handicapped school children, disabled adults, mentally ill patients, elderly people, unmarried mothers or young offenders. Moreover, community care was supported, not only because it seemed therapeutically sound, but because it also had the additional advantages over institutional care of involving less expenditure of public funds and of easing the acute problem of finding suitable people to staff institutions.

In summary, then, economic circumstances in the county in the early sixties were favourable. Employment was expanding, housing was more than keeping pace with rapid population growth and poverty due to unemployment and low wages was insignificant. The county as measured by the proportion of the population which was middle class was becoming more prosperous.

Nevertheless, pressures upon the social welfare services were increasing. Newcomers to the county brought not merely proportionate increases in the demand for most kinds of welfare provision: they also brought with them problems of adjustment to the new environment. The numbers of the elderly were growing and with them the problems of chronic illness, frailty, inadequate means, loneliness and bereavement. Among young people, there were increasing signs of social disorientation. The rate of conviction for indictable offences among juveniles and young adults rose, as did the number and proportion of illegitimate births to young people.

CHAPTER III

The Social Welfare Services and their Staff

The changing composition of the population of Bucks, as well as new ideas and concepts of welfare needs and how they should be met were, during the period of study, making their impact upon the social welfare services. The popularity of marriage had brought a substantial reduction in the number of unmarried women under 60 and consequently in the numbers available to staff residential institutions. Increasing emphasis was placed on community care both as a more humane and effective way of caring for the handicapped and the deviant and as a solution to the increasing costs of all kinds of social welfare services.

The organisation of each of the social welfare services available in Bucks is described in some detail in the chapter dealing with the work of its staff. In this chapter a brief account is given of the general administrative framework, within which the various services operated. It is followed by a description of some of the social characteristics of those who staffed the services.

The major statutory authority in the social welfare field was the Bucks County Council, the elected representative body, with jurisdiction over the whole area. Through its health and welfare department it provided home nursing, domiciliary midwifery, health visiting, ante-natal and infant welfare clinics, services for the care and after care of illness, and for the community and residential care of the mentally ill and subnormal and the severely physically handicapped and the elderly infirm. Responsibility for the day to day administration of these services in three areas of the county was vested in divisional medical officers located in Slough, High Wycombe and Bletchley, who were also medical officers of health to the local borough, urban or rural district councils.

The County Council's education department had some social welfare functions as well as educational ones. It provided a special service for parents of children ascertained as needing special schooling and a child guidance service for disturbed children. It also ran the County's youth employment service and employed youth leaders to organise clubs and other leisure facilities for young people. It had school attendance officers to ensure that parents fulfilled their statutory obligations.

The school health service was also the statutory responsibility of the education department. It was closely linked to the county's health services through the person of the County Medical Officer of Health, who was also the Chief School Medical Officer, and through the medical and health visiting staff who worked in both services.

The County Council was also responsible through its children's department, for the care of children deprived of a normal home life, and, through the Standing Joint Committee, for the police force. Its responsibility for the probation service was a more limited one. Probation officers were paid by the County Council but were appointed by and responsible to the magistrates of the courts of law in Bucks.

Housing welfare in Bucks was not the responsibility of the County Council but of the councils of the four boroughs, eight urban and eight rural districts which the county comprised. These councils, like the County Council, were elected representative bodies. The London County Council which owned and managed two estates in the south of the county was also concerned with housing welfare.

Besides the local authorities, three central government departments were responsible for welfare services which came within the scope of the study. The National Assistance Board, which gave financial assistance to applicants whose resources were inadequate for their needs, had four area offices in Bucks. These offices were responsible to the Board's regional office situated in Reading, which in turn was responsible to the national headquarters. The Ministry of Labour's disablement resettlement service was provided at six employment exchanges in the county. The Ministry of Pensions and National Insurance had several branch offices in the county, but their staff were not included in the survey. However, the Ministry was responsible for a War Pensions Welfare Service, and its office in Reading, Berks, served the Bucks residents who were entitled to benefit from it. In providing the service, the Ministry's staff was advised and assisted by the Bucks War Pensions Committee, a voluntary body whose chairman was appointed by the Minister.

Some of the social welfare services available to Bucks residents were based on hospitals in or near the county. The administration of these hospitals was in the hands of five hospital management committees, four of which were responsible to the Oxford Regional Hospital Board. The fifth, the Windsor Group Hospital Management Committee, was in the North-West Metropolitan Hospital Board region.

The general practitioners, whose role in the field of social welfare was also examined, were independent professional people under contract to the Bucks Executive Council to provide medical services for patients who registered with them. The Executive Council, like the Hospital Management Committees, was a statutory body whose members were appointed by the Minister and were broadly representative of local opinion. Many matters concerning general practice were determined, however, by the Local Medical Committee composed almost entirely of general practitioners, which was a sub-committee of the Executive Council.

In addition to the statutory bodies there were many charitable societies providing social welfare services. Most of these societies were organised by committees or councils composed of members who gave their services voluntarily. The constitutions of the voluntary societies generally provided for the election of officers and committee members by the membership, but elections were usually uncontested and new committee members nominated by existing ones.

Some of the voluntary organisations had a close working relationship with statutory bodies, while others had very little contact. For example, the six local branches of the Bucks County Association for the Blind worked with the home teachers of the blind employed by the county's welfare department, and the Oxford Diocesan Council for the Deaf employed directly a missioner who carried out the county welfare department's responsibility to the deaf and hard of hearing as well as his pastoral work for the Council. Marriage Guidance Councils, on the other hand, had little formal contact with statutory bodies.

Social welfare services came into being at many different times to help many kinds of people with many kinds of personal problem. It is not surprising, considering the complexity of many individuals' needs, that the staff of two or more bodies should sometimes be dealing simultaneously with the same individual or household and from time to time hold divergent views as to the best way of helping.

Recognition of the need to co-ordinate action and conserve effort produced various attempts to bring different social welfare services together. In Bucks in 1961, a number of committees existed to co-ordinate the work of other organisations or to promote discussion of problems of mutual interest. In some instances, the initiative had come from a statutory authority, and in others from voluntary bodies.

In the four divisions of the county, centred on Aylesbury, Bletchley, High Wycombe and Slough, co-ordinating committees representative of statutory and voluntary bodies with an interest in family welfare, met regularly but infrequently under the chairmanship of the divisional medical officer. Their main function was to consider how best to deal with individuals or households known to at least two agencies and whose problems seemed to be intractable. The staff who were in contact with the families whose affairs were to be discussed would be invited to attend the committee meeting, if they were not already members.

There were also Old People's Welfare Committees in the twelve principal towns in the county. These were co-ordinating committees representing all the statutory and voluntary bodies which helped the elderly. Their purpose was to stimulate community activity, but at the same time prevent duplication of effort.

In Slough, efforts to co-ordinate the work of local voluntary and statutory bodies had gone a stage further. An All Good Causes Fund had been established and the representatives of all the bodies involved met to consider the best use of local resources. The availability of the Community Centre on the Slough Trading Estate as a headquarters and meeting place for voluntary organisations helped to promote collaboration.

B*

Sex, age and marital status of social welfare staff

Nearly three quarters of those serving in the social welfare field in Bucks in 1960–1961 were women.[1] Health visiting, almoning both in hospitals and in the county, home help organising, home teaching and occupational therapy were done exclusively by women and there were only two men among the county's 118 district nurses. Only amongst welfare officers were men in a majority in the health field; but outside there was a slight balance in favour of men. Women filled all the moral welfare posts and the majority of posts in the children's department and voluntary welfare societies other than the N.S.P.C.C. However, in the N.A.B., Ministry of Labour disablement resettlement service, the youth service and school attendance section of the education department, in housing welfare and in the probation service, they were in a minority. Significantly, the emphasis in the departments where men predominated was as much on the protection of the public as on the welfare of the individuals served. The term 'officer' was more commonly used and the staff, unlike those working in the health field, usually possessed compulsory powers.

Nearly half the staff were aged 45 or more in 1961. There were relatively more younger women than men, but the age differences were not substantial. The differences in marital status of the men and women were, however, substantial. Eighty-five per cent of the men had been married (2 per cent were widowed), but only 26 per cent of the women, and of these latter nearly a third had subsequently been widowed or divorced. The unmarried men were almost all young ones in their twenties or early thirties. By contrast, there were relatively as many single persons among the older women as there were among the younger. Moreover, among the married, most of the men had children, whereas half the women had not.[2]

Social class origins and education

About a third of the staff could be described as working class in origin, because their fathers were manual workers, generally in

[1] General practitioners are not included in this analysis (see Chapter IX). Nor are voluntary workers (see Chapter XIX).

[2] It was the widows, on the whole, who had children: the still married women were with few exceptions childless. Appendix E. Table 38 and 39.

skilled occupations.[1] Apart from a few for whom information was lacking and some whose fathers were in the war-time armed forces, the others had fathers who did non-manual work (Table 4). The range of occupations represented in this broad middle-class grouping was, however, wide. Fathers in professional and scientific occupations like medicine, architecture, science, engineering, the law and the administrative branch of the civil service, which carry most prestige in the community, were outnumbered three to one by fathers in a range of occupations including school teaching, clerical work, retail trading and other jobs which normally have a lower standing.

There were some differences in the social origins of men and women. The latter were more likely to have had fathers in professional work, and less likely to have had a working class background. The staff of different branches of the services also had different origins. Almoners and psychiatric social workers were predominantly middle class and from professional groups within the middle class. Workers in other occupations requiring social work qualifications were also mainly middle class, but were less likely than almoners to have had fathers in professional work. There was also a contrast between the social background of district nurses and health visitors. The latter were more likely to have had a middle class and particularly a professional background.

Differences in social class origin paralleled if they did not entirely occasion differences in schooling. More men than women left school before their sixteenth birthday and twice as many women stayed on beyond their seventeenth. There was little disparity, however, in the proportion of men and women leaving school with a certificate. Equal proportions of men and women had taken a full-time university degree or diploma course; but if nurses and health visitors are excluded relatively more women than men had been to a university. (See Table 5.)

Not all those who took a university course matriculated while at school. Eight of the 49 who had been to a university left school without gaining a certificate of any kind. They reached university as mature students either by a qualifying examination later in life or by being accepted for a social science course on the basis of their experience. On the other hand, six of the 17 men and 43

[1] Very few had fathers who were semi-or unskilled workers.

Table 4

THE SOCIAL CLASS ORIGIN OF SOCIAL WELFARE WORKERS IN BUCKS

| Father's Occupation at worker's birth | | | | | | | Staff Category | | | |
Broad category	R.G. Social Class	All Workers	Men	Women	Almoner and p.s.w.	Other social work qualifica-tion*	No social work qualifica-tion	District Nurse	Health Visitor
		%	%	%	%	%	%	%	%
Non-manual									
Higher professional, business administra-tion, scientific	I	16·5	6·0	20·0	47·0	26·5	8·5	8·5	30·5
All other non-manual	II & III (non-manual)	41·0	47·0	39·0	37·5	57·0	42·5	37·0	32·5
Manual	III (manual) IV & V	34·5	43·0	31·0	12·5	10·5	39·5	46·0	28·0
Armed forces		4·5	1·0	6·0	—	4·0	5·5	7·0	—
Unclassified		3·5	3·0	4·0	3·0	2·0	4·0	1·5	9·0
Total Number = 100%		389	102	287	32	57	136	118	46

* Occupations include child care officer, probation officer, moral welfare, home teacher, deaf missioner, N.S.P.C.C. inspector.

Table 5

THE SCHOOLING RECEIVED BY SOCIAL WELFARE WORKERS

Formal schooling	All workers	Men	Women	Almoners and p.s.w.	Other social work trained	No social work training	District Nurse	Health visitor
						Category of staff		
	%	%	%	%	%	%	%	%
School leaving age								
Under 16	34	43	30	3	20	42	45	15
16	29	34	27	29	27	30	25	33
17 and over	36	21	43	68	49	28	30	52
Not recorded	1	1	—	—	4	—	—	—
Total	100	100	100	100	100	100	100	100
With school certificates or 5 G.C.E. 'O' levels or above	47%	43%	49%	65%	63%	45%	39%	50%
Full-time university course	13%	13%	13%	61%	39%	8%	—	—
Total Number = 100%	389	102	287	31	49	144	118	46

of the 73 women who matriculated at school did not go on to
take a full time university course. In other words, more than half
those who had minimum university entrance requirements never
took a full-time university course.

Occupational experience

It is difficult to provide a clear picture of the many and varied
occupational channels through which the social welfare staff
reached their present jobs. Some entered early in their working
life, others late. Some had had experience in different work,
others in work which bore a considerable resemblance to the work

Table 6

AGE OF ENTRY TO PRESENT OCCUPATION

Age of entry	All Non-nursing staff	All men	Women outside nursing	Non-nursing staff		Nurse trained	
				Those with social work qualification	Those with no social work qualification	District Nurses	Health Visitors
	%	%	%	%	%	%	%
25 or less	31	28	34	30	32	23	13
26–30	21	22	20	24	19	37	33
31–40	33	34	33	36	31	36	44
41 or more	15	16	14	8	17	3	6
Not known	1	—	2	2	1	1	4
Total	100	100	100	100	100	100	100
Average age of entry	30·8	31·1	30·5	28·9	31·7	29·5	32·3
Numbers in groups	225	102	123	89	136	118	46

they were doing at the time of the survey. Some had spent most
of their working life in Bucks or in areas close to it; others had
moved from one area of the country to another while remaining
in the same kind of work; still others had changed occupation
and address at the same time. Nevertheless, distinct patterns

could be seen in the occupational histories of the staff of different social welfare services.

First, most district nurse-midwives had embarked upon their initial nurse's training before they were 21 and three-quarters became district nurses within six years of becoming state registered nurses. Nevertheless, four out of ten did not take up district nursing until after the age of 31. (See Table 6.) Health visitors too for the most part began their nursing career before the age of 21, but half of them only became health visitors after the age of 31.

Outside the nursing field, patterns of employment were more varied, and it was not possible to say precisely when some of the staff first began the kind of work they were doing in 1961. For example, some clerical or administrative workers began to deal with those requiring assistance before any formal change was made in their working status. A gradual phasing of one kind of work into another was a commonplace in those central and local government departments in which social welfare work had been traditionally carried out by those in general civil service or local government officer grades. It was also found in hospitals where almoners' clerks or secretaries began to deal with patients' problems and were later given the status of almoner or almoner's assistant.[1]

Allowing for some inaccuracies in the recorded age of entry, under a third of the non-nurse trained staff had entered their occupation before their 26th birthday. At the other extreme, one in six was 41 or more years old.

Relatively more women than men were young entrants, but there was hardly any difference in the proportion of the two sexes who entered their occupation after 40. There were differences in the age of entry of the staff in posts normally requiring a social work training and those in posts where no such training was required. There were relatively twice as many entering the latter as the former after the age of 40.

Certain common features could be discerned in the careers of the staff before they entered their occupations in the social welfare field. Those who entered early had usually done so in one of two

---

[1] In all such instances, the age of entry was taken as the age the individual was first employed in his present occupation or a recognised junior grade of it.

ways. Either they entered after a period of full-time further
education or training, intended to qualify them for work in the
field, or they joined the clerical or executive classes of the civil
service or local government in their late teens and chanced upon
social welfare work in the normal course of their career.

Late entrants came from many occupations, but about a half
had been doing secretarial or administrative work. This was
truer of men than women. The women were more often already
working in occupations providing personal services, such as
nursing, teaching, or forms of social welfare. A few came from
domestic work in private households or residential institutions
and a few had been housewives for many years.[1]

A substantial majority on joining their present employers had
already worked in central or local government institutions or in
public utilities. This was particularly true of those entering
occupations where a social work qualification was normally
required. Those in other jobs were more likely to have worked
in private industry.

Religious observance and participation in voluntary work

The majority of the staff said their religious affiliation was to
the Church of England. Eight per cent were Roman Catholics,
21 per cent Non-Conformists, two Jewish and 3 per cent agnostics
or atheists. There were more Roman Catholics and Non-Conformists among those with a nursing background, and, as a consequence
fewer Anglicans and more Roman Catholics among women than
among men.

There were substantial differences between men and women in
the frequency of their religious observances as measured by
attendance at places of worship. Half the women compared with
only a third of the men called themselves regular attenders,
whereas three times as many men as women said they never
attended.[2]

Two-thirds of the staff had at some time done voluntary social
welfare work, although at the time of the survey only a third were
still active voluntary workers. Men were more likely than women
to have done some voluntary work; but the differences between
them were almost entirely accounted for by nurses and health

---

[1] See Appendix E. Table 40.   [2] See Appendix E. Table 41.

visitors, who were much less likely to have done such work. There were also differences between those in jobs requiring social work training and the others. Over three-quarters of the former had done voluntary social welfare work compared with less than two-thirds of the latter.[1]

Training

Staff in some sections of the social welfare services were expected to have a certificate or diploma awarded after a recognised training and examination which was regarded as qualifying them to work in the field. In most cases, the training course was a full-time one taken by recruits before entry. This was true of sections employing district nurses, health visitors, almoners, psychiatric social workers, probation and child care officers, home teachers of the blind, occupational therapists and moral welfare workers. Staff of housing departments were expected to qualify while employed by spare time study and subsequent examination.

Other sections of the services did not recruit people with recognised qualifications; but some gave recruits a training on appointment and most had some form of in-service training. The courses were usually short, of one or two weeks only; but N.S.P.C.C. officers and policewomen had systematic full-time training of three or more months. Some of the staff of these sections had taken university diplomas or degrees in social sciences.

Not everyone working in sections employing qualified staff had the recognised qualification. Some were older workers who had entered before formal qualifications had been established and had held their posts for many years. Some probation officers and almoners, a child care officer and a moral welfare worker fell into this category. A few, especially in hospital and county almoners' departments, were younger people who usually began

---

[1] Voluntary work was undertaken in many different fields. Youth leadership, especially of church organisations, was a common field for both men and women especially in the early years of their working life. Later on, however, men usually undertook the clerical or administrative work involved in running voluntary charitable organisations, while women were more likely to help those in need directly by visiting, nursing, helping to provide food at outings, teaching in Sunday school and so on. (See Appendix E. Table 42.)

by doing secretarial work in a social welfare field and were taken on to the social worker staff because they showed aptitude and interest. The comparative numbers of formally qualified and unqualified workers are shown in Table 7.

Table 7

NUMBERS OF STAFF WITH AND WITHOUT RECOGNISED QUALIFICATIONS*

Qualification Requirements	Numbers of staff			Per cent of staff	
	With qualification	Without qualification	Total	With qualification	Without qualification
Queen's district nursing and/or health visitor certificate	142	19	161	88%	12%
Other recognised diploma or certificate, after full-time course	63	22	85	74%	26%
Diploma or certificate after part-time study	17	9	26	65%	35%
No certification required	—	108	108	—	100%
	222	158	380	58%	42%

* Excluding youth leaders.

Career choice

Only seven people among the 389 social welfare staff participating in the enquiry said they were sorry they had entered their present occupation. One of them was a health visitor, one a probation officer and one a policewoman and the others were in central and local government jobs which did not require a social work qualification.

Just over 14 per cent, however, had mixed feelings when asked whether they were glad or sorry they had taken up the work they were doing.[1] An ambivalent attitude was more common among men than among women. It was also more common among nurses, health visitors and those doing work requiring no social work training than it was among those in jobs normally requiring a social work qualification. Even among those who were pleased with their career choice there were some who, given the oppor-

[1] See Appendix E. Table 43.

tunity, would choose another career. Nearly half those in jobs with no social work qualification mentioned a preference for another kind of career compared with only a third of those in jobs normally requiring a qualification and a quarter of those in nursing professions.

The district nurses who said they would choose to do other work usually specified health visiting or another branch of nursing. Health visitors who wanted to change, on the other hand, chose a branch of social work rather than of nursing. Jobs requiring a social work training were also the most common choices of women in occupations not requiring such training. Most of the women with a social work qualification who wanted to change also specified another branch of such work. For example, there were almoners and probation officers who wanted psychiatric social work and child care officers who wanted to become probation officers. Indeed, with only three exceptions, all the women who wanted other careers mentioned those which have to do with the care of individuals in need, that is, medicine, nursing, social work or teaching.

Men were more likely than women to want a change, and their choices of alternative careers were very different. Of the 47 men who wanted other careers, two-thirds mentioned work in science, technology, manual work, administration or business management. The third who named occupations in social welfare, specified either medicine or probation work.

Job satisfactions and dissatisfactions

A number of features of employment unique to each of the services led to complaints or expressions of particular satisfaction by the staff. These are discussed in later chapters. Certain themes, however, cropped up frequently in interviews with staff from every branch of the services, and they permit some generalisations to be made about the nature of the satisfactions which work in social welfare yielded or was expected to yield and about the actual or potential sources of dissatisfaction.

Nearly everyone interviewed suggested that a major, if not the principal source of job satisfaction was the opportunity afforded to help their fellow men.[1] They felt lucky to be in jobs where

[1] See Appendix E. Table 44.

they could devote all their working time and energy to helping those in trouble. Hence, dissatisfactions with jobs were often expressed in terms of the limitations imposed on that capacity to help.

Heavy caseloads, in particular, were a source of disgruntlement because they prevented the staff from giving enough time to helping each individual. A few people, including several health visitors, suggested that caseloads were unnecessarily heavy because they included some who did not need help. A few believed that some of their cases did not deserve help and directed their resentment against the offending patients or clients whose selfishness deprived deserving people of help. This kind of reaction was more commonly expressed by those who had not been trained in social work and who were dealing with people with social rather than health problems.

Some of the staff believed their ability to help clients was limited by the lack of essential services, particularly for the temporary residential care of elderly or handicapped people. Others blamed poor organisation and in particular unnecessary 'paper' work for restricting the time they could spend with their cases. The routine completion of official returns giving an account of the work done over a week, month or year, was particularly disliked by many of the staff. Although some of them were prepared to cede that it was a necessary if distasteful task, a substantial proportion was clearly not convinced that the records kept were essential.

While major satisfactions were derived from opportunities for altruism, few said these were the sole attractions of their work. Some, for example, felt that rewards were considerably enhanced when patients or clients showed appreciation for the help given or when they could see the results of their labour. They were depressed when their efforts were taken for granted or when there was little to show for them. It was generally those without a social work or nursing qualification who seemed to be most affected by their clients' indifference or ingratitude.

Satisfactions derived from the appreciation of colleagues and superiors were not often mentioned. It was more common to hear complaints of the lack of appreciation or understanding shown by those in authority. A considerable number of the staff felt that their work was not assessed at its true value nor its difficulties understood either by their own superiors or by others in social welfare work.

Indeed, there seemed to be widespread uneasiness among staff from many branches of the social welfare services about their public image. District nurse-midwives seemed to be least affected by this kind of uneasiness; probation officers, almoners working in the county, welfare officers, disablement resettlement officers, home help organisers and some others, too, were unlikely to express concern on this score; but many health visitors, school attendance officers, youth leaders, hospital almoners, N.A.B. officers and some others believed that the value of their work was generally underrated.

Financial rewards in all the branches of social welfare work surveyed were not great. A minority were earning more than £1,000 a year and very few indeed over £1,200. Salary differentials between the staff of different branches of the social welfare services were not great; nor were the salary ranges within each occupation.

Comparisons with other occupations suggested that men with comparable length of schooling and educational qualifications employed in commercial or industrial work were earning considerably more, but that they had shorter holidays and smaller pension provision.[1] Women, on the other hand, were not likely to be paid substantially less than their educational equals in other forms of employment.

In these circumstances, it was not surprising that almost no man expressed positive satisfaction with his salary and that twice as many men as women complained of poor financial rewards. Men sometimes mentioned that the burden imposed by small salaries fell more heavily on their wives than on them, and gave the impression that there was a conflict between their liking for the work on the one hand and their obligations to their family on the other.

Two other features of work in most branches of the social welfare field from which many derived great satisfaction were inter-related. First, much of the work offered considerable

---

[1] The average weekly wage of adult male industrial workers in April 1961 was £15 1s. 4d. or roughly £760 a year.

variety. It was seldom that two consecutive days were passed in the same kind of work. Many enjoyed the opportunity to be out of doors frequently and disliked work which was confined to a single office. Secondly, most of the staff had considerable freedom in arranging their own working schedules and appreciated the independence and responsibility it gave them. Only one or two felt that they had too much responsibility, were left too much on their own by their superiors or were isolated from their colleagues.

Summary

Social welfare services in Bucks were provided by a number of statutory and voluntary bodies who between them employed some 400 staff in 1961. The largest employer was the County Council with social welfare staff in its health and welfare, education and children's departments and in the police and probation service. The borough, urban and district councils were concerned with welfare primarily through their responsibility for housing.

Three central government departments, the Ministry of Labour, the Ministry of Pensions and the N.A.B. and hospitals in two Regional Hospital Board areas (the North-West Metropolitan and Oxford) also had social welfare responsibilities in the county.

Besides these statutory authorities, a number of voluntary societies employed staff to assist people in need, and many more organised voluntary helpers. Many of these bodies worked closely with the staff of statutory bodies.

Attempts to conserve effort by co-ordinating the activities of the many bodies providing services for the elderly, the handicapped and the so-called problem family brought into existence a number of co-ordinating committees.

Most of the staff of the social welfare services were between 35 and 55 and had entered their occupations in their late twenties or early thirties. Typically, the men were married with dependent children; the women were usually single and those who had married were generally childless. Those in jobs not requiring social work training were typically the sons and daughters of manual or clerical workers. Those in jobs requiring social work qualifications and especially the women among them were usually the offspring of professional people.

More than half the staff left school without formal qualifications. Only 13 per cent had had a full-time University course; but the same proportion had gained minimum University entrance requirements before leaving school.

Just under a third of the staff entered their occupations before their twenty-sixth birthday; but nearly half did not start until they were more than thirty. Men were slightly older on entry than women.

Most of those in posts requiring social work or nursing qualifications were already established in their occupations before coming to work in Bucks. Those working in other jobs were more commonly local men and women who began their present careers in Bucks.

The majority of the staff were anglicans, but not regular church goers. Most had been active voluntary workers in the social welfare field. Very few regretted their career choice; but a considerable number, especially of the men, would have preferred other work. Most of the men stated a preference for work outside the social welfare field. Women, on the other hand, chose occupations which had much in common with their present ones.

The main source of job satisfaction for nearly all social welfare staff was the opportunity to help people in need. Variety, the freedom to arrange the working day and responsibility were other attractive features of the work. Dissatisfactions commonly centred round low financial rewards and heavy caseloads. It was also widely felt that administrative heads and the public at large were insufficiently aware of the value of the work or the difficulties of those who did it.

CHAPTER IV

Clients and Client-worker Relationships

In Chapter II some indication was given of the changing conditions which were putting new stresses on the social welfare services in Bucks, and Chapter III described the services and the characteristics of those who staffed them. This Chapter presents some of the main characteristics of the actual clients of the services in 1960–61, and of their relationships with the staff.

Social welfare staff were usually dealing with the affairs of a single individual in a household who could be described as the client. Some workers dealt habitually not with a single individual, however, but with several people or the entire household. In these instances one member of the household was considered the worker's *main* client and the other members *subsidiary* clients.[1] The staff most likely to have several clients in a single household were health visitors, child care officers, school attendance officers, child guidance workers, N.S.P.C.C. officers and housing welfare staff—in short, those concerned with children and their families.

The description of those helped by social welfare workers, therefore, is mainly of the characteristics of the *households* of which the clients were members; but it is preceded by a brief outline of some of the personal attributes of those who were designated the workers' main clients.[2]

Main clients' sex, age and marital status

Seventy per cent of the main clients seen by the staff of the social welfare services in a typical week were women or girls—

[1] In order to assist and standardise the process of distinguishing the main from subsidiary clients certain rules of precedence were established. Generally, the application of these rules did not seriously distort the real picture. For example, normally the mother was called the health visitor's main client and any children under five subsidiary clients, but the father and older children whom health visitors rarely saw were not described as clients. In some instances, for example those involving the child care officers, procedures for identifying the *main* client, although standardised, produced some distortion. (See Appendix A for a description of the general rules used and Chapter XI on child care officers for the modifications introduced.)

[2] See Appendix A for an account of the methods used to analyse the characteristics of clients seen in a normal working week.

compared with only 51 per cent of the county's population in 1961. Two factors were responsible for the excess of females in the social welfare workers' clientele, the number of clients from the population aged 65 or more (among whom there were three women to every two men), and the number of young married women who were visited in their role of mother. There were some social welfare workers, however, who saw more male than female clients, among them the D.R.O.'s, youth employment officers, child guidance workers and probation officers.

The comparative concentration of social welfare staff visits to the elderly is illustrated in Table 8.[1] Thirty-five per cent of those seen were 65 or over, although they formed less than 11 per cent of the population. Teenagers and 60–64-year-olds were clients roughly in proportion to their numbers in the population.

Table 8

AGE OF MAIN CLIENTS SEEN BY SOCIAL WELFARE WORKERS IN A TYPICAL WEEK IN 1960/61, COMPARED WITH THE AGE DISTRIBUTION OF BUCKS POPULATION, APRIL, 1961

Age group	Percentage of social welfare workers' main clients	Percentage of population of Bucks.*
0–4	2	9
5–14	6	16
15–19	7	7
20–44	38	34
45–59	8	19
60–64	4	4
65 and over	35	11
All ages	100	100
	no.=4,488	no.=488,233

* G.R.O. Census 1961. County Report for Buckinghamshire. 1964. H.M.S.O.

Those who were less commonly *main* clients were children and middle-aged people. Children, however, were subsidiary clients in nearly all the households where women of 20–44 were described

[1] See also Appendix F. Table 45.

as main clients, so that altogether they figured as clients in 37 per cent of the clients' households.

It was the fact that there were so many elderly clients which accounted for the comparatively high proportion of widowed compared with the proportion in the county's population. (See Table 9.) There were not significantly more divorced people in the survey clientele; but the staff indicated that for every one they knew to be divorced there were twice as many who were still legally married but living apart from their spouses.[1]

Table 9

THE MARITAL STATUS OF ADULT CLIENTS COMPARED WITH THE BUCKS POPULATION AGED 16 AND OVER IN APRIL 1961

Marital status	Percentage social welfare workers' main clients	Percentage Bucks population
Single	16	21*
Married	61	71
Widowed	22 ⎫	8
Divorced	1 ⎭	
Total	100	100

* A fifth of the single in the Census age group 15–19 have been excluded to account for the 15-year-olds and allow comparisons with the survey data.

As far as education went, four out of five adult clients were believed to have left school at the minimum school leaving age, providing a rough indication of their social class origins.[2] The social welfare staff of most departments had an even greater proportion of clients with minimal full-time schooling; but district nurses and health visitors who between them saw 55 per cent of the clients in the typical week, had rather greater proportions of clients with longer schooling. Among clients of secondary school

[1] The staff may not always have known the exact marital status of their clients and have indicated some merely separated when they were divorced. But it is probable that divorce was less common among the working class who formed a larger proportion of the clientele than they did of the population.

[2] In England and Wales, about 25 per cent of those reaching their 16th birthday in 1961 were still at school. The proportion is likely to be considerably smaller in populations born earlier. Source: Annual Report for 1961. Ministry of Education. H.M.S.O.

age (11–15) three-quarters were attending secondary modern schools; only 6 per cent were grammar or technical school pupils.[1]

Over 40 per cent of the main clients seen in a typical week were known to have a chronic illness or disability and some of these had conditions affecting more than one system of the body. Rheumatic, heart and circulatory, and neurological diseases including, most commonly, partial paralysis following a stroke, each occurred in about 8 per cent of the clients.[2] A good deal of this illness was accounted for by district nurses' patients; but chronic conditions were even more common among the clients of other health and welfare workers with the exception of health visitors.

Characteristics of the clients' households

Housing circumstances of social welfare clients compared unfavourably with those of the county's population.[3] Social welfare clients were disproportionately drawn from those living in poorer conditions and from less well-to-do sections of the community. For example, there were fewer owner-occupying households among social welfare clients, more living in caravans and more sharing or doing without the basic housing amenities. Over-crowding, as measured by the proportion of households with more than one person per room, was twice as common. House-holds of social welfare clients were also more likely to be single person households, reflecting the greater number of elderly in such households. At the same time, there was a considerable excess of households with over six members, and households of at least eight were relatively four times more numerous than in the county as a whole.[4]

[1] The per cent distribution of 226 children aged 11–15 among secondary schools was as follows: Secondary modern, 75 per cent; special schools for handicapped, 11 per cent; approved or residential schools, 4 per cent; grammar or technical, 6 per cent; occupation centres, 4 per cent.

[2] See Table 46, Appendix F.

[3] See Table 47, Appendix F.

[4] It was possible to check the consistency of information about households when two workers reported on the same ones. Comparisons indicated that there were sometimes minor discrepancies in reporting household composition, e.g. in one instance a district nurse reported a household as consisting of a married couple and four children, whereas a N.A.B. officer reported a single woman and three illegitimate children. This case suggests that clients sometimes conceal the real facts from social welfare staff.

Exact comparisons between the social status of clients' and the county's population were not possible, since the Census provided data only on the socio-economic group distribution of occupied and retired males, whereas the survey information lent itself better to an analysis of the occupations of male chief economic supporters. Moreover, 20 per cent of the survey households were headed by women, many of them of retirement age, whose social status is impossible to determine adequately in occupational terms. But bearing these points in mind, a comparison between the population and the clientele suggested that clients were disproportionately drawn from families of unskilled or semi-skilled manual workers.[1]

Social problems

Forty-four per cent of the households of clients seen by the social welfare staff in a typical week did not seem to the latter to present any of the 21 categories of social or economic problem which the staff had been asked to report. Those without problems were mainly the clients of health visitors and district nurse-midwives.[2]

Among clients considered to have social problems, three-quarters were described as presenting one or two kinds of problem only and a quarter three or more kinds. Broadly speaking, staff whose main concern was with the elderly reported only one or two problems in the households they saw, generally of adjustment to chronic illness and disability, loneliness or inadequate income.

---

[1] Thirty-one per cent of the population of occupied and retired males were in unskilled, semi-skilled and personal service occupations, compared with 37 per cent of the male chief economic supporters of clients' households. On the other hand, there were roughly comparable proportions of Social Class I and II socio-economic groups among the adult males in the total population and the male chief economic supporters of clients' households (see Table 48 in Appendix F).

[2] Attention has been drawn (see Chapter I, page 6) to the subjective nature of the social welfare workers' assessments of social problems and the consequent difficulty of using them as measures of the prevalence of social problems among clients seen during a typical week. Comparisons between the reports of workers visiting the same households indicated that district nurse-midwives as a group often did not report problems recorded by others. Home help organisers also reported fewer problems and it was generally true that workers with no training in social work reported fewer difficulties than those with social work or health visitor training.

Staff concerned with law breaking, anti-social behaviour, and deprived or maladjusted children, however, tended to report many difficulties in their clients' households, particularly personality problems, disturbed marital and parent-child relationships, children's behaviour and housing. The proportions of all households seen in a typical week in which different problems were reported are shown in Table 10.

Table 10

PERCENTAGE OF HOUSEHOLDS IN WHICH DIFFERENT CATEGORIES OF SOCIAL PROBLEM WERE REPORTED BY SOCIAL WELFARE STAFF

Type of problem	Percentage of households	Type of problem	Percentage of households
Adjustment to physical or mental disability, or chronic illness	19	Juvenile delinquency	3
		Excessive job changing	3
Personality problems or inadequacy	14	Bereavement	3
		Child neglect or cruelty	2
Inadequate means	13	School truancy or refusal	2
Housing	10	Adoption	2
Loneliness	8	Rent arrears	1
Marital relationships	7	All others	1
Parent-child relationships	7		
Children's behaviour	6		
Finding suitable work	6		
Mismanagement of means	4	No problems recorded	44
Sexual behaviour	4	One or two problems	41
Criminal activities (adult)	4	Three or more problems	15
Intra-family relations (other than marital or parent-child)	4	All households	100

Client-worker relationships

One in four of the clients seen in a typical week were said to have taken the initiative themselves in approaching the service to which the worker was attached, or to have had the move suggested by another member of the public, usually a relative, neighbour or friend.[1] Rather over half were referred to the worker's service by health service personnel, the most frequent single source of

[1] See Table 49 in Appendix F.

referral being the G.P. No other service was responsible for the initial referral of more than a small proportion of the clients.

Little short of half the clients had first been referred to the service of the worker seeing them more than a year previously and 12 per cent had been clients for more than 5 years.[1] One in five, on the other hand, first became clients within a month before the recording period interview or were being seen for the first time. These averages conceal substantial differences between services. At one extreme, social welfare workers working with blind and deaf people and occupational therapists mostly had clients of many years standing: at the other extreme, over 90 per cent of the clients of policewomen, 81 per cent of those of marriage guidance counsellors and 64 per cent of those of hospital almoners had first been seen during the study week or less than a month before.

Most clients were seen in their own homes. Only 10 per cent came to the office of the social welfare staff and only 5 per cent were seen in hospitals, residential homes or elsewhere. The preponderance of home visits is chiefly accounted for by the large proportion of clients seen by local health service staff, whose contacts almost invariably took place in the home. The N.A.B. officers, school attendance officers and N.S.P.C.C. inspectors, too, nearly always visited the clients' homes. On the other hand, some workers almost always interviewed clients in their offices or in the hospital or clinic buildings in which they worked. This was true of hospital almoners and psychiatric social workers, child guidance workers and disablement resettlement officers. Staff whose contacts were more evenly divided between home and office were probation and child care officers, housing department staff and moral welfare workers.

A variety of services was undertaken at or arising directly from the contact between clients and workers during a typical working week,[2] the most common being either nursing or the giving of advice on health or the treatment and management of illness or handicap.

It was comparatively rare for social welfare workers, whether with a training in social work or not, to claim that part of the service they gave clients was help with emotional difficulties.

[1] See Table 50 in Appendix F.   [2] See Table 51, Appendix F.

Comparatively frequently staff claimed, and especially in the case of health visitors, that the purpose of the contact was merely to check on the circumstances of the client or family; when they thought no assistance was needed, they either recorded no action or suggested that the service lay simply in reporting the facts to their own service or to those who had asked them to call. Some of the other health service staff, i.e., district nurse-midwives and home help organisers, were the most likely to indicate that their activities were confined to a single specific service. County almoners and welfare officers, on the other hand, reported several services more frequently than they did a single one.

The workers visiting about two-thirds of the clients had made no contact with the staff of other social welfare services concerning these clients within the previous year, but they were sometimes aware that other staff were visiting. Most of the contacts were between staff of different branches of the health services, and these workers, especially if they were almoners, were more likely to make approaches to others than were non-health service staff. Outside the health services, the staff with some social work training had more contacts with others than those with no such training.[1]

Summary

In a typical week in 1960–61, social welfare staff saw clients drawn from many sections of the population, but tended to deal mainly with the elderly and disabled on the one hand, and with the young and their parents on the other. They saw more of those who occupied caravans, lived at high densities and had not the exclusive use of some domestic amenities than of those whose housing circumstances were more advantageous. Their clients lived more frequently in dwellings rented from the local authority and less frequently in owner-occupied houses than the relative numbers of such people in the population as a whole. The households were headed by men from all social classes, but, with the exception of some health service workers, were those of manual rather than non-manual, middle class workers and, amongst manual workers, of semi- and unskilled workers rather than of skilled men.

[1] See Table 52, Appendix F.

Rather more than half the clients' households were believed to have social problems. Nearly all those without problems were seen by health visitors or district nurses who between them saw more than half the clients. Some of these, especially elderly patients seen by district nurses, may have had social problems associated with illness or infirmity which were not recorded. Three-quarters of the clients had been put in touch with the social welfare worker by staff from another social service. The referring agencies were usually health workers, particularly G.P.'s. Nearly half had been clients for more than a year and only one in five had been clients for less than one month. Clients were nearly always seen in their own homes.

Workers performed a variety of services for their clients; but in a substantial number of cases the only action taken at or following the client-worker contact was the preparation of a report. In about a third of the cases, workers had been in touch with other services on behalf of their clients. Health service workers, especially almoners, were likely to make referrals.

In the chapters which follow, there is a description of the clients and the work of the staff of each of the services in turn. In the final chapter, the conclusions it seems legitimate to draw from the examination of staff and clients and their relationships to one another are given, together with suggestions for overcoming some of the problems which the analysis reveals.

CHAPTER V

The Social Welfare Work of the Health and Welfare Department

Bucks is one of 25 local authorities in England and Wales to have a combined health and welfare department. Consequently, the County Medical Officer of Health is also Chief Welfare Officer. The various sections of the department employing social welfare and nursing staff are shown in Table 11. The work of two of them, the Home Nursing and Midwifery Service and the Health Visiting Service, are considered in Chapters VI and VII. Other sections, however, had much in common and activities of their field staff are consequently considered together in this chapter.

All the workers dealing regularly with cases were interviewed, including the heads of the county medical social work and occupational therapy services who carried cases as well as administrative duties. The analysis which follows relates to 210 clients seen by eight home help organisers, 202 seen by eight almoners and social workers, 196 seen by nine welfare officers, 150 seen by eight home teachers of the blind and 104 seen by four occupational therapists.[1]

Characteristics of the health and welfare departments' clients

The majority of clients served by health and welfare workers were elderly. For example, three-quarters of the home help organisers' and home teachers of the blind and over half the county almoners' and occupational therapists' visits were paid to those over 60. Welfare officers dealt with fewer old people (42 per cent) and nearly a quarter of their clients were less than 20.

Because much of their work was with elderly people, the staff were generally dealing with households consisting of one or two people only. In particular, over half those seen by home help organisers were living alone and only a quarter in households

[1] One worker subsequently asked us not to use the information she gave about herself but did provide information about individuals seen. Three others, two welfare officers and one occupational therapist, did not provide records of their cases.

C

Table 11

THE SOCIAL WELFARE AND NURSING STAFF OF THE LOCAL AUTHORITY
HEALTH AND WELFARE DEPARTMENT

Sections	Section Heads	Field Workers	Numbers of Field Workers
Home Nursing and Midwifery Service	*Superintendent* *Nursing Officer*	District nurse-midwives District nurses, District nurse-midwife-health visitors	119
Health Visiting Service	*Superintendent* *Health Visitor*	Health visitors	47
Home Help Service	*Senior Home Help Organiser* *	Home help organisers and assistant home help organisers	8
County Almoning Service	Senior County Almoner	Almoners	6
		Social welfare assistants—	2
Mental Health Service	*Administrative* * *Assistant*		
		—Welfare Officers	11
Welfare Service	*Administrative* * *Assistant*		
		—Home teachers of the blind	8
Occupational Therapy Service	Senior Occupational Therapist	Occupational therapists—	5
			206

* These section heads were normally engaged solely in administrative duties and did not deal directly with patients or clients. They did not, therefore, participate directly in our survey of social welfare work.

of more than two. The exceptions were welfare officers' clients, few of whom lived alone.

Over-crowding was less common among health and welfare staffs' clients than it was amongst the clients of most other social welfare workers and especially amongst those dealing with children. Nevertheless, there was a ratio of more than one person per room in 12 per cent of the households seen by county almoners and in 14 per cent of those seen by welfare officers.

Judged by the age they left school, over four-fifths of the staffs' clients were of working rather than middle class origin. Judged by occupation of the occupied or retired head of household, manual workers or their dependents constituted the majority, ranging from 68 per cent of home help organisers' clients to 82 per cent of welfare officers'. Home help organisers were the most likely to deal with owner-occupying households,[1] representing in all probability the more middle class section of the population.

Most clients had a chronic illness or were severely and permanently disabled. Just over a third of those of welfare officers were described as mentally subnormal and rather less as mentally ill or senile. Occupational therapists and county almoners most commonly saw those with strokes or rheumatic diseases but also had a substantial minority of mentally disordered clients. For all these workers and home teachers, patients with multiple disabilities were the rule rather than the exception. Only home help organisers who helped maternity cases as well as those who were ill or disabled saw many households where there was no chronic health problem.

Most of the social problems identified by the staff were directly associated with physical illness or disability. In the case of welfare officers personal difficulties of mentally ill or subnormal patients were more commonly listed. Most health department staff reported widespread difficulties which could be described as consequences of illness or age, for example, loneliness, employment difficulties and inadequate incomes. Home help organisers reported least difficulties of these kinds.

Comparisons of the reports of workers who visited clients from the same households as health department staff[2] indicated that if the latter were county almoners, occupational therapists or welfare officers they were more likely to record difficulties than the other visitor unless the other visitor was a trained social worker or health visitor. Home help organisers, on the other hand, consistently reported fewer social difficulties than other workers whether or not the latter had trained as social workers.

Staff-client relationships and services provided

The purpose of referrals to the home help and occupational therapy services needs no elaboration, and in referring blind and

---

[1] 37 per cent of their clients' households were owner-occupiers compared with 17 per cent of the welfare officers' and 48 per cent of the county's households in 1961.   [2] 205 sets of comparisons were possible.

partially sighted to home teachers, the welfare department was taking the first step to fulfil its statutory responsibility. Reasons for referral to welfare officers were varied. About one third of their clients were referred following an ascertainment by the school health service of ineducability or educational subnormality. A tenth had been referred for emergency admission to mental hospital, and a quarter to consider their need for permanent or temporary residential care. Another third were referred either for social investigation or because anti-social behaviour suggested they needed help or supervision.

County almoners' clients too were referred to them for a variety of purposes including general investigation of home circumstances, assessment of need for home nursing, mechanical and domestic aids, arrangement of convalescence, temporary hospital care or residential holidays so that relatives might have a respite, permanent institutional care or re-housing in sheltered circumstances.

Most clients were referred to health and welfare social workers by other branches of the health service, and in particular by general practitioners and hospital almoners.

There were considerable differences in the time clients had been known to the workers of different sections. Nearly two-fifths of the home teachers' clients had been known to them for more than five years and nearly nine out of ten for more than one year. Only one per cent were being visited for the first time.

Occupational therapists too rarely visited people referred recently. Three-quarters of their clients had been seen first more than a year earlier and most had been visited regularly since.

On the other hand, about a fifth of the clients visited by county almoners, home help organisers and welfare officers were being seen for the first time. These sections, however, had a core of clients known to them for a year or even longer. Welfare officers and home help organisers had known nearly half their clients for more than a year and about one in seven for more than five years.

Workers from different sections had different patterns of visiting once a referral had been made. Nearly half the occupational therapists' clients were being visited once a week, and only slightly fewer once a fortnight. One in eight of the home teachers' clients were seen at least weekly; but the majority only had visits every two months or every quarter. Welfare officers had less of a set pattern of visiting, but a third were seen at roughly quarterly intervals. Emergency cases could be seen daily for short periods of time.

Home help organisers had been visiting some clients with surprising frequency, 29 per cent being seen more than ten times during the previous year and 60 per cent four times. County almoners, on the other hand, saw most patients infrequently. Eighty per cent had been visited on fewer than ten occasions in the past year. One in five, however, had been visited with greater frequency.

Staff were asked why they visited the recorded cases and what services they provided. Most gave a single reason for visiting but performed several services. For example, home teachers almost always labelled their visit 'a friendly call', but did some teaching in half the cases as well as considering financial circumstances, housing and domestic help in many others. Welfare officers and county almoners, in particular, dealt with many problems, both material and emotional. Home help organisers, on the other hand, seldom claimed to give the household any service other than the provision of domestic help.

The services undertaken by county almoners and welfare officers frequently consisted of referring clients for specialist services or advice. Consequently, they were often in touch with the staff of other services. Home teachers, occupational therapists and home help organisers had initiated fewer contacts with others but had themselves been contacted by many others, particularly by those employed in health services.

The social characteristics and training of the social welfare staff

All the county almoners, occupational therapists, home teachers and home help organisers, but only two of the eleven welfare officers, were women. Sixteen of the 28 women and three of the nine men were single. Among the 12 women who had married, nine had children. Only one married woman worked in the almoners' section, but amongst home help organisers only one was single.[1]

---

[1] The woman in the almoner's department married since her appointment.

Home teachers were rather older than the staff of other sections, the youngest of the six workers approaching forty, while two were in the forties and three over 50. Occupational therapists tended to be younger than other workers. Only one of the five was over 45 and three out of the five were not yet 35. The widest age spread was amongst welfare officers, those under 40 being in a minority of five to six.

The social class origins of the staff of the sections were rather different. Of the 13 county almoners and occupational therapists, eleven had been born into middle class families. The majority of home help organisers and welfare officers, on the other hand, had fathers in manual work. Four of the six home teachers' fathers were self-employed men.

Recruitment and training

Six of the county almoning section had trained as almoners, one had taken a course for home teachers of the blind and one had no social work training but had worked as a policewoman. Two had been over 30 before taking up social welfare work. With one exception they had some years of hospital experience before joining the county health department. The decision to leave hospital was taken either to enlarge their experience by accepting new, challenging work, or because they believed that the greatest need for social casework was in the domiciliary field.

Four of the five occupational therapists had taken a three year course leading to a diploma, and the fifth was recognised as a qualified worker by the Association of Occupational Therapy by virtue of long experience. All of them had had hospital experience, either with mental patients or physically disabled adults and children, or both.

All the home teachers had had considerable working experience before taking the training. Two became home teachers in their 20's, two in their 30's, and two only after 40.[1]

Three of the 11 welfare officers had social science diplomas, but no other training in social work. None of their colleagues had a recognised social work qualification, although one of the three

[1] One of the late entrants was a widow with children who had worked most of her life but only felt free to train when the children had grown up.

men who had been a local government officer before the war had then obtained the relieving officer's certificate.

While so few had academic qualifications, five had had relevant work experience. Three, for example, had been duly authorised officers under the Lunacy and Mental Treatment Acts, until their repeal by the Mental Health Act 1959, and dealt with compulsory admissions to mental hospital. They had also been guardians to the mentally defective under the Mental Deficiency Acts. One had been a mental nurse.

Home help organisers had not been trained in social work and only one, starting the work in another county, had had any formal in-service training. Most of them had been housewives bringing up children before joining the service. The previous working experience of four had been clerical; one had some nursing experience and one had been in domestic service and herself worked as a home help.

Views on training

The almoners were in no doubt of the value of social work training, but had detailed criticisms of their own. The most critical felt that recent changes in training courses had remedied the deficiencies of the courses which they had taken before 1955. The two social welfare assistants without training in the almoner's section felt handicapped by the lack of it. One suggested that training was helpful in explaining clients' behaviour, but also that a lack of it vitiated her relationship with some hospital almoners.[1]

Two of the occupational therapists felt their course had given them a good preparation for their social welfare work and two did not. The main criticisms were that domiciliary and family problems were hardly considered. The only therapist without formal training in the subject felt her own training and experience in nursing were more valuable in 'helping you to answer patients' queries about their illness and help them overcome their anxieties'.

Three of the home teachers felt their training in social welfare was adequate but three were more critical. The former were those

[1] She said, 'Not being qualified can be very difficult. I get on well in my own office but I'm resented by many almoners who feel it's an unwarrantable intrusion. I've felt extremely humiliated in the past but now I'm much more self-confident.'

whose main interests were in teaching handicrafts, while the latter tended to be more interested in human relationships. One strongly advocated a general two year social work course for younger people. 'I don't think youngsters can do social work', she said. 'You must have some maturity; but something like the Young-husband course would help. Specialisation is wrong. Blind people are no different from sighted. Everyone needs to be helped to make the best of life.'

Only one welfare officer felt that the work could be done effectively by someone with in-service training and did not need a full social worker training. Those who had taken social science diplomas found the courses useful but not adequate. In particular they wanted more training in aspects of mental health.

Six of the seven home help organisers felt that their work required some training, although they had not all considered seriously the form it should take. When pressed five suggested a full-time social worker course in medical, social and psychological problems. One thought 'a short course in social administration plus in-service training would be the best'. Only one felt that the work did not require special training. 'For home help work', she said, 'commonsense and practical experience are essential. You don't need theoretical study.'[1]

Satisfactions and dissatisfactions

All the almoners were convinced they had chosen the right career and the social welfare assistants wished they had a full almoner's training. Their rewards stemmed from contact with individuals needing help; but there was also greater freedom to arrange work in local authority service compared with hospital. Another advantage was working closely with general practitioners. One almoner felt she could do more for her clients because she was less dependent on approval from medical consultants than in hospital. Several mentioned that they could follow their cases through and keep longer contact with them than in hospital-based social work.

Working independence was one of the attractions, but several felt there were drawbacks to work with the county. One complained

---

[1] She concluded rather inconsistently, however, by saying she could not do the work efficiently, if she had not had prior work as a clerk in the department.

there was too little consultation by headquarters with those working outside Aylesbury. Changes were sometimes made which were unsuitable for those working in different circumstances.[1] Several spoke of difficulties stemming from pressure of work—a complaint common to many services. One said she could not maintain standards with the numbers referred to her. Two felt they were too often asked to undertake work which should have been referred elsewhere, resulting in a misuse of their skills.

There was some discussion of future trends in almoning. One resented finding out about patient's income before seeing what help they needed with personal problems. On the other hand, two almoners were critical of many colleagues for placing too much emphasis on casework and too little on dealing with patient's material needs. 'We're becoming negative,' she said, 'so keen to improve professional standards that we're becoming the profession that says what it won't do, not what it will'.

With one exception, who felt she should have stayed in bedside nursing, occupational therapists were all satisfied with their career choice. Satisfactions came from helping people.[2] That part of the work which involved persuading employers to find suitable outwork or finding markets for disabled people's handicrafts was not popular, especially since success often depended on local economic conditions.[3] Other complaints were of pay and travelling expenses. Car allowances were criticised by all and two considered salaries for experienced occupational therapists too low.[4]

[1] 'It's difficult to get access to superiors and I think this leads to lack of understanding at the top of what the work involves. When I discuss things at County office I find we speak a different language. It may be my inability to seek help in the right way', one said.

[2] Typical comments were: 'It's a thrill when they (the patients) go back to work when they never thought they would'. 'It's rewarding to see a brightening of personality, to see people begin to enjoy life and to make the most of what they've got.' 'By finding outwork, I can often make a significant contribution to income.'

[3] Two comments: 'I dislike the hawking of patients' work and the searching for job opportunities amongst employers. It could be done better by a specially conceived plan of campaign at headquarters'. 'I can't get enough outwork in the time I'm left to search for it.'

[4] 'The salary isn't a positive drawback—certainly not to entry; but it's amazing that the most responsible occupational therapist receives just over £1,000 a year. The scale of pay is just about tolerable for a single woman and is helpful as additional income for a married woman; but it would be impossible for a man, and unthinkable if he'd had three years' intensive training.'

C*

Members of the section displayed a notable sense of comradeship and of loyalty to the head of their section. Two, however, complained of insufficient interest by health department chiefs. One described the support as 'ludicrous in comparison with the support I had in hospital where my work was regarded as an essential part of a patient's treatment. It's every bit as important in domiciliary work but they don't seem to see it'. Another felt health department officials did not appreciate that domiciliary work was more difficult than hospital work because 'it's work with people who are virtually incapable of being rehabilitated'.[1]

In describing the satisfactions of their work some home teachers stressed the pleasure of teaching. Others laid more stress on forming a relationship which gave comfort and pleasure. One said this was her 'compensation for not being married. I get the emotional satisfaction of giving, which is especially significant for the single woman'. Another single woman made a similar point. 'I've gained a great deal of personal insight and help with my own problems from my contacts with blind people. It's enriched my life and experience.'

Talking about difficulties of the work, three distinct points were raised. The first was the size of caseloads. 'I'm skimming the surface the whole time. If I do a lot for one, it's at the expense of someone else.' The second was the relationship with the administration. One complained that 'the administration is too mechanised—people are just names to them'. Another felt too much responsibility was left to her. 'You have to work on your own and it's lonely. I find it quite worrying to be left on my own so much.' The third was the inadequacy of facilities, for example, lack of suitable office and storage space, delays in obtaining materials, difficulties of finding regular buyers for articles made by the blind, and the scarcity of transport to bring those from rural areas to meetings in towns.

Five of the 11 welfare officers had no regrets about their careers and would choose the same again. Four would have preferred another branch of social welfare work. Two of them only would have liked quite different occupations.

[1] One illustrated her allegation of remoteness: 'One of the doctors from the county health department visited the occupational therapy centre recently. His name and face were unknown to me although he'd worked in Aylesbury for a number of years'.

Like other social welfare staff, welfare officers enjoyed helping people. 'The old saying that it's better to give than receive is really true, I find' was one man's way of expressing it. As a group they did not mention the advantages of independence and variety as frequently as some. On the contrary three suggested they were simultaneously subject to too rigid administrative control and left to work too much alone.[1]

Many frustrations were laid at the door of clerical and administrative staff.[2] The latter were represented as 'not appreciating the value of social work'. Some complained of conflicting pressures inherent in being responsible to both welfare and mental welfare sections of the department.

All the home help organisers were pleased they had come into this branch of the social services, and five out of seven said given a choice again they would take up social welfare work, although only one specified the home help service. The other two, if free to choose again, would nurse.

The home help staff in common with others enjoyed their work primarily because they were helping people. Some mentioned other sources of satisfaction, for example, visiting and meeting different people, and contact with colleagues, staff from other branches of the social welfare services, and with home helps 'who take an interest and do much more than is required'.

Some organisers were frustrated by the demanding behaviour of some clients, and tended to divide clients generally into those who were deserving and those who were not. 'You need to differentiate', said one, for example, 'between those who are in trouble and those who merely *think* they are.' Another suggested that 'the home help service is being used increasingly by people who could find their own domestic help. Home helps rather resent

[1] One young welfare officer said, 'It is often useless to go to them (my superiors) for advice. The psychiatrists and psychiatric social workers are the most helpful and I've learned a lot from them'. Another suggested he had 'a galaxy of bosses' but no real personal contact with them. A third resented as time consuming 'making stupid detailed monthly returns', and complained of 'having to conform to a rigid procedure when to help people you need to be flexible'.

[2] Administrative staff were accused of having 'an inferiority complex due to their lack of qualifications even in administration', and consequently of being slow to press for the appointment of trained social workers or for the secondment of staff for training.

having to go to maternity cases. They feel, and I don't blame them, that these people can afford to make their own arrangements.' 'People do not seem to help relatives these days,' said a third. 'They shirk their responsibilities and rely on the welfare state. We are expected to run about too much after people—in the evenings, for example. They seem to expect us to suit their convenience.'[1]

General summary of findings and conclusions

With the exception of welfare officers most of the staff were dealing predominantly with the elderly who were chronically ill or permanently handicapped. Most patients lived either on their own or with one other person, usually an elderly spouse, who might also have impaired physical or mental capacities. Whatever the nature of their disabilities or social circumstances, most of them needed a gamut of services, including constant or periodic medical attention, home nursing and domestic help, ways of occupying their time fruitfully, and assistance in leaving their homes for an outing or holiday. Some required financial assistance regularly, others to meet particular emergencies; to achieve maximum mobility some needed alterations to their homes and others needed temporary or permanent sheltered accommodation.

Almoners of the health and welfare department visited mainly to assess the needs of clients who had not been handicapped all their lives, their disabilities developing in middle or old age. The laudatory comments of general practitioners and health and welfare workers who had referred patients to them suggested that the service had justified itself.

Those with longstanding handicaps tended to rely for help on welfare officers and home teachers of the blind. The majority of these officers believed they could provide a better service for their patients if they had had a social work training. Welfare officers, whose work was increasingly in the field of mental welfare, were particularly anxious for training in mental health. Home teachers thought there was too little emphasis in their training on helping

---

[1] There were also distasteful but unavoidable aspects of the work. One person said, 'It can be a dirty job. Well, handling the laundry of incontinents is hardly a job for the likes of us. We are not refuse collectors. But we can't expect home helps to do jobs we don't show we can do.'

the blind to overcome difficulties experienced by those who were ageing whether or not they were blind. In my view the work of these officers calls for a two-year social work training.

Welfare officers faced additional problems. Nine of them combined mental welfare with general welfare duties, and were responsible to two separate sections of the health and welfare department. This divided responsibility undoubtedly added to the stresses of officers dealing constantly with difficult cases. Some felt, in addition, that they could not obtain enough specialist help from the administrative heads of the sections who had field experience but no social work training.

Where health and welfare duties are carried out by a single department and not by two, it should be easier to plan staff requirements, organise appropriate in-service training and deploy social worker staff according to objective assessments of need. The sectional framework of the combined department in Bucks in 1960–61, however, had some inherent weaknesses. Welfare officers, home teachers, almoners and their social welfare assistants and home help organisers usually had clients with similar demographic and social characteristics and similar needs. Each group had some comparatively simple and some complicated cases to deal with and similar aims. Yet, because they were responsible to different administrative sections, had different training for their work and different degrees of supervision and guidance in carrying it out, the best use was not made of their services or of limited facilities for in-service and further training.

Field staff might be better deployed if all staff at present working for the welfare section, the mental welfare section, the almoner's section and the home help organisers' section were brought into a single social welfare division, headed by a trained social worker working with specialist medical officers in mental health, geriatrics and rehabilitation.

Such a radical re-organisation in the internal structure of the health department could only be carried through smoothly with the goodwill of the administrative and social welfare staff. Staff must be convinced the scheme would improve the quality of their work, and not affect adversely their own salaries or prospects of promotion.

Social workers should not be difficult to convince, but administrative staff may be. Expanding county council responsibilities will provide increasing opportunities for promotion to administrators, so that fear of demotion should not be a factor in opposing change; but in local government the distinction between administration and social welfare work has only recently emerged, and the value of training both for administrators and for social workers is not completely accepted.

The provision of domestic help is often crucial if those who cannot manage themselves are to remain at home. Introducing someone else into the home when the housewife is no longer able to clean, wash or cook, however, is likely to touch upon many sensitive areas. Many housewives are individualists, hypersensitive about their homes and vulnerable to implied criticisms of their housekeeping capacities. Home help organisation is not therefore a job which can be done by anyone with administrative ability. Organisers need to know something about the social and psychological problems of ageing and handicap, and about domestic workers' difficulties in other people's homes. Information supplied by home help organisers suggested, however, they were often unaware of social difficulties reported by other social welfare workers in households both were visiting.

A two-year social work course should provide a satisfactory basic training for home help organisers. While numbers with social work training are limited, however, priority should be given to the demand for them in the general health and mental welfare services. If home help organisers work closely with the rest of the social welfare division under the general direction of the principal social welfare worker, as suggested earlier, the service could be provided by those with administrative experience and an interest in the welfare of elderly and disabled persons. In the meantime, however, home help organisers and their assistants should be encouraged to participate in systematic in-service training courses.

The potential value of occupational therapy for the temporarily or chronically ill or handicapped is still being uncovered. In the past, most emphasis was given to the therapeutic value of handicraft. Today, much greater importance is attached to teaching disabled persons to cope with the activities of daily living, and in order to do this, occupational therapists need to know what effect various kinds of disability have on the capacities of individuals, and how the physical and emotional environment can be modified to help disabled persons maintain their independence and self-respect. Consequently, more emphasis should be given in courses for occupational therapists to understanding the physiological and psychological aspects of illness and disability and the social factors affecting adjustment.

Occupational therapists in Bucks spent much time trying to find suitable paid work for handicapped people. This part of the job was thoroughly disliked by some of the occupational therapists and would probably be better done by other staff. The latter would have to have some knowledge of the effect of different disabilities on the capacity of individuals, be conversant with the work done in local firms, and maintain friendly relationships with employers and trade unions.

Such work might be done by D.R.O.'s at Ministry of Labour Employment Exchanges with whom occupational therapists need to work closely, since both are concerned with disabled people.

All the recommendations made in this chapter could be carried through without major changes in the structure of the health and welfare department. They would not, however, provide a fully integrated domiciliary health and welfare service which I believe necessary. Such a service would require a radical re-arrangement of staff and functions, and its possible shape is considered in Chapter XX.

CHAPTER VI

The Health Visiting Service

In its origins and until the advent of the National Health Service in 1948 health visiting was predominantly concerned with the saving of child life. A great deal of the credit for the spectacular reduction in infant and child mortality and in the number of children permanently crippled by serious illness or nutritional deprivation between 1900 and 1948 must be given to the educative work of the health visitors. Rising real incomes, better nutrition, effective immunisation and antibiotics, especially during the second World War, provided the base for an improvement in health, but the health visitors helped to change customary child rearing practices. It was they who urged mothers to immunise their babies and to avoid gastro-intestinal and chest infections by attention to diet, food hygiene, clothing and ventilation.

When the National Health Service was being planned it was assumed that health visitors would still need to play the same role if further reductions in infant and child mortality were to be achieved. At the same time, since they appeared to be successful advisers on infant health, it was intended that they should concern themselves also with the health of older children and adults. A circular from the Ministry of Health forecast that 'after the Appointed Day she (the health visitor) will be concerned with the health of the household as a whole, including the preservation of health and precuations against the spread of infection, and will have an increasingly important part to play in health education'[1] Her task, it was suggested, would be with the whole family.

At first all seemed to be well, but within a few years doubts began to be voiced on many sides about the value of the health visitor's work and in 1953 the Minister of Health appointed a Working Party which reported in 1956.

It made no proposals, however, for radical changes in the service. Although it acknowledged that less of the health visitor's time needed to be given to the physical care of mothers and young

[1] Quoted in *Report of the Working Party on Health Visiting*. 1956. H.M.S.O., p. 3.

children, it saw a growing role for them in mental hygiene and in the after-care of hospital patients, and considered that more health visitors were required. It saw the health visitor's function primarily as providing health education and social advice, and considered that she was admirably placed to help the general practitioner directly in his practice. It rejected the view that the health visitor should undertake bedside nursing or complicated social casework.

The Minister of Health accepted these conclusions and urged local health authorities to give health visitors a larger part to play in preventing the break-up of 'problem families', the supervision of the care of elderly people in their own homes, the home management of handicapped children and the prevention of mental illness.[1]

In many ways the Working Party Report was disappointing. The opportunity was not taken to make a detailed study of health visitors' work, nor to examine its impact on those they were trying to help. No systematic attempt was made to discover what relations they had with other social welfare workers or with general practitioners, nor to suggest the kind of organisational changes needed to improve these relationships. As a result, many of the misgivings and much of the scepticism about their effectiveness remained.

The Report of the Working Party set up to examine the staffing of local health and welfare authority departments (the Younghusband Report, 1959) brought no further clarification of the health visitors' role largely because its terms of reference precluded anything but incidental discussion of her work.[2] Indeed, if only unwittingly, the effect of the Report was to put still further in question the health visitor's future in the social welfare services.

In 1960–61 there were 47 full-time health visitors in Bucks. In addition, 16 district nurse-midwives in rural areas in the north undertook visiting as well. There was also one part-time health visitor who was employed as a moral welfare worker for the other part of her time. One health visitor worked exclusively with households in which there were tuberculous patients.

[1] For example Ministry of Health circulars. Nos. 7/59, 26/59, 23/61.
[2] *Report of the Working Party on Social Workers in the Local Authority Health and Welfare Services.* H.M.S.O. 1959.

Each health visitor was allocated a district and her main duties were with children under five years. Rapid housing development called for frequent re-alignment of districts in some areas. Some health visitors, especially in the south of the county, had as many as 1,100 pre-school children in their districts. Others, mainly in the north, had only five or six hundred. The average number for the county was about 700.

In addition to work with pre-school children, health visitors acted as school nurses and, if necessary, visited the homes of school children in need of medical treatment. They also paid visits to expectant mothers to arrange ante-natal care and confinements. Some visited patients with tuberculosis and occasionally those who were chronically ill, and they would call on other people

Table 12

HEALTH VISITORS' WORKING WEEK BASED ON ESTIMATES
FROM 42 FULL-TIME HEALTH VISITORS

Activity	Average No. of hours	Average hours as percentage of total time	Range of hours recorded
Visits including travelling	23·5	55%	18·0–28·0
Clinics including school exams and ante-natal classes	7·0	16%	4·0– 9·0
Administrative clerical, telephoning, discussion, meeting with colleagues, superintendents, other social welfare personnel	11·5	27%	8·0–13·5
Reading books, circulars, bulletins, periodicals	1·0	2%	0·5–11·5
Total time	43·0	100%	38·5–51·5

if asked to make special enquiries by hospital staff, child care officers, general practitioners or others. They also worked in child welfare clinics where many undertook group teaching on various aspects of pregnancy, maternal health and child development for expectant mothers and for young parents. Some gave talks on health to secondary school children, and some spoke to mothers' clubs.

There were considerable differences between individual health visitors both in the total amount of time worked during a typical week and in the proportion of that time spent in home visits.

The estimates provided by 42 health visitors are summarised in Table 12. They indicate that, after allowing for travelling, roughly two-thirds of the health visitors' working hours was spent in contact with mothers and children or with patients.

Visits usually lasted about 20 minutes each; but about one in five was over 35 minutes and one in 20 took over an hour. The average time spent in travelling to the home, in writing a report of the visit subsequently and in taking any action arising out of the visit was rather less than 20 minutes. But about one in ten of the visits resulted in work which health visitors calculated took as much as one hour of their time in a week.

The health visitors' clients

Household composition

In 1961, Bucks health visitors visited mainly households where there were dependent children.[1] In 87 per cent of the households visited there was at least one dependent child, and in all but 2 per cent of these at least one of the children was of pre-school age. The visits were fairly evenly divided between households in which there were one, two and three or more children.[2]

Typically, the household visited consisted of a married couple and their dependent children. Occasionally, there was a lone older relative as well. Very few households consisted of a single parent with dependent offspring and in only one per cent were there foster children. Rather more common were households of two related families. These were usually ones in which the tenant or householder had a married son or daughter who as a result of shortage of housing accommodation was still living in the parental home. (See Table 13.)

[1] The survey was of the work of social welfare staff with individuals rather than groups. Health visitors only recorded details of those seen in home visiting and when mothers came to consult them outside normal clinic hours. Altogether, 46 health visitors provided information on 1,137 households visited.

[2] Of the households with dependent children, 36 per cent had one, 30 per cent two, 26 per cent three or four and 8 per cent five or more.

Elderly people formed only a small proportion of the clientele of health visitors. One in 20 of their visits were paid to people over 60 and only one in 50 of the households visited consisted of elderly people living alone. Some of their visits were to younger adults in poor health, and some to married couples expecting their first baby.

Housing and social circumstances

A rather larger proportion of the households visited by health visitors than of those seen by many other social welfare staff owned or were buying their own houses. Nevertheless, health visitors visited more households with some kind of housing problem than did most other workers.

The problem which affected most of those with housing difficulties was overcrowding. Rather more than a third of the households were living more than one person per room and as many as 7 per cent had three or more persons per room. It was comparatively common for health visitors to see those sharing the lavatory and bath with another household.

Another feature of the housing circumstances of those seen by health visitors was that they were often occupants of furnished or unfurnished rooms rented from private landlords, of tied cottages or of caravans.[1] They were also more often newcomers to the areas in which they were living.

These findings must not necessarily be taken to imply that health visitors were more likely to visit those families which had

---

[1] Comparative figures were as follows:

Persons per room	Households of clients of:	
	all social welfare workers	health visitors
1 or fewer	62%	81%
More than 1—less than 3	31%	16%
3 or more	7%	3%
	100%	100%

Comparative figures for housing		
Owner-occupation	34%	43%
Furnished rooms, tied cottage, caravan	9%	14%
Shared bath and lavatory	4%	7%
On housing list	6%	9%
In present residence less than 1 year	19%	39%

Table 13

COMPOSITION OF HOUSEHOLDS VISITED BY HEALTH VISITORS

Composition	Percentage of Households
Married couple only	7
One married couple plus dependent children	79
Married couple plus dependent children and other relatives	3
Two related married couples plus dependent children	6
Lone parent and dependent children	2
Lone individual aged 60 or over	2
Unrelated adults only	1
All households visited	100

housing difficulties than those which had not. They are more likely to mean that the brunt of the housing shortage tended to fall on young married couples with children of pre-school age.

Since there were married couples in most of the households visited by health visitors, the chief economic supporter was almost always a man. Only 4 per cent were headed by women and half of these were over the age of 65.

In most households, the chief economic supporter was the only earner in the household. Only 7 per cent of the housewives in the households visited by the health visitors were known to work—just over half of them on a full-time basis and the rest part-time.[1] In 6 per cent of the households, however, there was no current income from earnings. These were usually the households of retired men and women; but a few of those headed by young people were dependent upon national insurance sickness or unemployment benefits, national assistance or both.

Judged by the occupation of the male chief economic supporter, the households visited by health visitors were more often middle class and less often manual workers' households than the households seen by many other social welfare workers. Moreover, among manual workers' households, they visited more of those

[1] Recent surveys indicate that in many areas up to 20 per cent of married women with children under five work—mostly part-time—outside their homes. If this percentage held in Bucks, it implies that health visitors saw working mothers less frequently than non-working mothers.

headed by skilled than unskilled or semi-skilled workers.[1] These findings suggest that health visitors, unlike most other social welfare staff, visited a fairly representative social cross section.

Health and social problems

In 20 per cent of the households at least one individual suffered from either chronic physical disability, mental illness or sub-normality. Health visitors were more likely to record chronic conditions in housewives than in male chief economic supporters, and even more in other household members, that is, in elderly people or among children.

Since so many of their visits were to young married couples with young children, they saw much less chronic illness than district nurses or social workers from other branches of the health and welfare services. On the other hand, they saw more than policewomen, probation officers, school attendance officers, N.S.P.C.C. officers and moral welfare workers whose work was usually with socially deviant people.

In about two out of every three of the households health visitors were not aware of any difficulties serious enough to be categorised as social problems. Among the other third, about half were considered to have one problem and the remainder two or more. The average number of problems described was 2·3 per family, or very close to the average (2·2) for all social welfare personnel.

There were considerable differences between health visitors in the extent to which they reported problems. Eight of the 46 reported problems in less than 20 per cent of the households they visited, and three reported them in more than 80 per cent. There was a slight tendency for younger health visitors to report more problems than older ones, which could reflect the increased emphasis in training on social problems in recent years. Neither heavy nor light reporting of problems was confined to particular areas. Thus, there were no differences between those working in rural and urban areas, nor between the north and the south of

[1] Health visitors did not know the male chief economic supporter's occupation in 6 per cent of the cases and in another 4 per cent women headed the household. Amongst the remainder the distribution was as follows: Social Class I and II=20 per cent; III non-manual=11 per cent; III manual=42 per cent; IV and V=27 per cent. See figures for all clients. Appendix F. Table 48.

the county. Differences between health visitors could have been due to differences in the character of the households within health visitors' districts, or to differences in their perception of what constituted problems or to fortuitous sampling biases. Probably all three factors contributed to the individual differences.

The two categories of problem most frequently noted by health visitors were housing difficulties and personality problems. In both categories, 11 per cent of the households were considered to present such problems. No single other category of problem was recorded in more than one in 20 of the households, but all of the 21 specified categories of problem were recorded at least once.

Collectively, just under two-thirds of the problems could be described as problems arising from unsatisfactory social relationships or behaviour. The other third seemed basically due to material difficulties such as the housing situation, the lack of jobs suitable to an individual's mental or physical capacity or the practical domestic difficulties occasioned by the nature of an individual's disability. The distinction between the two types of problem, however, is not clear cut. Gross material difficulties can place unbearable strains on individuals and help to undermine their relationship with others. Equally, material difficulties can be the consequence of personal inadequacies of various kinds.

Some further light may be shed on health visitors' judgments as to the problems in the families they visited by comparing their accounts of some of the families with those of other social welfare staff who had visited the same families.[1]

In the majority of instances where the district nurse-midwife was the other visitor, neither worker was aware of any social problems in the household. The midwife had helped at a normal domiciliary confinement and the health visitor was paying her first visit soon after the baby's birth. Where problems were reported, however, it was the health visitors rather than the district nurse-midwives who recorded them.[2] The district nurses, pre-

[1] 78 of the households seen by health visitors had been seen by one other, 5 by two others, 3 by three other workers.
[2] In 24 of the 40 households seen by a health visitor and a district nurse, neither reported problems, in 3 the district nurse-midwife reported more difficulties, and in 3 they agreed on the nature of the difficulties. In 10 the health visitor reported more difficulties than the district nurse-midwife.

sumably because their training placed little or no emphasis on the social consequences of chronic illness or disability, were less likely to see social difficulties which arose from chronic illness or less likely if they did to describe them as problems with which an individual might require social assistance as well as nursing care. In general, it seemed that health visitors were more likely to be sensitive to the social difficulties of the chronically disabled and of those with difficult personalities than were the nurse-midwives.

There were also many differences in reporting problems when the health visitor reported on the same household as the staff of other branches of the social welfare services, but they were by no means so clear cut. It was usual for both the health visitor and the other worker to report several social problems.[1] If the other worker had had no social work training, however, it was relatively common to find that he or she and the health visitor reported different kinds of problem. The health visitor tended to report difficulties of parent-child or marital relationships, of aggressive or inadequate personalities and of sexual behaviour. The other worker reported housing difficulties or inadequate means or recorded school truancy.

When the other worker reporting as well as the health visitor had had some form of social work training, e.g. an almoner, psychiatric social worker, child care officer or probation officer, there was less disparity in the type of problem recorded. A slight tendency existed for the other worker to report rather more social problems in each household;[2] but, with a few exceptions, their reporting showed that the health visitor and the trained social worker had a similar picture of the household and approximately the same view of its problems and its needs. One or two examples may serve to illustrate the approach typical of health visitors and the attitudes which distinguished the social welfare worker without training in social work from the trained social worker.

---

[1] All but two of the 54 families visited by someone else as well as the health visitor were considered by one or other of the workers to have at least one problem. In five the health visitor did not record a social difficulty whereas the other worker did, and, alternatively, two other workers saw no difficulties where the health visitors did.

[2] Among 34 families health visitors recorded 106 problems and trained social workers reported 135.

The first example is of a family visited in the same week by a health visitor and an N.A.B. officer. The health visitor called to see the wife of a van driver with three children, the oldest of whom was an asthmatic boy of 16 and the second educationally subnormal. The wife's mother was also a member of the household. The health visitor described an extremely complicated situation in which unhappy marital and parent-child relationships were accompanied and aggravated by the problems of chronic illness, behaviour disorders and juvenile delinquency. In addition to all these difficulties, the inadequate wife was unable to care properly for her elderly mother who was sharing a room with the youngest child. The health visitor called to see whether arrangements could be made to admit the old lady to welfare accommodation in order to ease the strain on the overwrought wife. She described her purpose in visiting as one of talking to the old lady as well as helping the wife. As a result of the visit she also contacted the D.R.O. to enlist his help in obtaining suitable employment for the asthmatic boy, and the general practitioner to discuss his medical condition.

The officer who was visiting the elderly lady to see whether her financial circumstances were still the same, did not record any of the more general family difficulties. He indicated the problem of over-crowding in the home in addition to the problem of the old lady's inadequate income, but not those with which the family as a whole were confronted.

In another instance, the other visitor was a school attendance officer who visited the wife of a semi-skilled factory worker to find out why two of the children were not attending school. He found that the mother had recently had another baby and suspected that the oldest daughter had been kept at home to help with the housework and with the other five children. He described his reason for visiting as the need to inform the mother of her legal obligations. Apart from the problem of school absence, he recorded no social problems in the household.

The health visitor's visit to the house was made some three months earlier and followed the notification of the birth of the new baby, the mother's sixth. Although she had called only once before that year, the family had been known to her department since 1948 when the oldest child was born. The health visitor in her account of the family situation indicated that there were persistent problems of behaviour disorder in the older children and suggested that the mother's inadequate personality and low intelligence were factors both in these disorders and in the alleged sexual promiscuity of a 13-year-old daughter.

The comparability of approach of health visitors and trained social workers is illustrated by the example of a family seen by a health visitor and a child care officer within three months of each other. The health visitor reported that she had visited an unmarried mother aged 17 who had recently given birth to a coloured baby. The girl's own mother, who also had young children, was thought to be a prostitute, and the health visitor described the problems as those of the sexual behaviour of mother and daughter. She recorded the family's reception of her as 'hostile' and found 'it impossible to help this family'. She added that 'the police and children's department are watching the situation'. Her own role was confined to trying to ensure that the young mother gave adequate care to her baby. Nevertheless, she also visited to keep in touch with a family which she felt might well break down at any moment.

The child care officer's description of the family was similar but fuller. The father had recently been in gaol and had had several labouring jobs since his discharge. She thought all four girls of 17, 15, 12 and 8 were in moral danger, and family relationships, including those of husband and wife, disturbed. The question, as she saw it, was whether society could permit the parents to keep the children in such a home. The case of the older three girls was coming up to court, and she, the child care officer, had called (unsuccessfully, she thought), to persuade the mother to attend the hearing. She was trying to tell the mother what the court might propose and what she would have to do if she wanted to keep her family together. She did not indicate, as the health visitor had done, whether the family was hostile to her; but her narrative implied that she was not sanguine about the future of the family.

The Nature of the work

Nearly all the families seen by health visitors had originally been referred to them through the county health department office. The first visit occurred either when the health visitor was asked to call on an expectant mother to see whether she should be confined at home or in hospital, or when a baby's birth was notified. Only one in ten of those visited were referred initially from another source, which was almost always the general practitioner. Some of the mothers, however, had made the first approaches themselves.

A quarter of the households visited during the study period had been known to the health visitors for less than a month and 21 per cent of the calls were first visits. Altogether, just over half had been visited for less than one year. Most of those visited had been seen only once or twice in the year; but one per cent had been visited as frequently as once a week for a year or more, and a quarter at least monthly.

Most of the visits were undertaken on the initiative of the health visitors; but 5 per cent were initiated by either a general practitioner, hospital almoner, district nurse-midwife, children's officer or a neighbour, and 9 per cent by the individual to whom the visit was paid.

Generally speaking, visits were paid not because health visitors anticipated difficulties, but in order to see that all was well. Nearly 80 per cent were described as routine calls or friendly visits, although once there health visitors would often give advice on infant feeding or some other aspect of child-rearing practices. About half of these 'friendly' calls were routine visits soon after a baby's birth. Eleven per cent of the visits were made to discuss arrangements for an expectant mother's confinement, and 10 per cent to help a mother with some mental or emotional difficulty. From time to time, however, there was a specific problem of fostering or adoption, housing, domestic help or financial assistance to be considered.

In the event, in about a quarter of the visits, health visitors considered that no service of any kind was necessary; but in a third they gave instruction about some aspect of child-rearing and in a fifth advice about a definite health problem. They also considered that in about 12 per cent of their visits they had given mothers support or encouragement with an emotional problem. Only a small proportion of those visited received other kinds of help.

Contacts with other social welfare services

As a direct result of their visits, health visitors got in touch with other social welfare staff on behalf of 7 per cent of the families seen in the study period, but contact with others had been made sometime during the previous year in connection with a further 22 per cent of the households.

Most of the workers who referred families to health visitors were employed by a health service of one kind or another. Usually they were from other sections of the local health and welfare department or hospital almoners, but there were some referrals from G.P.'s.[1] The children's department, the education department, housing authorities, the N.A.B. and voluntary organisations also had each contacted health visitors in connection with one or two per cent of the families.[2]

When the health visitors initiated contacts, these were also more likely to be with the staff of the local authority health and welfare department than with other social welfare agencies.

Health visitors were often aware that other social welfare services were interested in the families they visited, but had no reason to make personal contact with them. This was particularly the case with G.P.'s and the maternity services. Home help organisers and other workers from the local authority health and welfare department too were known to have visited 18 per cent of the families without contacting the health visitors.

In most cases when health visitors knew that others were in touch with the families but not with them, there was no reason to consider that contact was really necessary. The families did not appear to present difficult or persistent problems. In some instances where no contact had been established, however, it seemed that everyone would have benefited if the two workers had been in touch with each other as well as with the family.

An instance of this kind involved a Jamaican couple. The man had worked for some years in London and had been joined more recently by his wife who had left four children behind when she

---

[1] 4 per cent of all families seen had been referred to G.P.'s sometime in the previous year.

[2] Neither probation officers nor police had referred any of the cases seen to health visitors. Health visitors contacted the probation department about 1 per cent.

came to join him. Shortly after her arrival they moved to Bucks, she became pregnant and he was discovered to have active pulmonary tuberculosis. The husband was admitted to hospital and his wife remained at home in the single furnished room in which they lived. There, shortly before the baby was due, at the request of a general practitioner, she was visited by a county almoner, who found that the expectant mother was shortly going to give up work and would need financial help. She was worried about both her husband and her children in Jamaica. As a result of the visit, the almoner contacted the N.A.B. and the minister of the local Baptist chapel and wrote to a London society dealing with the welfare of Jamaican families to enquire about the other children.

Three months later, the health visitor called at the house when she had been notified of the birth of the baby. She had first visited the mother several months earlier at the request of the consultant at the chest hospital and had been a weekly visitor to the house ever since. She laid more emphasis than the almoner on the unsatisfactory home conditions, pointing out that, in addition to the baby, the mother was looking after a 16-month-old child whose mother went out to work. The curtains were drawn and the electric light on when she called, although it was day time. The couple were not on the local authority list for rehousing and would be unlikely to find more suitable accommodation. As a result of her visit, she gave advice on infant care and contacted the N.A.B. and a local charitable organisation. She had not been in touch with the county almoner, nor did she indicate that she knew that the latter had visited the family.

The health visitors

Health visitors were, on average, rather younger than district nurse-midwives and rather more of them were married. In social terms, more of them had been brought up in middle class families and stayed at school beyond the minimum school leaving age.

Like the district nurses, most had entered the nursing profession before the age of 20, and by the age of 21, 39 out of the 46 were in one or other stage of nurse training.

Some of the older health visitors told us they went into nursing not so much, as one put it, 'as a matter of conscious choice, but for lack of other opportunities'. Two had the necessary qualifications to enter university but had been dissuaded from doing so by their parents.

The decision to specialise in health visiting was taken by the majority between the ages of 25 and 34; but a minority postponed the decision until their late thirties or early forties. Only one had already had health visiting in mind when taking up nursing. 'My parents lived for social work and I grew up in the atmosphere', she told us.

Many chose health visiting because they did not like institutional life. As one health visitor put it, 'I went into it to escape the rut of hospital life'. Nearly half the Bucks health visitors, however, did not go straight from work in a hospital ward to health visiting. For 21 of them district nursing and/or midwifery was an intermediary stage between hospital nursing and health visiting, and some had done private nursing. They usually left district nursing for health visiting either 'because the hours are shorter and you're not so tied', or because they wanted to help prevent some of the illness or unhappiness which they saw as district nurses. They felt that the answer lay in health visiting and went in hoping to assist mothers to bring up healthy, well-adjusted children who would not need medical and nursing care.

The training courses

Thirty-seven of the health visitors had taken courses at one or other of the London centres for health visitor training, that is, at the Royal College of Nursing, the Institute of Education or the Battersea Polytechnic. Half had taken the course between the end of the war and 1954: the other half were equally divided between those who had trained before or during the war and those who had trained since 1955.

With the hindsight gained from experience, two-thirds felt that their course has been good in providing them with a necessary understanding of mental health, social and psychological problems. A third were not enthusiastic, and of these the majority considered that the teaching was inadequate.

The most critical were those who had completed their courses before the end of the war.[1] There have been substantial changes in the syllabus for health visitor training in the last decade in the direction of increasing the teaching of psychology and social factors in the emotional development of children. These changes have clearly been appreciated by those who have taken the course recently. Nevertheless, six recently trained health visitors felt that practical work placements during training had been unsatisfactory and three complained of inadequate training in teaching methods both for adult groups and for health education in schools. Indeed, these criticisms came more frequently from recently qualified health visitors than from those who trained earlier.

Health visitors as a group were more conscious of the need to extend their knowledge and keep in touch with new developments in their field of work through refresher courses, than the staff of other social services. Some did not specify the particular subjects they would like to study in refresher courses; but 19 made suggestions, and among these the most frequent were for courses in mental health, geriatric problems, the principles of social casework and health education methods and teaching practices.

Health visitors' views on their jobs

Thirty-five of the 46 health visitors, or rather over three-quarters of them, told us that they were glad they had come into health visiting and, on the whole, found their work satisfying and absorbing. However critical they might be, they felt there were positive rewards in their chosen career.

Most of the conscious satisfactions arose from the opportunity to understand and help other people. A number talked about the pleasure they had in seeing the results of their work or in being thanked for their services; but most said that they liked working in a job where they could help others and which was valuable to the community.

One health visitor refused to say that there were any drawbacks to her job. She was working in a small well-to-do country town and its rural outskirts, and had been there for eight years. 'I love the work,' she told us. 'I enjoy it from getting up in the morning

[1] Four of the 11 trained before the end of the war felt that they had been poorly prepared and one had mixed feelings. None of the 11 who trained since 1955 felt it was poor and only two had mixed feelings.

until going to bed at night. I think I'm the right type for my area. I'm very happy with the type of community I'm in. I'm in a rut and I love it.' She was, however, unique in finding nothing to complain about.

Compared to district nurse-midwives comparatively few health visitors stressed the advantages of living in the community rather than in hospital—presumably because many of them had come to health visiting by way of district nursing or midwifery and not direct from hospital life. Again, compared with district nurses, few emphasised the variety of their work, the independence of judgment they could exercise in its performance, the security of employment or their standing and prestige in the community at large. It seemed, therefore, that the satisfaction most health visitors derived from their work came first from the feeling that they were contributing to a worthwhile aim—the prevention of ill-health and emotional disturbances—and secondly, from the opportunities afforded to get to know and understand people.

Although the majority expressed general satisfaction, there was comparatively a larger minority of dissatisfied people in health visiting than in district nursing or in various kinds of trained social work. In contrast to the latter groups, almost all of whom said that they would choose the same profession again if given the chance, 22 health visitors said they would choose something else. Six of these would have chosen another branch of nursing itself, eight would have gone into social work, four would have become teachers and two doctors.

Some complaints were made by health visitors with about the same frequency as they were by almoners and other trained social workers. Thus, between one in five or one in six of all three groups complained about the burden of clerical and administrative duties which they had to undertake and felt they should be provided with adequate secretarial assistance. Similarly, about three out of ten of each of the groups bemoaned large case-loads and their inability to devote sufficient time to families who needed more of their help. For example, one health visitor said, 'I've hardly any time to visit at all the families who I know could be helped by frequent visits'. Another said that 'Just scratching on the surface you cannot do justice to the job'. Compared with district nurses or workers with no social work training, few health visitors as well as trained social workers felt that ungrateful patients, the inability to see results or apparent failure with some cases were major drawbacks to their work.

In some respects, health visitors as a group complained less frequently than other groups. For example, one in seven health visitors expressed dissatisfaction with pay or some aspects of the conditions of service which, if anything, was a rather smaller proportion than from other groups of social welfare workers. Only one in five talked about red tape, criticised the way in which their work was controlled or supervised or complained of lack of support from superiors. This compared with one in three of the trained social workers and a similar proportion of those with no social work training. Health visitors were also less likely to express frustration with the lack of facilities available for their clients than either social workers or district nurses, largely because the frustrations of the latter so often centred around meagre provisions for the elderly and chronic sick who formed only a small proportion of health visitors' caseloads. And, unlike many district nurses and some other social welfare staff, only one health visitor complained of the difficulty of escaping from work and achieving a life outside it.

In three important ways, however, clearly related to each other, health visitors' dissatisfactions significantly exceeded those expressed by any other group of workers interviewed. The first was the inability to use in practice the techniques and knowledge acquired during training; seven health visitors made such a complaint compared with six workers in the rest of the study. One health visitor said 'my imagination was fired by the health visitor course, particularly by the sociological approach. Unfortunately, the work in the field does not allow me to practice what I learned. It has not matched my ideas or aspirations'. Another commented, 'I think my training was wasted. A good deal of the work I do doesn't need such a lengthy training'.

Secondly, seven health visitors compared with only five in all the remaining services put together, complained that their job was not clearly enough defined. One, who had changed from district nursing to health visiting because she wanted to work more regular hours and not feel so tied, felt she preferred district nursing because 'the job is more clearly defined. You know what

D

you're supposed to be doing and so does everyone else'. By implication, she did not feel confident that either she or other people knew what the functions of the health visitor were. Another health visitor said, 'I do a bit here and a bit there, but never do anything really properly. I used to have bad dreams about not finishing anything'. A third said, 'It's too ill-defined. Whenever a problem crops up it must be transferred elsewhere'; and another commented, 'There's a lack of definition in the job. We're all things to all men. We're not regarded as social workers as such, yet we deal with all kinds of social problems'. A fifth said, 'The job has widened and increased in scope in recent years. Something must go to make way for all the new duties, but no one will decide what'. And yet another, expressing her uneasiness, said, 'We just dabble'.

To the feeling that the functions of the health visitor were ill-defined was added the belief that some of the tasks they were being asked to do were valueless. Three out of 10 described one or other of their duties as useless, and one in six went as far as to suggest that the county health visiting service was run on mistaken lines.

There was not complete unanimity, however, among those who were critical. One or two felt that too much emphasis was placed upon mental health to the detriment of the primary function of health visiting—preventing neglect of the child's physical needs. One suggested, 'We sometimes go so deeply into the psychiatric causes that we fail to see the commonsense and practical causes of ill-health'. These were comparatively isolated voices, however, and most of the criticism was levelled at the routine hygiene examination of school children, the handing out of welfare foods and routine home visiting of families with children under five.

In so far as school health inspections went, one health visitor said, 'You don't do six years' training just to look for nits', and a second also confessed that she resented this 'menial' aspect of her job. She thought it made her into more of a policewoman than a health visitor. 'The children call me "nitty lizzie" behind my back, I know they do', she told us. One of the causes of the resentment in connection with welfare foods was that making arrangements to order and hand it out at the clinics 'entails a lot of work'.

Those who complained of 'unnecessary' work in this connection, however, were also of the opinion that the service itself was no longer of value. 'I'd much rather give that cheap milk to the old people. They don't get anything', one health visitor suggested.

Criticism of even minimum routine home visiting to mothers with babies came from health visitors all over the county. Some argued that it was clear that some mothers would not require a health visitor's assistance, e.g. doctors' wives, and that all visits to them were a waste of time. One of the health visitors who suggested cutting down severely on visits to more well-to-do families, said, 'We can let them know where to find us if they need help'. She felt that this would also reduce hostility, because some families resented the health visitor's call, interpreting it as 'interference'. Another echoed her when she said, 'A health visitor is not necessarily welcome and when this is the case we're not likely to be very effective either'.

Implicitly or explicitly those who complained of the lack of opportunity to use skills and insights gained in training, of the lack of definition in the job or of valueless tasks felt that more of the health visitors' time should be devoted to work with families who did display social and psychological problems, to organised health teaching in schools or in classes for parents and to being available to give advice on children's feeding or behaviour if it was sought. 'A great deal of lip service is paid to the preventive aspects of mental health', said one health visitor, 'but very little is actually done. A superfluity of trivial little duties prevents one from getting on with the main job'.

Concern with status

Uncertainty about the content of the work and the contribution it was making to the welfare of mothers and children seemed to lie behind the concern displayed by some health visitors about their status in the community and their relationships with the staff of other branches of the social services and especially with doctors. Health visitors were not alone in expressing concern about such matters; some trained social workers, and especially hospital almoners, also expressed much resentment at the lack of recognition of the value of their services on the part of some specialists. However, few of the latter and none of the district nurses made the kind of sweeping statement about their status which was expressed by six of the 46 health visitors.

For example, one health visitor, who had two sisters who were teachers, one a graduate and the other emergency trained, said, 'Both spent less time in training than I did, but their status in the community is much higher than mine. Nursing is regarded by many people as only a glorified form of domestic service'. Another said, 'most people think one is an odd bod, who is doing the work more or less voluntarily. They don't realise you're highly qualified'. And a third complained of the 'lack of status, despite the lengthy training—and status does matter to me. I feel strongly about this'.

For some, however, the bitterest pill was the lack of respect shown for their work by general practitioners. One told us that she had left district nursing because she felt that it was too limited a career and wanted work which would call for more thought and initiative. To her astonishment, she found that her services as a health visitor were not highly valued by the local G.P.'s. She noticed a big change in their attitude to her as a health visitor compared to when she was a district nurse. Another complained that doctors only had a use for nurses as long as they acted as handmaids. As soon as a nurse tried to make an independent contribution, her services were ignored or belittled.[1]

Comments and criticisms such as these suggest that there were many health visitors with lively and critical minds seeking to improve their service to the community. They also suggest, however, that a substantial minority, that is, about one in four, were extremely frustrated, disillusioned and indeed doubtful about the value of health visiting or their own future in it. Some of the comments made by this minority will serve to illustrate this discontent.

'I really doubt the value of health visiting as it is at present', said one health visitor, 'and feel that I would have been more useful if I had stayed in hospital nursing'. Another said, 'I doubt whether I made a wise decision to move out of practical nursing'.

'Many of us feel very frustrated', said yet another. 'In recent years we have been going round in small circles. We need fresh

[1] Further evidence of the considerable strain in the relationship between doctors and health visitors is discussed in Chapter IX.

air and more stimulation from headquarters.' A fourth made a somewhat similar comment. 'There's a lack of opportunity to extend one's activities and widen one's professional horizons.' Finally, one health visitor who had given a good deal of thought to the issues which she wanted to discuss with the research team told us, 'Health visiting as a profession is missing the boat altogether and falling between all manner of stools. It would have been much better if most health visitors were still bedside nursing except for a minority who should become either social workers and have the training recommended by the Younghusband Working Party, or specialists in health teaching in which case they should take a course like that provided by the Institute of Education'. She added, 'At present, we're not giving the public a good service. The question is how to change it. I'll be grateful if the survey shows us a way out'.

Some conclusions

In Bucks in 1960–61 health visitors were predominantly engaged in their traditional work of visiting mothers with children of pre-school age and in making recommendations for the ante-natal care and confinement of expectant mothers. Only one visit in 20 was to a household where there was a person of retirement age. Only to a limited extent, therefore, had there been any extension in the type of household which they visited compared with the situation before the National Health Service came into being.

Most of the health visitors' calls were to mothers who were not facing difficulties serious enough to warrant being called social problems. However, health visitors, especially those who trained most recently, were aware of social problems among a considerable minority of the families they visited. In some such instances, they did little more than maintain a 'watching brief'; but usually they tried to give emotional support and mobilise help from other community resources.

As a group, health visitors seemed more aware of the social problems families may encounter than district nurses. They also emphasised personality difficulties more than workers who had had no form of social worker training and deficiencies of the physical environment more than workers with a social work training.

Morale among a sizeable minority of health visitors was not high. Satisfactions derived from feeling that the work helped individuals and was of value to the community; but many felt that their contribution was not given the recognition it deserved by general practitioners or the community at large. Some expressed doubts about the value of their work, felt their functions were ill-defined and believed much of their lengthy training had been wasted.

When a service with as long and honourable a history as that of health visiting is under scrutiny, a reluctance to suggest drastic changes is justifiable. Evidence that the present situation is unsatisfactory must be overwhelming before wholesale changes—which may or may not be remedies—can be introduced. Moreover policies cannot be abandoned simply because those who carry them out are unhappy or because the community at large does not show much appreciation of them; and health visitors need not feel that because many general practitioners under-value the importance of providing mothers with advice and support on infant feeding and a variety of difficulties, real or imagined, encountered in the child's first years of life, this is the definitive judgment on their work. It may be, rather, a judgment on the doctors themselves.

Nevertheless, the survey team felt that a radical reorganisation of health visiting in Bucks was needed in order to provide both a more clearly defined and better service to the community and a more satisfactory career for those undertaking it.

Many of the tasks the health visitors were asked to do at the time of the study were either too simple or too complicated for someone with their training and they should be relieved of them. It does not, for example, require a nurse's training or a health visitor's course to see whether children's heads are clean. On the other hand, the health visitor's training is not sufficient for her to be able to give individuals of all ages and conditions who are emotionally disturbed, mentally ill or thoroughly inadequate and their families the help they need.[1] If it were clear that health visitors would not be responsible for tasks of either of these two kinds, some of their feeling of frustration would go.[2]

[1] It was significant that nearly all the families of this kind being seen by health visitors were also being visited by other social welfare personnel.

[2] It is not possible or desirable to eliminate all simple routine tasks from the work schedules of even the most highly trained administrative and professional staff.

Secondly, I believe there is and will always be a need for an expert to advise mothers on an individual basis about difficulties encountered in bringing up their children, especially during the first years of life. Most mothers need to discuss their problems from time to time, not only with their informal sources of help—their own mothers and sisters, for example, or their more experienced friends—but with someone who has a sounder and wider range of knowledge and experience in all aspects of child rearing, from dealing with infant feeding difficulties and minor ailments, to toilet training and manifestations of sibling rivalry. Sometimes, mothers may require little assistance of this kind from the community services, but in other cases, because they are isolated from kin, have a rather limited intelligence or for other reasons, they may require a good deal of support. The present training of health visitors, although it may require modification, is basically appropriate to meet these needs.

This kind of service to individual mothers, however, should be given by someone who is working closely with the family's general practitioner, who is likely to be consulted on both the major and minor ailments of the early years of life. It is essential to ensure that his activities and those of the health visitor neither duplicate nor conflict but are integrated and complementary. This can best be achieved if health visitors are given responsibilities for patients registered with certain general practitioners, rather than for those living in a defined area.

Such a scheme has many advantages. It provides a more formal organisational framework for collaboration between the general practitioner and the health visitor which should make it easier for the two to work together by helping to break down residual suspicions and hostilities. In this way it can restore to the health visitor her feeling that the doctor considers her work important. It enhances her status in the eyes of the general public. It also gives those doctors who at present have little interest in preventive medicine an opportunity to learn what health visitors can achieve in promoting health and handling illness in its early stages. Again, the health visitor's knowledge of the social services and community resources can be used to mobilise help for patients whose illnesses or disabilities have led to financial or social difficulties.

Difficulties may arise in operating this scheme. For example, the health visitor may become isolated from her own professional colleagues and from an important source of new ideas about child-rearing and development. She may find herself under pressure, from a general practitioner who is not interested in preventive medicine, to undertake other work for him—for example, keeping his records up to date or acting as a receptionist during busy surgeries. Moreover, difficulties may occur when members of the same family register with different doctors.[1] In my view, however, it should be possible to spot difficulties of this kind.

There is one weakness in health visiting today, however, which cannot be overcome by such an arrangement. When a nurse becomes a health visitor, she abandons bedside nursing and nursing supervision, and many of the skills which have taken years to learn. At a time of acute shortage of nurses, she loses the respect of many doctors who believe that to do preventive and educative work only is a waste of a skilled nurse's training. She may also lose some self-respect, and question her own motives for abandoning work more physically exacting and, as at present organised, requiring greater personal sacrifices. However intellectually convinced she may be of the value of her educative work, her confidence can recede, especially when she does not receive so many clear indications of gratitude as she did when she was nursing the sick or delivering beloved offspring.

In this connection it was noticeable that those who combined health visiting with district nursing and midwifery seemed both happier themselves and more highly valued by the general practitioners than those who were solely health visitors.

Health visitors, therefore, while maintaining their primary function in preventive rather than curative medicine, should retain a recognisable nursing function. This might best be arrived at by giving health visitors responsibility for supervising the home nursing of patients in a doctor's practice. Much domiciliary nursing is routine and does not require the skills of a state registered nurse; but someone with a full nurse's training should be available to determine with the doctor what nursing and social care are needed. The health visitor's training should fit her particularly well for such a role.

[1] Cf. Allister and McPhail, *Lancet*, 63, ii.

Some of the weaknesses inherent in the organisation and functions of the health visiting service at the time of the survey would probably be removed if the comparatively simple step were taken of basing health visitors' work on doctors' lists rather than on geographical areas.[1] Ideally, however, more radical changes are needed in the deployment of medical, nursing and social work skills in the domiciliary health services and these are discussed in Chapter XX.

[1] Since the survey, health visitors in several areas of Bucks as well as elsewhere, have been responsible for visiting children registered with particular general practitioners and not those resident in a particular area. The change appears to have been welcomed by both doctors and health visitors.

D*

CHAPTER VII

The District Nursing and Midwifery Service

In Bucks, district nursing and domiciliary midwifery were combined. Of the 125 full-time staff, 92 undertook district nursing and midwifery duties and 17 acted as health visitors as well. Nine, including two men, had nursing duties only and six were midwives without nursing duties. Half the 25 part-time staff were nursing only.

In his Annual Report for 1961, the County Medical Officer of Health drew attention to difficulties of staff recruitment. There were then vacancies which had been advertised without success for six nurse-midwives, for one nurse-midwife-health visitor for combined duties in the north of the county, for three relief staff and for an assistant superintendent. These staff shortages occurred against the background of an increasing population of elderly people and of women in the child-bearing years. The consequent pressure of work was bound to affect the services which district nurses could give to both their elderly patients and the mothers they delivered.

The first priority of the home nursing and midwifery service was to maintain and improve professional standards of bedside nursing and midwifery—a particularly difficult task when staff is short and under pressure. However, those responsible for the service believed that the district nursing staff were well placed to observe social problems which might accompany chronic illness or occur in homes where women were delivered, and to alert other social welfare staff if they themselves could not help. District nurses, consequently, were included in the survey.[1]

The district nurse-midwives' patients

Half the patients seen by the district nurse-midwives during the recording period were over 60 and nearly 40 per cent between 20 and 44. In the areas where the district nurses were also health visitors these proportions were reversed. In all areas, dependent

---

[1] 119 full-time workers were interviewed. 109 of them provided records relating to 2,570 patients.

children were rarely patients; but between 10 and 14 per cent were people of 45 to 59.

Most of the young women were booked for home deliveries and were not suffering from chronic illnesses or disability; but there was a great deal of such illness among the district nurses' elderly patients, many of them having multiple diagnoses. Every third individual in the over 60 group had a heart or circulatory disease, one in six had rheumatic disorders, and approximately the same number were suffering from the after effects of a stroke or a diseases of the nervous system. Roughly equal numbers, that is, about one in twelve, had chronic respiratory conditions, diabetes, disease of the digestive system or senile confusional states. One in 15 being nursed had a malignant tumour, and one in 20 had lost either sight or hearing or both.

About one in four of the district nurses' elderly patients were living alone and about double that number were living with their spouse only. The other quarter were either living with younger relatives or unrelated persons. Few of them were in over-crowded dwellings; but many, especially in the rural north, were in houses which lacked domestic amenities.[1]

Measures of social class based on the occupations of chief economic supporters of households are particularly unsatisfactory when the population consists of elderly women. A better indication of the social standing of district nurses' patients was the level of formal schooling which the nurses considered their patients had had. Four out of five had left school at the minimum school leaving age, a proportion roughly comparable to that found among clients of other social welfare staff.

The district nurse and social problems

Since district nurses were visiting either to provide nursing care or a midwife's help and not in the first instance to deal with some social problem or difficulty, it was not surprising that they were much less likely to report social difficulties than were workers whose main reason for visiting a household was to give help or

[1] For example, 17 per cent of the households of district nurse-midwife-health visitors' patients had no water closet and 29 per cent had no bath, compared with 8 per cent and 15 per cent respectively of the households visited by all other social welfare personnel.

advice with a social or psychological difficulty. In only 30 per cent of the households which the district nurses visited did they report a social difficulty of any kind, whereas social welfare personnel (other than health visitors) reported problems in 87 per cent of their clients' households. Health visitors were the only other group of workers who reported households with problems about as frequently as district nurses.

There are obvious reasons why many households visited by domiciliary midwives should not be expected to present social problems. Pregnancy is not a pathological state, and normal childbirth, when the child is desired, has a welcome and happy outcome. Indeed, since serious housing difficulties or other obvious social or psychological difficulties are usually taken as important indications for *hospital* confinement, the domiciliary midwife is likely to deliver mainly those mothers who live in households where such difficulties are not apparent.

On the other hand, in her other capacity of nurse, the district nurse-midwife was dealing with elderly people and with chronic illness, and as a result was likely to visit more households where incomes were small and derived almost entirely from pensions and assistance grants than staff of other social welfare services. Moreover, the district nurse was more likely to visit her patients at frequent intervals than any other group of workers, and would, therefore, have had greater opportunities to get to know about difficulties.[1] A comparison of their reports with those of other workers who visited the same households during the survey[2] suggested, however, that they were less likely to perceive social difficulties than most other visitors.[3]

Most cases in which there were considerable discrepancies between the district nurses' views of patients' difficulties and those of other workers were elderly people. In one case, for example, an occupational therapist and district nurse were both

[1] A third of the nurses' patients had been on their books for over a year, and nearly all of these were being visited at least once a week. No fewer than 45 per cent were seen at least twice weekly and 13 per cent (including maternity patients) had been seen once daily or even more frequently.

[2] 146 households seen by district nurses were reported on by 153 other social welfare workers.

[3] Only home help organisers reported fewer social problems than district nurses in households seen by both.

visiting an arthritic old lady of 75 who had led an extremely active life and had only recently lost her husband. The occupational therapist described the woman as suffering from the loss of her husband, loneliness and boredom. 'I visit,' she wrote, 'to show her how her old skills and new ones she has since learnt can be adapted to her disability'. The therapist had been in touch with the woman's general practitioner and knew she was being visited by the district nurse and taken out occasionally to an Old Folk's Club. She also knew something of the old lady's financial circumstances.

The district nurse, on the other hand, wrote she was visiting to give the old lady nursing care, but did not report social difficulties.

There were also some households of younger patients where district nurses reported few if any difficulties where other workers saw many. One such instance concerned a widow with an adolescent daughter and two sons. The district nurse called to do dressings, but felt she gave the woman, who had cancer, emotional support in her long drawn out ordeal. She did not mention other difficulties in the family.

A policewoman and a child care officer were the other reporters. They were concerned with the 15-year-old daughter who had been picked up by the police late one night and, on examination, was found to be pregnant. The putative father was barely older than the 15-year-old girl. The policewoman had referred the case to the child care officer who arranged with a moral welfare worker for the girl's confinement, and was working to reconcile mother and daughter. This situation, which had developed by the time the district nurse reported her cases, seemed unknown to the district nurse despite her frequent visits and her sympathy for the mother's own plight.[1]

In a few cases, the district nurse seemed more aware of difficulties than the other worker. One such case concerned a mother with eight children, the youngest not yet a year old. The district

[1] The child care officer gave the fullest description of the situation. 'Girl desperately in need of attention and affection, receiving little support during adolescence. Mother unable to look after girl because of physical handicaps. Mother unwilling to accept child back with girl after confinement.' The object of her visit was 'to discuss with client and mother arrangements for the stay in Putnam House and to help them to understand their own feelings towards each other and towards the putative father'.

nurse thought there was friction between husband and wife, the wife often threatening to leave home, and the husband not able to keep a job for long. The children had free milk and school meals and the oldest boy of 11 had been in trouble with the police. The wife was in poor health through frequent child-bearing and was unable to get help from relatives in London.

A hospital almoner saw the mother two months later when she booked a maternity bed for her ninth confinement. She reported only that the patient was 'anxious about the care of her children during her confinement. Husband unable to take time off work as he has only just moved to this job and all their relatives are in London'.

In this instance, the district nurse seemed to have more awareness of the complex family situation than the almoner, perhaps because she had seen the mother several times and always at home, whereas the almoner was seeing the mother for the first time and in hospital. The case shows that opportunities to get to

Table 14

COMPARISONS BETWEEN THE WORK OF DISTRICT NURSE-MIDWIVES, DISTRICT NURSE-MIDWIFE-HEALTH VISITORS AND HEALTH VISITORS

Bases of comparison	District Nurse-Midwives	Nurse-Midwife-Health Visitors	Health Visitors
Cases with one or more problems reported	27%	40%	36%
Cases with three or more problems reported	4%	13%	11%
Average number of problems per case (when at least one problem)	1·6	2·3	2·3
Total no. of cases seen	2,152	418	1,137
No. of workers in group	90	17	46

know families in their home surroundings were sometimes used by district nurses to draw a fuller picture of the family than a trained social worker could if the time spent with the patient was limited and the interview took place outside the home.

In this case it was noteworthy that the district nurse had a health visitor training and comparing *all* district nurse-health visitors' cases with all those visited by district nurses without health visitors' qualifications, it was apparent that the former reported more social problems. This is indicated by figures in Table 14. Their additional reporting was not confined to any one type of social difficulty. They were more likely to report problems of housing, inadequate means, adjustment to disability, loneliness, child behaviour, disturbed marital or other family relationships and personality than their colleagues with no health visitor training. It seemed legitimate to conclude, therefore, that the differences between district nurses and others was related in some way to their past experience and training or to the kind of person they were.

The district nurse-midwives, their social background and training

The age structure of the district nursing service was very similar to that of the health visiting service and of all social welfare staff, that is, just under half were over 45. The proportion nearing 60 and due to retire was rather greater among nurses than among health visitors (16 per cent compared with 11 per cent). Like other services staffed mainly or entirely by women, too, district nursing relied over-whelmingly on single people. Over three-quarters of the staff were unmarried and a further 6 per cent who were widowed, separated or divorced were living as single people.[1]

Only four of the married women working full-time had dependent children. Full-time district nursing, in short, was rarely combined with child-rearing; but this was no less true for women in other social welfare fields.

District nurses were more likely to be from families of manual workers and to have left school at the minimum school leaving age than health visitors and the women staff of other services, with the exception of home help organisers and wardens of old people's settlements.[2] The differences between district nurses and health visitors seems to imply that choice of career within nursing is partly determined by early social and educational influences.

---

[1] The team did not interview part-time staff, however, and 20 of these were married women.   [2] See ante. Table 4 and 5.

Clues as to how these influences may work were contained in the responses of those interviewed to questions about their careers.

For example, a number of older district nurses said they would have liked to go into health visiting, which they felt would be less physically tiring, but had been deterred by having to undergo more training. It may be that those with longer schooling early in life and more experience of formal examinations are more able to tackle new courses in their middle years than those who lack this experience.

Secondly, many district nurses, talking about their jobs, emphasised the satisfaction from 'practical work'. They enjoyed working with their hands. It is possible that those brought up in middle class homes find it less easy to be entirely satisfied by practical nursing and midwifery, and are more likely to look for careers which involve less manual work which, in our society, tends to carry less social prestige than so-called 'brain work'.

Most district nurses made their choice of profession early in life. By the age of 21, two-thirds of them had begun a career in nursing.

By far the most frequent reason given for wanting to nurse was the desire to help sick people.[1] Some entering later did so because they found office jobs dull and felt nursing would be more worthwhile. The decision to go 'on the district' was usually taken within five years of becoming a fully qualified nurse, that is, an S.R.N. It was taken generally for several reasons, the most common being the desire to leave the communal life of the nurse's home and the restricted hospital environment, the opportunity to learn more about patients and their families in their own homes, the wish for greater independence and the need to provide a home for ageing parents.

Satisfactions and dissatisfactions

Nearly all district nurses felt they had made the right choice of career and, if called upon to start work once more, would do

[1] For some people, however, nursing offered the only way out of a difficult home situation. An older nurse, for example, was only allowed to leave home, where she was unhappy with her stepmother, because her father felt she would be 'safe' living in a nurse's home. Another had only achieved her ambition of going to London from Ireland by becoming a student nurse.

the same work again. Ten per cent expressed some doubts, but there were none who wholly regretted their choice.

Satisfactions were often expressed by enumerating the advantages of district over hospital nursing and midwifery. One put it, 'district nursing means nursing the patient rather than the disease'. Two who liked domiciliary midwifery particularly, said their rewards were, 'being able to give individual attention to patients in their own home', and 'seeing the case through and meeting the rest of the family'. Another liked 'belonging to the village' and another 'not living in a home with a lot of other women. I can have a full personal life'. One midwife said 'No one chivies me about. I'm my own boss. I couldn't stand all that silly red tape of hospital now', and another, 'I'm left to get on without someone breathing down my neck. I'm a bit of an individualist and I like a responsible job'.

Despite their general satisfaction, 92 per cent of the nurses felt their jobs had at least one or two drawbacks, the major ones centering round the work schedule.[1] Six out of every 10 nurses complained of the hours they had to work or be 'on call', which seemed unavoidable. As one nurse-health visitor put it, 'It's 24 hours a day, six days a week. But I can't see how else it can be done, especially as I'm not awfully keen on other people doing my cases'. She and others making the same complaint were at pains to point out that they considered themselves 'well looked after in Bucks'. Those who were approaching retiring age seemed to find the working hours most onerous. One, who hated losing a night's sleep on a maternity case, said, 'I've become a proper old stick-in-the-mud. It must be old age creeping on'. Many nurses found record-keeping tedious. Some of these admitted 'form-filling' was necessary; but many complained that much of it was not essential. One nurse remarked, 'Nursing is becoming almost a sideline. It's pushed aside while one does a lot of unnecessary paper work'.

Some complaints were about pay and status. Nurses who had joined the service late in life, after holding responsible posts in other branches of the service, felt they had been penalised for making the change. As one nurse put it, 'I resent each time I take

---

[1] Dissatisfaction with working hours was voiced more commonly among district nurses than among other workers.

a new qualification having to drop salary for the training and then having to start at the bottom of the scale'. She and others felt more allowance should be given for experience and training elsewhere.

Others complained that, though they had had substantial salary increases these had not kept their incomes above those of women in work requiring much less skill and training. One said, 'I can't help comparing the pay with that of shop girls'. Another felt that low salaries had affected the district nurse's status in the community: 'People don't realise how well-trained we are. I'm not snobbish but the only way I can put it is that our status is not recognised'.

Some nurses made criticisms of other branches of the social services, and most commonly of hospitals. They were not always informed of the treatment needed for a discharged patient or given supplies of special dressings 'to tide a patient over'. Many midwives also resented having to look after mothers and babies discharged from hospital within a few days of the delivery. They missed the very special satisfaction of helping to bring a wanted baby into the world.

There were many complaints of the shortage of home helps, especially at weekends and on public holidays, which increased their own work. One prepared meals and cleaned on Christmas Day for old people who were living quite alone. Another felt that much of the care she gave old people such as washing, shampooing hair and nail cutting did not require a trained nurse. She described herself as a 'mobile crane' and her training as largely unnecessary for the jobs she did.

Health visitors, too, came in for criticism from some nurses. One potential point of conflict was the health visitors' duty to interview expectant mothers to see whether they needed hospital confinement on social grounds. 'The midwife should have more say in deciding whether or not a patient goes into hospital for her baby.' One asked rhetorically, 'Why do they make so much of health visitors today?', and went on to say, 'Health education is important, but today it's carried to extreme lengths. The cult of the health visitor increases the shortage of district nurses'. Tension was not confined entirely, however, to relations with staff of other services. Nurses who were either not midwives or had not a

Queen's Institute of District Nursing training complained of social discrimination by their colleagues with these qualifications.

It was noticeable that a larger proportion of district nurses than of health visitors or trained social workers said they found patients' lack of gratitude or tendency to take things for granted a major drawback in their work. Fifteen per cent of the nurses felt that some of their patients made the work less pleasant than it should have been, and a few made sweeping generalisations about all their patients. One nurse expressed a commonly held view: 'The welfare state is superb, but I sometimes feel people are given too much. They come to your door for the slightest service. They expect too much because they're given too much'.

The training of district nurses in the social aspects of home nursing

Most nurses were satisfied with the teaching they had had on social aspects of their work in the Queen's Institute of District Nursing training course, many because they felt that a nurse should not be concerned with anything beyond the immediate nursing task, but others because they thought their courses had dealt adequately with the social and psychological problems they met in their day-to-day work. Only 12 of the 81 who had a Queen's qualification but no health visitor's certificate were critical of the course, usually on the grounds that mental health problems were inadequately dealt with.[1] Those who had taken the health visitor's certificate after the Queen's training were all critical of the latter, as were many full-time health visitors who had previously done district nursing.

The records completed by district nurses during the survey period indicated that training had not made many of them aware of the complexity of social and psychological difficulties which elderly and chronically ill patients may face. Nor had it helped some to bear with the ingratitude of some patients. Assuming it is desirable that nurses and midwives should be more aware of difficulties and better prepared to tolerate 'awkward' patients, what needs to be done?

The most obvious suggestion is to make these social and psycho-

---

[1] Nineteen of the 118 district nursing staff had neither the Queen's Institute nor health visitor's certificate.

ogical aspects of the work the subject of the week-long refresher courses held once a year in the county.

The formal lecture to a large audience is not the best way to try to teach problems of human relations, however, particularly in this field, where its value is probably slight. A method likely to have greater value is the small group, meeting regularly with an experienced tutor to guide discussion, which should centre around cases met in the normal course of work.[1] If the county were to appoint an experienced tutor in social work, as recommended in Chapter XX, he or she would be able to lead such group work or arrange that it should be done.

Whatever methods are used, the lead must come from those responsible for the administration of the service. For many reasons, it cannot be left to the initiative of district nurse-midwives to obtain further insights by study outside their working hours. In other branches of the social welfare services some of those without formal academic qualifications were taking evening classes or correspondence courses in psychology or social science either for general interest or to obtain a formal qualification. Among nurses, however, only 4 per cent had taken an evening or correspondence course at any time during their career and only one was undertaking any systematic course of personal study in the survey year. Indeed, district nurses' duty hours virtually preclude evening courses; and their work was too exacting to permit systematic individual study in off-duty periods. The time needed to enlarge horizons and increase insights must come out of the nurses' normal working hours, and while there is serious pressure on the service and a shortage of staff it will not be easy to secure sufficient time and high enough priority to accomplish these ends.

The first priority of a home nursing and midwifery service is to maintain and improve the quality of nursing and midwifery skills of its staff. New methods of treating disease are constantly calling for changes in nursing techniques, and staff must be informed of new developments and trained in their use. Moreover, while the demand for home nursing and for midwifery services grows, staff providing these services will be working

[1] Since 1961, consultant psychiatrists in child guidance have set aside a number of sessions for such discussions with district nurses.

under considerable pressure. Nevertheless, if the substantial advances made in techniques for preventing or treating illness are to be successfully applied, some priority must be given to the study of human behaviour in both basic and in-service training of professional workers like district nurses.

CHAPTER VIII

The Hospital Social Services

Most of the hospitals serving Bucks were within the Oxford Regional Hospital Board area; but people living in the south of the county were covered by the North-West Metropolitan Regional Hospital Board. One hospital took mental patients and three had provision for long stay geriatric patients. In another there was a special unit for spinal injuries which treated patients from all over the world. There was also a Medical Rehabilitation Centre serving a whole hospital region. All these and most of the general hospitals employed social workers. During 1960–61, 22 people were employed in these hospitals as almoners, almoners' assistants, or psychiatric social workers, and 21 of them were interviewed.[1] The almoners[2] and their assistants provided records of 337 patients. The two social workers in the mental hospital recorded details of 49 cases.

Patients seen by almoners and psychiatric social workers

Almost half the 49 psychiatric social workers' clients were male; only one was a dependent child and eight were over 65. Half were married, a quarter single and a quarter widowed, separated, or divorced.

Sixty-one per cent of the hospital almoners' clients were women or girls and 4 per cent dependent children. Nearly a quarter were more than 65. Like the clients of the psychiatric social workers about half those of the almoners were married. Among the rest, however, there were slightly fewer single, divorced or separated people and rather more widowed.

Only a few of the psychiatric social workers' patients had chronic disabilities besides their mental disorders. The almoners' clients often had chronic and multiple disabilities, the most commonly recorded being rheumatic and muscular complaints (15 per cent), diseases of the central nervous system (11 per cent), and diseases of the heart and circulatory system (10 per cent).

[1] Two of those seen did not provide information about cases seen.
[2] Since 1964, almoners have changed their name to medical social workers.

Information on patients' households and their domestic circumstances was often lacking from the records of hospital based almoners and psychiatric social workers in contrast to those supplied by staff from the local authority health and welfare department, especially when the latter had had social work training.[1] It would have been easier for staff visiting homes to make their own observations, but it is possible that hospital based staff were less clear about the significance of household information than those who regularly visited homes.

An additional circumstance also perhaps partly explained the relative inadequacy of data provided by almoners on their clients' households. It was that about two thirds of the clients had been known to them for less than one month and had been seen once, twice or three times at most. In the case of the psychiatric social workers' clients, not quite half were new patients seen for the first time within a month of the recording period; but over a third (34 per cent) had been known to them for at least a year.

Nearly all clients seen by hospital almoners were referred by doctors or ward sisters, and in the mental hospital it was common for the superintendent psychiatrist to ask the psychiatric social worker to investigate the home circumstances of all new patients. Sometimes, the patient himself asked for a consultation with the almoner or psychiatric social worker.[2]

The services undertaken and the problems presented

The psychiatric social workers almost always described the purpose of the first referral in general terms: investigating home circumstances or the need to deal with problems arising from an

[1] Almoners and psychiatric social workers did not record the occupation of the chief economic supporter in the households of 24 per cent and 18 per cent respectively of their clients; almoners did not know whether 30 per cent of their clients normally lived in a rented or owner-occupied house, and for over half their clients did not record how many rooms there were or whether the house had certain basic domestic amenities such as W.C.'s, bathrooms, and hot water taps. The psychiatric social workers were unable to provide this information for a quarter of their clients.

[2] Ten per cent of the almoners' cases and one of the psychiatric social worker's came initially through self-referral. There were also instances where the patient was referred by someone outside the hospital. Relatives in a few cases got in touch with the almoner as did health visitors, county almoners and the N.A.B. In one instance, the psychiatric social worker was contacted initially by a magistrate's clerk.

emergency admission. Sometimes, however, the referral seemed to be for a more specific purpose, for example to arrange for home nursing or occupational therapy.

The reasons why patients were referred to the almoners were far more diverse and in less than a third was the reason given as general investigation. In 20 per cent of cases the almoner was asked to arrange convalescent care, 9 per cent of referrals were concerned with employment and 8 per cent with home nursing or medical care. Some cases were referred so that arrangements could be made for ante-natal care, the adoption of illegitimate children and the care of unmarried mothers and their babies. Some referrals were due to housing difficulties and a number were to arrange the permanent institutional care of elderly infirm patients.

Since the enquiry covered the work of only one trained and one trainee psychiatric social worker over little more than a week of their working year, the clients seen may not have been a representative group, but it was surprising to find that only 30 of the 49 clients were considered to present social problems. Problems of marital or parent-child relationships were among those most often noted. Material difficulties related to housing or inadequate means were rarely observed.

Almoners were much more likely to record social problems. Only 10 per cent were considered to have none. The most common problems listed were those arising out of illness itself. Next in importance (25 per cent) were problems arising from the difficult personality of the client or another member of his household. Problems of marital or parent-child relationships, loneliness or social isolation, finding suitable employment, inadequate means, and housing were also noted frequently. Indeed, almost every kind of social difficulty specified occurred in more than 5 per cent of their cases. Only those associated with children—truancy, child neglect or juvenile delinquency—were not observed or were mentioned in only one or two of the clients' households.

Four cases reported on by the social workers from the mental hospital were also seen by other social welfare staff, and the reports of one of them illustrate a difficulty which could occur in using the hospital as a base for helping people when they return to their homes.

The case was that of an elderly widow seen by the psychiatric social worker in hospital. She lived on her own and was depressed and senile, but the psychiatric social worker did not record material or personal difficulties. Nine months later, the old lady was seen in her own home by a home help organiser who was trying to arrange domestic help for her. The organiser did not mention that the old lady was senile or depressed, or note her recent hospitalisation, but she did suggest that she had not enough to live on and was on bad terms with a daughter who lived near. The problems may only have developed between the old lady's admission to hospital and the visit paid after her discharge by the home help organiser; but it seems more probable that these were long-standing difficulties, a knowledge of which was vital to the old lady's care.

Fifty-three other workers reported on cases seen by hospital almoners. Fourteen of them were district nurses and the cases they had in common with almoners were mostly elderly patients needing nursing care. The district nurses' accounts tended to be brief and to show awareness only of the need for nursing care, and on average they reported only one difficulty to every two noted by almoners.[1] Home help organisers, too, reported fewer difficulties than hospital almoners in the five cases they both saw.

Most other workers reporting cases seen by hospital almoners reported as many or more problems than the almoners. Health visitors reported more fully and more comprehensively in three cases, as fully in four and less fully in one of the eight common cases. County almoners reported more fully in four out of their five common cases. Staff from outside the health department tended to report more problems than almoners if they were trained social workers and about the same number if they were not. Since most of the other workers, whether trained or not, were concerned with the welfare or behaviour of children, they naturally gave more emphasis than almoners to problems of child behaviour, school truancy, delinquency and parent-child relationships.

[1] There were exceptions, provided by the district nurse-midwives in the north who were also trained health visitors. Two of their three reports made similar comments on family social circumstances to those of the almoners. In the third case it was the district nurse who seemed to have a more intimate knowledge of the family. A description of this case is given in Chapter VII, p. 93–4.

Contacts with other services

Only in a small proportion of their recorded cases had the almoner recently been consulted by outside social welfare agencies. The local authority health and welfare staff were the most likely to have been in touch (in 7 per cent of cases), and it was also to these workers that almoners were most likely to refer patients. In most of the cases reported on by others as well as by almoners (except those handled by district nurses) contact had been established between the reporting workers, joint consultation occurring most frequently when the other worker was a health visitor. The psychiatric social workers were less likely to have had referrals from outside the hospital or to have referred their clients to others. When they did, like the almoners, they were most likely to be in touch with welfare officers or others employed by the local health authority.

A case reported on by a hospital almoner and three other workers, however, can be used to illustrate the potential danger of duplicating services to individuals. It concerned an old lady of 78, severely crippled with arthritis, widowed and living alone in a flat near Slough. She was visited weekly by a district nurse who had referred her to the G.P. on several occasions, to the county almoner to arrange a seaside holiday, to the home help organiser for domestic help, to the optician for glasses and to a dentist for dentures. She was also being visited by a county almoner who was aware of the interest of other services, and who was trying to prepare the old lady for the time when she would have to go to a county welfare home or geriatric hospital ward.

The third worker paying regular visits was a N.A.B. officer, who had visited her five times in the past 12 months. He reported that the old lady felt friendless in Slough and had applied to her landlord, the L.C.C., for a transfer back to London. Meanwhile, he had approached the L.C.C. welfare officer to see whether they could order extra fuel, and had asked the Slough All Good Causes Fund to get her a fireguard.

The hospital almoner, the fourth worker to report, saw this client in the out-patient department of the hospital. She needed special surgical boots and had attended the hospital regularly for two years. The almoner, who had seen her six times in 12 months, reported that the old lady 'cannot accept or adjust herself to her physical limitations, has difficulty in making friends and leads a solitary life. She is constantly complaining and tends to neglect herself and her flat, and is, therefore, ostracised by the local club for the aged'. The almoner described her own efforts as 'directed at improving her morale, by catering for her material comforts and arranging for regular visitors'. She reported the patient as 'adamant that she does not want welfare accommodation'.

From the accounts of these four workers it was apparent that six others were regularly visiting, including a home help organiser, a general practitioner, the L.C.C. housing welfare worker, the British Red Cross Society, the Slough All Good Causes Fund and the W.V.S. It seems on the face of it both extravagant and inefficient that workers attached to ten different sections and branches of the statutory and voluntary social welfare services should actively concern themselves with a single old lady— especially since there seemed to be much overlap in the kind of service some of them gave.

In particular, the question arises whether in cases like these the hospital almoner's service is essential or even desirable. The old lady was already well known to domiciliary health and social services. She had not been hospitalised and was using the out-patient service only for limited, specialist advice and help. This woman's difficulties could only be resolved—if at all—by those who were already visiting her in her own home. When there is so grave a shortage of trained social workers in the hospital service they should work entirely with patients not dealt with by the domiciliary services.

The social background and work experience of hospital social workers

All the almoners and the one trained psychiatric social worker were women. The only man was a trainee psychiatric social worker, a University graduate still undecided about his future.

Eighteen of the 20 women were single, one was married and another divorced. Two were under 25 and another two between 25 and 34. Seven were between 35 and 44 and another seven between 45 and 54. Two were in their late fifties. As far as family background was concerned, the almoners were more frequently of middle class origin than nurses, health visitors or other social welfare workers. Fourteen had fathers in business, administrative or professional occupations (Social Class I and II) and no fewer than five had fathers who were doctors of medicine.[1] Only two had fathers in manual work, both of these skilled and self-employed. None left school before 16, and 15 stayed to 17 or 18, eleven of them matriculating. Sixteen of the 21 almoners had done extensive voluntary social work in their late teens, twenties and early thirties, in this respect resembling probation officers and child care officers, who also take a recognised social work training. Almoners were more likely than these two groups to admit to deep religious convictions.

Recruitment and training

The Institute of Almoners determines the suitability of individuals wishing to qualify as almoners, and supervises their professional training, which lasts a year and normally follows a university course leading to either a degree or a diploma in social science.[2] The Association of Psychiatric Social Workers does not itself select trainees for psychiatric social work, this task being left to the four universities which run one-year mental health courses. The diplomas awarded are recognised by the A.P.S.W. Normally, universities will only accept for training those with a university degree or diploma and some practical experience in social work; but exceptions are sometimes made of suitable individuals with a good deal of relevant experience.

Nine of the 21 hospital social workers had had either a full almoner's or psychiatric social worker training. Four of these had made up their minds early to take a university social science diploma and had followed it immediately by an almoner's training. The other five fully trained almoners had all had considerable working experience before going to university as mature students. Four almoners had taken emergency courses arranged by the

---

[1] Amongst the 46 health visitors only one had a doctor as father and there were none among the 119 district nurses.

[2] In 1964 the Institute of Almoners became the Institute of Medical Social Workers.

Institute of Almoners and they too had had considerable experience before qualifying.[1]

Nine of the 13 trained workers had, therefore, had considerable working experience before training in their late twenties or thirties. All 13 had worked in situations which brought them into close touch with almoning: six had worked in hospital—one as a nurse, and five in secretarial posts in almoners' departments; nine had worked for voluntary organisations such as Settlements, the Invalid Children's Aid Society and the British Red Cross Society, and one in youth employment. For none, therefore, was an almoner's career a shot in the dark.

Eight of the hospital social service staff were working as almoners, assistant almoners or welfare assistants without formal training; but like the trained staff their previous working experience had brought them into contact with almoning. Six had a secretarial training and eventually found work in an almoner's department, and gradually began to take on more and more of the almoner's work. Their translation from the role of secretary to that of assistant almoner, almoner and, in two instances, to almoner-in-sole-charge (a position carrying special responsibility and differential pay) followed.

In terms of formal education qualifications and previous working experience the untrained almoners in Bucks resembled those with the almoner's emergency training. There was no difference in the length of full-time schooling; and their working experience was similar.[2] The significant difference between them was the year's formal social work training which one group had had and the other had not.

Views on training

The four emergency trained almoners were unanimous in thinking their course useful, particularly perhaps because, in the words of one, 'It brought together an older, more mature group

[1] At the end of the war and immediately afterwards, the Institute accepted some individuals without university background for emergency training, discontinuing this special arrangement and reverting to the former position in 1949. Since 1956 the Institute has also recognised the generic social casework course taken at postgraduate level at some universities.

[2] Five of the eight, compared with one of the four emergency trained almoners, had obtained school-leaving certificates. Two of the nine fully trained almoners had also left school without formal educational attainments.

who could share their experiences'. The criticisms against it were that it was too short and dealt over simply with the casework relationship.

There was less unanimity among those who had taken the full training. Five of the seven who had taken courses before 1955 suggested they were not an adequate preparation for their work in the 60's, because the nature of almoning itself had changed. One summed it up: 'It was a reasonable preparation for the job of almoning as it was then, not for the type of work expected now— that is, case-work'.[1] The two more recently trained almoners expressed greater satisfaction, but made some detailed criticisms.[2]

Three of those without an almoner's training did not regret it. Two of them had social science diplomas, one after two years at university and the other after four years' part-time evening study at technical college. Both believed these courses, together with their experience in various branches of social work, were sufficient. One said: 'No training is ever adequate. Mine (the social science diploma course), for its time, was an excellent basic training but the chief preparation for any job is the job that went before it'. The third who did not regret her lack of training was working under the close supervision of a trained almoner, took a limited view of her work and was not anxious to accept more responsibility.

Five untrained workers said they would have liked to take a full almoner's (or in one case, generic social casework) training. One had a degree in economics with sociology, and had found the sociology 'marginally relevant'. Another felt unsure of herself. 'I've picked up a good deal on the job; but I feel inferior about my knowledge of casework when I talk to trained almoners.' A third regretted not having a training earlier 'only because *not* being trained is a disadvantage with other almoners and from a career point of view. You reach a certain level and can't get further,

---

[1] Another almoner criticised the pre-1955 course for being 'a little precious'. 'I felt they were watching every step I took. It made me self-conscious for a time, which I'm not convinced is a good thing.' This criticism was also levelled against the course by an almoner who had taken her training since 1955 and had been generally pleased with it. 'You're very conscious of being watched all the time', she said. 'It made me feel rather insecure. There was a critical atmosphere.'

[2] For example, one thought that teaching on marital problems, given that most almoner trainees were young single women, was not well done.

yet I know many of those of my age *with* training feel that it was not of much use and that they've learned all they want to know since. For the younger ones, this is less true because the training itself has improved immensely'.

Relationships between trained and untrained almoners

Comments made by trained and untrained almoners suggested there was some tension between them, especially in the south of the county where staffing problems were most acute. Trained almoners expressed concern about the employment of untrained persons in posts of responsibility, suggesting that, in intensive casework in particular, they might do more harm than good. Untrained almoners showed they were aware of their colleagues' disapproval, five of the eight spontaneously suggesting that they had suffered slights at the latter's hands. One of these said, 'I've no illusions about my own skills. I do not do complicated case-work, and I regard my work as mainly administrative. I do not consider my lack of training is a great drawback in my day-to-day work, but feel at a considerable disadvantage when I have to discuss cases with almoners from other hospitals, who seem to go out of their way to remind me of the difference in our status'. Another alleged that 'some of the trained almoners have given me an inferiority complex. One even refused to give me informa-tion or refer patients to me'. Another suggested that she and other untrained almoners ought 'to stick together in a kind of mutual protection society since the other almoners are not particularly friendly or helpful'.

Satisfaction and dissatisfactions with almoning

Like most other workers in social welfare, most almoners were satisfied with their career and would have chosen almoning again if given the chance. Seventeen of the 21 responded in this way. Those who felt less wedded to almoning included three trained and one untrained almoner.

The three trained almoners were dissatisfied for different reasons. Two would have preferred academic careers, both finding almoning too restricted and frustrating in some respects. The third almoner, who enjoyed her work but felt that given the choice now she would not enter the profession, said, 'the forces which made me take up social work in the thirties no longer operate. There isn't the same poverty and ignorance. It is now the sick who need help above all, so I would choose medicine, which is potentially the most valuable of all professions now.'

Almoners often emphasised the satisfaction derived from helping people and from learning about them, in this way not differing from staff in other branches of social welfare. Almoners were more likely, however, to acknowledge that the work fulfilled certain personal needs or helped overcome personal difficulties. For example, one said, 'I've a very great desire to help people and I can satisfy it to a great extent in my job'.

Many comments on their jobs centred around the quality of the relationships they enjoyed (or failed to enjoy) with others in the hospital and the esteem in which their work was held. 'One of my greatest rewards', said one almoner, 'is being recognised, accepted and wanted by the rest of the hospital staff. I've seen this grow during my years at this hospital.' 'I gain self-respect from the job', said another, 'because I know it's appreciated'. 'There's a lot of fun here with both staff and patients', said a third, 'because we all feel we're working for the same purpose'.

Nine almoners (six trained and three untrained), however, complained about their relationships with at least some of the other hospital staff or about the low value which they felt some people attached to their work. Most of the complaints were about doctors,[1] but most recognised differences between doctors. 'The work varies with the attitudes of ward sisters and consultants', said an almoner with 15 years experience. 'By and large the surgical sisters and doctors are less interested. I try to visit these wards to enquire, but in the main I'm kept busy with patients from the medical wards where the doctors and sisters do recognise the value of our work.' 'It's much improved since I started', said another. 'There was great hostility, but after a time even the most benighted surgeons realise you're a human being. One or two sisters—especially those from provincial hospitals, where there has

---

[1] 'Doctors still regard one as a very subsidiary member of the team', said a young almoner with only two years experience. 'Doctors aren't the easiest people in the world to work with', said an older worker. 'I suffer from occasional frustration due to the inability of hospital staff—especially doctors—to use the almoning services well', said a third.

been virtually no almoning service—are a bit more distant than those who've had experience of almoners.'

Some almoners—including four out of five of the untrained—used the questions on hospital almoning as a career to discuss difficulties they faced in trying to solve patients' difficulties, and the future of hospital almoning as such.

The monetary difficulties of the families of manual workers when the breadwinner was ill was a practical problem discussed. 'Many families have taken the opportunity of high wages to make heavy H.P. commitments—something which didn't happen years ago', said one. 'So when the wage isn't coming in they're in severe financial straits even with improved national insurance benefits.' Another discussed 'absurd anomalies' in the treatment of the permanently disabled. 'Service or industrial disabled get various additional benefits such as constant attendance allowances. Those disabled from an illness or injury outside work can only get sickness benefit although their needs are often the same.' She went on to say, on the other hand, that it was sometimes easier to rehabilitate the latter. 'The compensation cases are, in my experience, the most easily demoralised and the least likely to make the effort.'

Most of the difficulties she faced in helping patients seemed to one almoner to arise from deficiencies in the domiciliary services, and she thought improvements were needed first in the home help service, especially extending it to cover weekends. She was also critical of delays at Ministry of Pensions and N.A.B. offices in dealing with hospital patients, much unnecessary distress being caused because families had no money coming in while investigations were being made into their circumstances. This almoner felt hospital almoning had reached a dead end. 'Its future seems uncertain. In fact, to be effective, almoners will, I think, have to go out into the community. It's there that they can be most effective. The future lies with the county services'.

Another almoner echoed some of these views. 'Almoning is too tied to the medical side. It is rather a narrow form of social work, in my view. But it is easier to criticise than to see how it could be altered and improved.' An emergency trained almoner, however, expressed the most doubt about the future of almoning.

E

'With the exception of the old, the welfare state has made more than adequate provision for most people's material needs. All that is needed in this sphere now is the will to co-operate. On the other hand, we need to develop services to help the mentally ill or ineffectual, and this is a job done more appropriately in the home by workers with an intensive training in mental health rather than in general almoning.'

General summary and conclusions

In 1960–61, the hospital almoning service in Bucks was under-staffed. There were several vacancies for almoners and p.s.w.'s, and eight of the 21 filled posts were staffed by those without the training recognised by the Institute of Almoners or A.P.S.W. Recruitment difficulties undoubtedly increased the pressure under which staff worked and accentuated the tension between trained and untrained almoners. Since recruitment of almoners and p.s.w.s. for full-time service in hospitals is likely to become more not less difficult in future,[1] it is important to consider whether the nature of the work in hospitals makes it desirable to recruit only or mainly social workers with the training recognised by the Institute of Medical Social Workers and A.P.S.W.

Much of the argument for employing fully trained almoners hinged on the need for staff capable of intensive casework with patients. The records provided by hospital staff suggested, however, that neither trained nor untrained social workers had time or opportunity to do intensive casework with more than a small number of patients. Only exceptionally were patients or their relatives visited at home. Interviews were generally short and often took place in wards where privacy was difficult to achieve. Patients were seldom seen more than once or twice. It was perhaps for these reasons that almoners often provided less information about their patients' social and domestic circumstances than workers in domiciliary services.

In short, the hospital was an unsatisfactory base for establishing close relationships between social workers and client. Almoners, whether trained or untrained, spent their time dealing with

---

[1] For example, single women will not be available to the extent that they were in 1960–61.

patients' financial and employment problems, their convalescence arrangements, their housing difficulties and need for domestic help. They did this mainly by contacting the staff of other branches of the social welfare services. It was not possible to judge the effectiveness of this work, but the records did not suggest substantial differences in the way it was tackled by trained and untrained almoners.

All this leads to the conclusion that some of the fears of trained almoners about the employment of untrained almoners, whose educational attainments, insights, interests in helping people and long experience in social service were equal to their own, were exaggerated.

It is, of course, right that trained workers should view with alarm any dilution or abandonment of standards of work which have proved valuable for the welfare of clients. Control of the quality of entrants and certification after training are both very important in maintaining professional standards; but their purpose can be forgotten and formalised standards used as barriers to further development or reconsideration of the work. This seemed in danger of happening in hospital social work.

The nature of the work led me to conclude that most of it could be carried out competently by social workers with a two-year training of the kind proposed by the Younghusband Working Party,[1] or by those who have worked in almoner's departments in a secretarial capacity for some years and have shown they have the temperament and skills for social work. There would still be a need for a few highly trained medical social workers in the hospital service to estimate needs, plan and direct work and supervise in-service training. These should have had a university training and a postgraduate course in social work; but in the future they might well be recruited from those who had already qualified as social workers in Younghusband courses.

However, because the demand for university graduates for social welfare services is likely to exceed the supply, most of them should be encouraged to enter the domiciliary based medical

[1] This recommendation is in line with, but goes beyond, that made by the Ministry of Health to Regional Hospital Boards in October, 1963 (Ref.: K/S. 20/01/T.F.1).

social work service rather than hospitals. Such a redistribution of university trained staff between services is further indicated if some of the work at present undertaken by hospital social workers is in future carried out by health visitors and social workers attached to general practice units.

CHAPTER IX

The General Practitioner and Social Welfare

The work of general practitioners is bound in many ways to that of the social welfare services. Many services are available to the public through G.P.'s; and since there is no definitive dividing line between health and social well-being, whether they like it or not, they will be consulted by some of their patients whose problems are as much social as medical.

There were several reasons, therefore, for including G.P.'s in the Bucks survey. The first was to find out what proportion of those seen in a typical day's work in general practice seemed to present social or psychological difficulties over and above strictly medical problems. The second was to learn what G.P.'s did when they encountered such difficulties, and the third was to obtain their views on the work of the staff of social welfare services.

A random sample of 70 G.P.'s was asked to give systematic information about every patient seen on a single day and also for their views on the statutory and voluntary social services available locally. Altogether 50 of them provided information about 1,367 patients and their views on the services. A further 16, who had had no consultations with Bucks' patients on the selected day, gave us their views about social problems and about the work of personnel of the social welfare services.[1]

Social and psychological difficulties seen in general practice

Just over a third of the patients seen in a typical day were believed by their G.P.'s to have or cause some social or psychological difficulty; but there were considerable differences in reporting between doctors. Since the definition of 'social problem' was left to them some of the variation in the frequency with which individual doctors reported patients with problems arose from differences in their assessment of what degree of difficulty constituted a social problem. Some of the variation could have been due to chance since only patients seen on a single day were in-

[1] A description of the methods used to draw the sample of practitioners and their patients and to record the information is given in Appendix C.

Table 15

REPORTING OF DIFFERENT SOCIAL PROBLEMS BY GENERAL
PRACTITIONERS

Rate per 1,000 consulting patients

Description of Problem	No. of patients	Rate per 1,000 consulting patients	Percentage of problems
1. Disturbed social functioning due to mental illness or sub-normality	181	134	32·1
2. Adjustment to chronic illness or disability	76	56	13·5
3. Marital relationships, sex in marriage, infertility or family planning	73	54	13·0
4. Care of the elderly, including domestic help, loneliness or housing (excluding inadequate means)	71	53	12·5
5. Child behaviour in pre-adolescents	38	28	6·7
6. Social incompetence or antisocial behaviour of an adult, including child neglect, low domestic standards, delinquency	33	24	5·8
7. Sexual problems in adults outside marriage, illegitimacy, homosexuality	27	20	4·8
8. Housing problems (other than for the old)	24	18	4·3
9. Inadequate means	20	15	3·5
10. Adolescent behaviour problems (excluding illegitimacy)	11	8	1·9
11. Social resettlement of immigrants	7	5	1·2
12. Other	5	4	0·9
All kinds of problems	495	364	100·2

cluded. Some seemed to be associated with the characteristics of
doctors themselves, doctors qualifying since the war reporting
more patients with problems than doctors qualifying earlier.

On an impressionistic level, the three research workers were often struck by the doctors' detailed knowledge of the family circumstances of patients they believed had social difficulties and their comparatively limited information on other patients. It seemed that doctors usually became familiar with the social circumstances of patients only if the latter directly confronted them with difficulties.

The problems mainly described were of four kinds: those associated with mental illness or subnormality; those concerned with care of the elderly; those of the chronically ill or physically handicapped; and those associated with sex, fertility and marital relations (see Table 15). Together, these accounted for 71 per

Table 16

PERCENTAGE OF PATIENTS WITH DIFFERENT PROBLEMS WHO RECEIVED HELP FROM DOCTORS DIRECTLY OR INDIRECTLY

Type of problem	Percentage of patients receiving help from a doctor		No. of patients consulting
Care of elderly	83·1		71
Social incompetence	76·0	greater	33
Adjustment to disability	75·0	than	76
Mental health	71·8	average	181
Child behaviour	71·0		38
All types of problem	62·8		495
Marital relations	59·9		73
Extra-marital, sexual behaviour	52·0	less	27
Inadequate means	50·0	than	20
Social resettlement	(2)*	average	7
Adolescence	(4)*		11
Housing	37·5		24

* Actual numbers.

cent of the problems reported. Most of the other problems reported fell into two main categories; those of deviant behaviour accounting for about a fifth of all problems and material problems of housing or income which accounted for approximately 10 per cent.

When doctors considered a patient or his family had or caused a 'social problem' they were further asked if they were doing anything directly or indirectly about it. Their responses showed that this depended very much on what the problem was. (See Table 16.) Doctors were nearly always helping directly or indirectly if the problem was one of making adequate arrangements for the care of elderly people. On the other hand, they were usually bystanders if the problem was a housing one.

Table 17

PERCENTAGE OF PATIENTS WITH DIFFERENT PROBLEMS WHOM GENERAL PRACTITIONERS KNEW TO BE VISITED BY OTHER SERVICES, AND ABOUT WHOM GENERAL PRACTITIONERS HAD BEEN IN TOUCH WITH OTHER SERVICES

Type of problem	Percentage of patients:		Total No. of patients
	where other service known to be in touch with patient	where general practitioner in touch with another service	
Care of elderly	57	40	71
Adjustment to disability	46	35	76
Housing	46	25	24
Child behaviour	37	18	38
Extra-marital sexual behaviour	37	15	27
Mental illness	35	28	181
Marital relations	33	25	73
Social incompetence	24	10	33
Inadequate means	(1)*	(1)*	20
Adolescence	(2)*	(1)*	11
Social resettlement	(3)*	(3)*	7
All problems	39	30	495

* Actual numbers.

While G.P.'s were directly or indirectly helping about two-thirds of the patients with problems, they were only aware of help provided by other social welfare services in about two-fifths of the cases, and were only in touch with other services in under a third (see Table 17). They were more likely, however, to be aware of other social welfare services' involvement when the problem was one of caring for the elderly, coping with physical disabilities or housing, and less likely when the problems were those of personal relationships.

General practitioners' views on social welfare services and their staff
(a) The district nursing service

General practitioners were more frequently in touch with the district nurse-midwives than with the staff of any other social welfare service, particularly in connection with the care of their elderly patients.[1]

The tradition of co-operation between G.P. and district nurse is long established, and does not owe its existence to the National Health Service. One doctor in a rural area looked back nostalgically to the time when district nursing was the only 'social service' available and he and the nurse coped with all the villagers' health and social problems. Some doctors told us that they still asked the district nurse to see to any extra-medical problems they felt their common patients might have. These nurse-midwives, however, worked in North Bucks and had also the training and duties of a health visitor. General practitioners in these areas were in favour of this arrangement, which made the same individual responsible for supervising the health of mothers and children at all stages of their development, and for the bedside nursing and social care of elderly patients. Some of their colleagues in other areas advocated the appointment of nurses with this triple function. To them it seemed both to be admirably simple and to make the best use of the nurse's training.

Not unnaturally, since the G.P. works so closely with her and is constantly reminded of her skills and her ubiquity, the district nurse came in for a great deal of appreciative comment. One G.P. said: 'With many of the other services one feels one could struggle on without them; but this one is essential'.

Much of the praise emphasised the nurse's devotion to duty and willingness to do any kind of practical job, however arduous. 'A race apart—the average district nurse is wonderful, absolutely selfless.' 'District nurses deserve halos. You can put that in big red letters. They work far harder than any doctor.' 'She just goes in and rolls up her sleeves and gets on with the job.' General

[1] See also Chapter VII—The District Nursing and Midwifery Service.

E*

practitioners even accepted with tolerance and humour a certain independence—both of spirit and of action—from district nurses, while a similar show of independent judgment on the part of staff of other services usually met with their disapproval.

Some doctors recognised that tension could arise between them and district nurses in the latters' role of domiciliary midwives. One regretted the almost total disappearance of his maternity practice—'the last thing left which we could do with our hands', and said, 'I know it is a point of pride with them (district midwives) to deliver the baby before the doctor arrives'. Another said, 'They seem to have a little practice on their own and only call me in when necessary'. He went on to say, however, that this situation suited him admirably.

The only anxiety commonly expressed by doctors about the service was that an acute shortage of nurses might arise. One doctor noted that, because the number of young couples in his area had increased greatly, midwives' caseloads had become heavier. Moreover, hospital provision for confinements had not kept pace with the increase in births, and in order to free beds domiciliary midwives were being asked to supervise mothers discharged from hospital on the third or fourth day after their confinement. Several doctors felt these measures placed midwives under great pressure which they could only meet by performing their home nursing work more perfunctorily.[1] District nurses, for their part, were also generally appreciative of G.P.'s and many said specifically that their relationships with local doctors was one aspect of their job which gave them a sense of satisfaction. 'You work with doctors as colleagues', said one nurse, 'more than is the case in hospital'.

Some of the nurses, like some of the doctors, spoke frankly about the possibility of conflict, especially with midwifery cases, but we did not get the impression that there was much feeling among nurses on this issue. Indeed, the midwives' good-humoured readiness to accept the G.P. in midwifery, and even to alter

---

[1] In their view, a shortage—perhaps a desperate one—could only be avoided if district nurse-midwives received a substantial increase in salary. As one doctor put it, 'The whole business of vocation has been pushed too far. If we want a decent service we must be prepared to pay for it'. This doctor put most of his views forcefully and said it was 'disgusting' that district nurses should be expected to pay rent for their houses.

their views about his ability to help, was illustrated by an experience related by one midwife. In a case requiring a forceps delivery, she had called in a G.P. new to the area, who turned out to be young and recently qualified. 'I thought to myself, another raw recruit', she said, but changed her mind when he delivered the baby with great competence. 'I told him afterwards what my first thought had been and we had a good laugh about it. You can always learn, and I learnt a lot from him that night.'

(b) The health visitor

The relationships of G.P.'s with health visitors were not nearly as close as those with district nurses. Nor, on the whole, were they so appreciative of each other's work. General practitioners expressed many diverse views about the health visitors. Three of the 66 doctors interviewed insisted they had never had any contact with the health visitors in their area. One said, 'I am quite prepared to work with health visitors; but so far none of them has contacted me'. Another doctor, a comparative newcomer to the area, blamed the Medical Officer of Health for failing to insist that the health visitor introduce herself.

Thirty, or nearly half the doctors, made either critical or very critical comments about the health visitors' work. Some of these criticisms related to the way in which a health visitor had handled a particular patient. 'She was meddlesome—frightened the patient', was the comment of one doctor who objected to a health visitor's advice to a nursing mother. Another elderly doctor suggested he had frequent clashes with a health visitor. 'Even if I am wrong', he said, 'I don't want it pointed out to the patient'.

Much of the criticism of these 30 G.P.'s was couched in vague terms and suggested there was a good deal of misunderstanding or ignorance of the health visitors' functions. Many doctors seemed to have started their practices with well-rooted prejudices against health visitors, and these prejudices were responsible, at least in part, for failure to establish fruitful working relationships.

An additional factor making for a certain coolness seemed to be the low valuation placed by many G.P.'s on the preventive health services in which the health visitors' main work lay. Both the infant welfare and the school health service originally came into existence to give advice to those with limited means and limited education. Although the concept of the services was that of prevention or early remedial treatment, inevitably many parents who could not afford to pay for medical advice or treatment if a child was ill, used them to obtain help in emergencies. On the other hand, the better off expected to pay for their medical advice and their children's education and were, therefore, not served to any great extent before the advent of the National Health Service by workers attached to the local authority's preventive health services.

The relatively sharp distinction existing before the war between those accustomed to seek advice from G.P.'s in sickness and in health and those who were the main concern of the local authority's infant welfare and school health service had a profound effect upon the character of these services and on the relationships between their workers and the general practitioners.

The coming of the N.H.S., with its emphasis on optimum preventive and curative services for everyone, irrespective of ability to pay, should have brought to an end the tensions between G.P.'s and local authority health services. The interviews in Bucks, however, 13 years after the establishment of the National Health Service, suggested that some old sores had not entirely healed, and that new uncertainties about the respective functions of G.P., assistant medical officer of health, and health visitor helped to keep them open.

Most of the 30 doctors who were critical of the health visitor were often expressing doubts about the services of which she was a part. Five, putting an extreme point of view, questioned the necessity for any preventive services. They considered that the greater prosperity of post-war Britain and the higher standard of living enjoyed by the majority of the population made the routine medical examination of all pre-school and school children unnecessary. Since the health visitor was mainly concerned with these two activities, these doctors felt that her work too was unnecessary. They believed that they themselves could do any educative work needed and that most of the patients requiring help were either already consulting them exclusively or would prefer to do so. They also often expressed the view that some of their patients resented the health visitor's call, feeling that it was made on the assumption that mothers must be held to be incompetent in child-rearing until the health visitor had satisfied herself to the contrary.

Most doctors did not hold this extreme point of view, and believed that the general educative and preventive work must go on both for the pre-school infant and for the school child. Nevertheless, a considerable number thought it a misuse of scarce resources to employ highly trained nurses exclusively on preventive work.

Although nearly half the G.P.'s made critical comments about health visitors, 17 had been favourably impressed with their work and four spoke of their local health visitors in terms as laudatory as those they used to describe district nurses. Three out of these four were young doctors who had qualified within the last ten years. It was noticeable, moreover, that the 17 doctors who praised health visitors usually gave an example of the kind of situation in which they had been helpful, in contrast to the often vague and generalised comments of those who were critical.

Health visitors were not asked specifically to discuss their relationships with G.P.'s, but many raised the matter spontaneously.[1] For example, 13 of the 46 said their work was not highly valued by general practitioners. This was a higher proportion of responses of this kind than was made by any other group of social welfare workers. One health visitor found the 'lack of understanding from G.P.'s a real drawback'. She had had previous experience as a district nurse, and was aware of a change in general practitioners' attitudes towards her. Another health visitor said she had hesitated to telephone one of the local doctors about one of his patients, as she had been urged to do by the Medical Officer of Health, because he (the G.P.) made her feel like an 'interfering busybody'. This was not the only health visitor who seemed loath to contact general practitioners because she feared a rebuff. But several health visitors who had been able to establish friendly contact and a relationship of mutual trust with general practitioners emphasised the satisfaction they derived from this and the difference it made to their work.

From both sides, therefore, there came evidence of tension or deliberate decisions to forego contact in order to avoid ill-will. In some cases, the health visitor herself may have been to blame

[1] See Chapter VI, 'The Health Visiting Service'.

for the low valuation which the G.P. put upon her services. Not all health visitors are paragons of virtue or of tact, and they start their work with mothers at a considerable disadvantage compared with district nurse-midwives. While the popular image of the district nurse endows her with a halo and a lamp and all the qualities of saintly devotion, the image of the health visitor is still derived in part from the somewhat authoritarian supervisory role which she played with mothers and children in the days of poverty and unemployment before the second world war.

Much of the tension seemed to arise because G.P.'s were not convinced of the value of health education, of instructing mothers in child development and in the management of a family in health and disease and of trying to support and encourage mothers who are under stress; today, these are the health visitor's main functions. Failure to appreciate the importance of preventive work can only be overcome if more emphasis is laid on it and on the part which social welfare staff of all kinds play in achieving it in the basic training of medical students. Some of the blame for the continued separation of health visitor and G.P. services also rested with the local health authority for failing to understand and therefore help overcome the obstacles which kept the two services apart.

Since the survey, steps have been taken nationally and in Bucks to try to remove all three barriers to co-operation. The Council for the Training of Health Visitors has been established, a new syllabus and system of examination for the certificate have been devised and training schools have made some radical changes in the content and method of teaching. Secondly, most medical schools have been reconsidering the training of doctors in preventive and social medicine and attempting to increase the status of the discipline among both clinical teachers and students. Thirdly, medical officers of health in many areas have been seeking to integrate G.P. and local authority health services by bringing the former into school health and infant welfare work or attaching health visitors and district nurses to general practices.[1]

[1] Since 1961, health visitors in several areas of Bucks have been visiting pre-school children registered with particular practices and not those living in particular districts. The experiment is reported to have been welcomed by both G.P.'s and health visitors and to have led to closer and more cordial relations between them.

The proposals which I have to make for furthering the integration of G.P. and local authority domiciliary health and welfare services are outlined in Chapter XX.

(c) The county almoning service

Although the county almoning service had been established for seven years at the time of the survey, some G.P'.s claimed they did not know it existed.[1] Most of these practiced from outside the county boundary and may have had few Bucks patients needing the almoners' services. Nevertheless, their ignorance of the service in the face of the considerable effort made by the County Medical Officer of Health to inform them of the whole range of ancillary services and methods of obtaining them needs further consideration.[2]

Where general practitioners had been in touch with the service they had been impressed with the speed and efficiency with which the almoners worked and with the almoners' willingness to accept responsibility for finding out what kind of arrangement would suit the patient best and then making sure they obtained it.

Some doctors used county almoners as they would information officers, confessing to confusion by the apparent multiplicity of services. One doctor said he no longer needed to discover the right person to meet his patients' non-medical needs. He simply rang up the almoner and left her to sort it out. Other doctors appeared to use almoners in this way and their eagerness to do so lent support to the suggestion made by a number of G.P.'s that there should be one designated person to whom the doctor could go if he wanted help in connection with any social problem.

It is impossible to say how far the doctor's confidence in the county almoner stemmed from the latter's social casework training, or from other factors likely to influence their attitude. Probably

---

[1] See Chapter V for a description of the county almoners' work.

[2] All G.P.'s on the Bucks Executive Council list were issued annually with a loose-leaf booklet listing and indexing services and the names, addresses and telephone numbers of those providing them. Changes during the year were notified on loose-leaf sheets so that the booklet could be kept up-to-date. Some doctors claimed they had not received the booklet. It is probable that it had been lost under piles of unopened envelopes from drug houses. Other G.P.'s had not read it and took the opportunity of the research interview to enquire about many services.

they did not feel that their skills clashed with hers as they might well have done with the health visitor.

Doctors showed appreciation of the 'practical help' almoners gave their patients and did not mention specifically their more time-consuming function of helping relatives to understand and meet the needs of disabled or ageing people. Perhaps social casework of this kind is never really apparent and, therefore, not fully appreciated if it is good.[1]

(d) Other social welfare workers

Doctors made few comments on the competence of home help organisers, most of their remarks concerning the adequacy of the provision. Nearly all of them felt that the service which was vital to the continuing community care of elderly and disabled people was only able to meet a small proportion of the need. Some, particularly in the more prosperous areas of the south, said they no longer made requests to the home help organisers for patients who could pay the full cost of the service, feeling that it was easier for such patients to obtain domestic help privately.

Doctors told us that they were seldom in contact with local authority welfare officers,[2] but most were full of admiration for their work with the families of severely subnormal people, with psychotic patients in acute phases of their illness when they needed emergency admission to hospital and with elderly senile people who were no longer able to remain in their own homes and had to be admitted to long-stay geriatric units. One doctor marvelled at the ability of the welfare officer in his area to calm down severely disturbed patients. 'He's really wonderful at dealing with loonies', he said. He and some others were pleased that they were relieved of the burden of coping with psychotic and severely subnormal people, which they admitted they themselves would find intolerable.

The work of moral welfare workers was also commended by

[1] None of the doctors accused almoners of dogmatism about patients' psychological needs or of concentrating upon meeting these at the expense of material needs. cf. B. Wootton, 'Daddy knows best', in *Twentieth Century*, 1960, p. 31.

[2] See Chapter V 'Health and Welfare Department Social Welfare Workers', for an account of the work of welfare officers.

most doctors.[1] One confessed to being surprised by a moral welfare worker's approach, because he had expected her to indulge in moralising and to emphasise the sinfulness of the unmarried mother's conduct. In fact, he found her tolerant, sympathetic and extremely helpful. Some doctors, however, believed there was a forbidding atmosphere surrounding the name and reputation of the Diocesan councils for moral welfare which made some unmarried mothers unwilling to seek help as soon as it was needed. One or two said that, for this reason, they referred unmarried mothers to county or hospital almoners rather than moral welfare workers.

Doctors were asked whether they referred patients to the clinics conducted by the Family Planning Association.[2] Those in the north of the county could not do so since there were no clinics available. Those in the Aylesbury area referred patients who felt they had enough children to the hospital out-patient gynaecological clinic, which also considered problems of infertility.

Doctors in the south of the county where Family Planning Association clinics were available fell roughly into four equal groups. The first referred any patient who asked for advice to the F.P.A. clinic. One doctor in this group said he did this rather than fit patients himself 'because if anything goes wrong, there won't be a comeback'. The second group liked to provide birth control advice themselves, feeling that it gave them an opportunity to get to know married couples, their family aspirations and possible difficulties. A third group, while referring middle class patients to the F.P.A., did not feel their clinics or the methods advocated were suitable for many working class women. The fourth group made up of four Roman Catholic doctors had objections on religious grounds to the use of mechanical methods of birth control and would only refer non-Catholic patients who strongly insisted to F.P.A. clinics.

Since there were so few marriage guidance counsellors in Bucks, there were few opportunities for doctors to refer patients to them.[3] Only one among the 66 interviewed had referred a couple. The

[1] See Chapter XVIII for a description of the work of moral welfare workers.
[2] See Chapter XIX for a description of the work of the F.P.A.
[3] See Chapter XIX for an account of the work of marriage guidance counsellors.

majority were somewhat critical of these workers whom they dubbed 'amateur psychologists' and 'do-gooders'. For this reason, one doctor referred cases to a London centre where all the counsellors were medically qualified, and two advised patients who could afford it to go to a psychiatrist outside the National Health Service.

Confronted with marital difficulties, which a G.P. suggested 'one suspects from the miserable appearance of the woman', most doctors did what they could themselves. But many emphasised that their capacity to help was limited: 'people come too late. They wait until the marriage is broken beyond repair before they seek help. Then all one can do is prescribe tranquilisers which do not get to the root of the problem at all'.

Summary of findings and conclusions

Collectively, general practitioners in Bucks were conscious of many social difficulties to which patients' physical and mental difficulties give rise. They thought that about one-third of the patients they saw in a typical day's work had social or psychological problems which impeded their daily activities or social relationships. About a third of these problems were associated with mental illness, usually of a psycho-neurotic kind. Doctors were also aware of many marital difficulties, problems of adjustment to chronic illness or disability and problems of caring for elderly people. Other forms of problem, which did not rise directly from the nature of an illness were less frequently observed.

On the whole, doctors did not seek help from the domiciliary social welfare services in dealing with social difficulties, sometimes because they were aware of the shortage of facilities, sometimes because they were not fully aware of available services, and sometimes because they doubted the competence of the available staff.

Despite health department efforts to inform G.P.'s of the range of services available, many doctors confessed ignorance of the services and how they could be mobilised on behalf of their patients. The circulation of a loose-leaf booklet seemed to be inadequate on its own as a source of information and it seemed desirable that G.P.'s who did not make use of the services should receive personal visits from the medically qualified staff of the county health department. More fundamentally, it appeared to be essential that new attitudes to other social welfare services should be acquired during medical training.

General practitioners were generally satisfied with the district nursing-midwifery service, although they anticipated increasing difficulties following the growth in the elderly and child-bearing population. They also appreciated the work of county almoners and welfare officers. They were divided, however, in their attitudes to health visitors. Just under a half were critical, often suggesting that the latters' skills were more needed in bedside nursing. These doctors did not rate preventive and social work or health education highly. More young doctors commented favourably on the work of health visitors and suggested ways of integrating the health visitors' work with their own. Much still needs to be done in medical education, however, to orient future G.P.'s to an approach in which health promotion, disease prevention and therapy are seen as integrated services to which many social welfare workers as well as doctors can contribute.

The local health authority in 1960–61 seemed insufficiently aware of the obstacles to co-operation between G.P.'s and health visitors. The measures taken since then to attach health visitors in certain areas to general practices are to be welcomed as experiments which may point the way to closer working relationships between G.P.'s and the staff of the local authority health and welfare department.

Some of the general implications of this review of the place of general practitioners in the field of social welfare are considered in the final chapter.

CHAPTER X

The Education Department's Social Welfare Services

In Bucks in 1960–61 the education department of the County Council employed a number of people concerned with the social adjustment of children rather than with teaching or school administration.

First, there were 14 school attendance officers, who investigated unexplained absences from school. In some areas the school attendance officers made the necessary enquiries into home circumstances, before arrangements could be made to provide children from poor homes with free school meals and allowances for clothing.

There were also four workers concerned with the welfare of children attending special schools and of those who had some degree of handicap but were attending the County's ordinary primary or secondary schools.[1] They were also responsible in some parts of the county for assessing the means of families whose children might need free school meals. One of the four workers was responsible for the administration of this work and only saw parents at their request or in special circumstances.

The education department ran two child guidance teams in the county, one at Slough and one at Aylesbury. The Aylesbury team also held two sessions weekly at High Wycombe.[2] Each team consisted of a consultant psychiatrist from the Regional Hospital Board, working on a sessional basis, a psychologist and a psychiatric social worker.

In Slough, an untrained social worker also assisted with the clinic's work.[3]

In Bucks the youth employment service was undertaken by the

---

[1] A fifth worker held a part-time appointment for a few months at the beginning of the survey period.

[2] Half way through the year the psychiatric social worker attached to the Aylesbury office left and her post, despite repeated advertisement, remained vacant throughout the rest of the year.

[3] Since the survey a third team has been established in High Wycombe, and the Aylesbury team has two sessions a week in Bletchley.

education department.[1] There were youth employment bureaux at Aylesbury, High Wycombe, Slough and Bletchley, and the officers from these bureaux were also available for consultation at offices in six other towns for a few hours each week, dividing their time between interviewing pupils in their last school year (if possible with parents), and keeping in touch with local employers. The bureaux also acted as employment exchanges for young people under 18 when they were unemployed, drew unemployment benefit or wanted advice on job opportunities. The youth employment officers dealt with any special problems, such as those of handicapped teenagers or of those who changed jobs frequently. Counter clerks dealt with most routine enquiries and issued young people with their national insurance cards.

The education department was responsible for the youth service which was organised in 14 districts, each of which was supervised by an organisations committee consisting of local representatives of voluntary youth organisations and employees of the education department. The committees considered the provision for young people's leisure, made grants to voluntary youth organisations and heard reports from the nine youth leaders in charge of the education department's own youth clubs.

It seemed probable that the staff of all these sections would to a greater or less extent be asked to advise or assist individuals with personal difficulties of an emotional or material kind. With the exception of the psychiatrists and psychologists attached to the child guidance clinics, therefore, they were all asked to participate in the survey.

In the event, although all the staff were interviewed, one school attendance officer and one special welfare section worker did not record any of their cases, and some of the information provided by three other attendance officers had to be excluded due to misunderstandings about our instructions. Altogether, we obtained information about 258 households seen by school attendance officers, 72 seen by child guidance workers and 48 seen by special welfare section workers.

Youth employment officers were asked to exclude from their recording all children still at school and those boys and girls who came to the youth employment bureaux simply to obtain an insur-

---

[1] It was responsible to the Ministry of Labour.

ance card or information about employment formalities. They recorded only those cases which the counter clerks passed on to them as requiring their special attention, or others which presented special difficulties. Altogether, the four officers recorded information about 103 young persons and their households.

As the survey was concerned with the help given to individuals as individuals or, at most, in family groups, it did not cover the general social provision for groups of children, adolescents or adults. For this reason workers employed by the education department who were responsible for community development and those undertaking administrative, teaching or leadership work for voluntary youth organisations were excluded. It was intended, however, to ask the nine full-time youth leaders employed by the county to participate in the enquiry on the grounds that they might be called upon to give individuals advice on personal problems falling within the scope of the survey's interest. But, although they were all interviewed and talked about themselves and their work, only one provided information on problems brought to him. Consequently, the report does not deal with the youth service.

The characteristics of the education department's clients

Two-thirds of the youth employment officers' clients were boys and one-third girls, and four-fifths had no disability likely to affect their ability to earn; but 9 per cent were considered to be mentally subnormal, 1 per cent to be subject to chronic mental illness, and 10 per cent to have a form of chronic physical disability. The most frequently mentioned category of disability after mental subnormality was that due to diseases of the central nervous system.[1]

In contrast to youth employment officers, other education department workers were seldom concerned with only one individual in a household. The school attendance officers, it is true, had usually only to investigate the absence from school of a single child in a household; but in over three-quarters of their cases the problem was a family one and could only be tackled through the parents. Their contacts, unlike those of the youth employment officers, took place almost exclusively in clients'

[1] This category comprised six with epilepsy and two with cerebral palsy.

homes. About half the children dealt with were boys and half girls. Twelve per cent of the school attendance officers' main clients had a chronic illness or disability, and a few had both mental and physical disabilities. Mental illness (4 per cent), mental subnormality (3 per cent) and respiratory illness (3 per cent), were the most common categories.

Child guidance clinic and special welfare section workers were generally concerned with one child in a family and one or both parents. In the case of the child guidance clinic, three-quarters of the child clients were boys and only a quarter girls. By contrast, two-thirds of the special welfare section workers' clients were girls and only one-third boys. The interviews conducted by the special welfare section were, with only one or two exceptions, in the clients' homes, in sharp contrast to those of the child guidance workers who only saw 6 per cent of their clients in home surroundings.

The child guidance workers recorded only two children with any form of chronic physical disability and one of these was an epileptic. They considered, however, that 14 per cent had a chronic mental condition. The special welfare workers' clients, on the other hand, were mostly children who were chronically ill or disabled and likely to remain so. The disabilities they recorded most frequently were mental subnormality, mental illness and diseases of the central nervous system including both epilepsy and cerebral palsy.

The social background of the clients

Nearly all the children seen by child guidance workers were living with both parents. Broken homes with one or other of the child's parents missing were much more common among the households visited by school attendance officers and special welfare workers.[1]

There was also something of a contrast between the social status of the households seen by the staff of various sections. A quarter of the child guidance clients were from Class I and II households, compared with only 8 per cent of those seen by

[1] No fewer than 23 per cent of the households seen by the former and 35 per cent of those seen by the latter consisted of a lone parent and unmarried children.

school attendance officers and special welfare workers. On the other hand, school attendance and special welfare staff saw twice as many children from semi- and unskilled workers' households as did child guidance workers.[1] In this respect, youth employment officers differed from both child guidance workers and school attendance officers. Their clients were overwhelmingly drawn from skilled manual workers' households (R.G. Social Class III).[2]

There were differences in the urban-rural distribution of clients as well as in social class background. Child guidance workers' clients were drawn predominantly from the municipal boroughs in the county, whereas school attendance officers' clients came mainly from rural areas. School absenteeism may well present a greater problem in rural than in urban areas. At the same time, it is only to be expected that the child living near the child guidance clinic is more likely to be able to use it than a child living at a distance.

Staff-client relationships

There were substantial differences in the frequency of contact between staff and clients and in the duration of the staff-client relationships. School attendance officers and special welfare workers had known over half their clients for more than a year; but were meeting other clients mostly for the first time. Child guidance workers, on the other hand, had known comparatively few of their clients for over a year, and were meeting few for the first time. Typically, they were seeing people at regular weekly or fortnightly intervals for periods of up to a year.

The children seen by child guidance workers were usually referred from one of four main sources, general practitioners, hospitals, schools and courts of law, either directly or through probation officers. A few were said to have been referred by the parents, although theoretically, direct access to the child guidance clinic service was not possible. Parent referral is likely, therefore, to refer to those instances where a parent asked the clinic to help with a child who had previously received treatment.

[1] Percent of child guidance staff's clients in Social Class IV and V, 31 percent, school attendance, 57 per cent, special welfare, 63 per cent.

[2] Only 5 per cent of youth employment officers' clients had household heads in Social Class I and II occupations and only 36 per cent in Social Class IV and V.

Little comment is needed on the school attendance officers' referrals. They were almost entirely from the school heads, who asked the officers to investigate unexplained school absences. In a few cases, however, a parent, a school medical officer or a children's officer was said to have made the first referral. The majority of special welfare section's clients, too, were referred by school heads or by school medical officers.[1] In all these instances, the special welfare section was asked to investigate the eligibility of the family for free school meals or assistance with clothing.

Forty-two per cent of the young people seen by the youth employment officers themselves took the initiative in coming for help about jobs or training, and school heads referred another 36 per cent. Most of the others were boys and girls from special schools for handicapped children who were likely to face particular difficulties in finding suitable employment and were referred by school medical officers.[2]

Table 18

SOCIAL PROBLEMS REPORTED BY EDUCATION DEPARTMENT WORKERS

Reporting officer	Percentage of households:		Average No. of problems reported	No. of records
	With no problems	With 4 or more problems		
School attendance	25	17	1·9	258
Special welfare	17	29	2·4	48
Youth employment	15	9	1·6	103
Child guidance	0	50	3·5	72

The problems presented

In about a quarter of the households visited, school attendance officers felt there were no difficulties serious enough to be called social problems. The absence from school which they were

---

[1] Only one of the 48 cases was referred by a general practitioner and two by hospitals. The National Assistance Board was responsible for referring six cases.

[2] One or two were referred by child care and probation officers.

investigating had a satisfactory explanation, and they then had only to report this to the school. Fewer of those visited by special welfare section workers and youth employment officers were said to be without problems, and child guidance workers felt that every individual seen had social problems affecting one or more members of the household. Moreover, they recorded more difficulties on the average than other education department staff. (See Table 18.)

Youth employment officers nearly always described the problems they encountered as matters of finding or keeping jobs suited to the skills or capabilities of the client; but, in some of their cases they considered that there were underlying problems of adjustment to a physical handicap. They were also aware of many other problems of both a material and an emotional kind, although only a small proportion of the households presented any single type of difficulty. (See Table 19.)

In just under half the households visited school attendance officers described one of the problems as school absence or truancy; but they were aware too of other problems of various kinds in a sizeable minority of households. The special welfare section workers saw an even greater proportion of households with economic difficulties. They were often likely to see school truancy, too, although not as frequently as school attendance officers.

The child guidance workers, on the other hand, did not indicate many problems of a material kind; but childhood behaviour problems, other than delinquency or truancy, were said to exist in at least 80 per cent of their clients' households and disturbed parent-child relationships in 74 per cent.

Reports from workers who had visited the same families as education department workers provided an opportunity to see whether there were any systematic differences in the ways in which household problems were seen or dealt with by the different staff.

Generally speaking, there was a tendency, noted elsewhere, for staff with some social worker training to present a more detailed and complicated picture of the household's problems than workers with no social worker training. The untrained social workers habitually confined their attention to the problem bringing them to the house, whereas the trained social workers took a wider view of situations presented to them.

Table 19

TYPE OF SOCIAL PROBLEM REPORTED BY EDUCATION
DEPARTMENT STAFF

(No. of cases—see Table 18)

Type of problem	Percentage of households seen by officers from:			
	Youth Employment	School Attendance	Special Welfare	Child Guidance
Childhood behaviour	3	18	29	81
Truancy or absence	1	47	21	19
Parent-child relationship	8	14	25	74
Personality defects	4	20	21	61
Marital relationships	3	12	17	15
Inadequate means	1	9	42	—
Mismanagement of means	2	13	19	3
Employment	98	4	8	6
Housing	4	9	13	3
Physical handicap or illness	17	13	23	21

An example of such a case involved a married couple and their three daughters aged 16, 12 and eight. A trained probation officer was concerned with the 16-year-old who had been found by the court to be beyond control and in need of care and protection, and had been placed under her supervision. The probation officer described the poor relationship of father and daughter, the erratic home discipline, 'alternating between indulgence and rejection', the girl's poor work record and her unsatisfactory associates. She did not mention the school truancy of the second daughter which had brought the school attendance officer to the house. On the other hand, the school attendance officer noted only 'truancy and repeated absences from school', and made the cryptic comment that he was employing his 'normal methods' of 'warning of action regarding continued absence from school'. In this case, neither worker showed an awareness of the problems the other was attempting to tackle, although the two sets of problems were clearly related.

Services given and contacts with other social welfare staff

Most of the recorded contacts of youth employment officers were arranged on the initiative of the client. Ten per cent of the contacts, however, had been arranged by a head teacher, school medical officer or employer. In almost every instance the contact was arranged to obtain suitable employment or training for it. On a few occasions, however, the youth employment officers did rather more than take steps to find suitable work for the applicants. For example, they referred one young person in 20 to the National Assistance Board, and in rather more cases considered that they personally provided some emotional support to those in personal difficulties. This was particularly true when the young person was handicapped.

The school attendance officers almost always took the initiative themselves in calling on people with a view to establishing the reason for a child's absence from school, and, in most instances, felt that they had discharged their duty once they had done this. In 30 per cent of their visits, however, they indicated that an additional purpose of their calls was to inform the parents of their legal obligation to send the child to school and the consequences of failing to do so, and in one case in every seven they took the first steps necessary to prosecute a parent.

They did not always confine their work to enforcing conformity. For example, in one in 20 cases they recommended free school meals for the children of the family visited, and in a few cases referred a lone parent to the National Assistance Board. In a few cases, too, they tried to obtain domestic help for a household during the mother's illness, and in others contacted health services on behalf of someone in the family in need of medical or nursing care. Moreover, in nearly one case in every 10 they felt that they had been able to provide help with emotional difficulties.

The special welfare worker's visits, like those of the school attendance officers, were almost always the result of a referral from a head teacher or school medical officer. Just occasionally, a parent asked the special welfare worker to call, and one case was referred by a hospital almoner. The special welfare workers had a greater variety of reasons for calling than school attendance officers. The reason most frequently given was the need to assess the financial position of the parents and their ability to make a contribution to the cost of the special residential schooling received by a handicapped youngster. In other instances, the worker called to help the family make arrangements for a child to be sent to a special school.

As a result of their visits, special welfare section workers gave many different kinds of service. For example, they made arrangements to give financial assistance to 18 of the 48 families seen and referred three to the National Assistance Board. In two instances child care officers were seen to discuss plans for fostering a handicapped child. In nine cases they took up an educational problem with a school head or referred someone who was about to leave school to a youth employment officer.

There were two main reasons for the child guidance workers' interviews, to obtain a social history from the child's mother and to give her support and insight. In only a few of the 72 cases did the staff refer their clients to other social services or discuss their difficulties with a third party.

There were substantial differences in the extent and kind of contact which the staff of the four sections had with other social service personnel concerning their clients. School attendance officers and special welfare section workers had contacts in the main with the school heads and only got in touch occasionally with staff from another branch of the social welfare services. The child guidance clinic workers' contacts, on the other hand, were most likely to be with personnel in different branches of the health services including the hospitals, general practitioners and the school health service. Youth employment officers were mainly in touch with school heads and employers and seldom approached other social service staff.

A number of the households reported upon by education department staff were also seen by another worker in the recording period. A comparison of the reports on the same family indicated that it was uncommon for workers to be in touch with each other. The two workers recording had only been in touch with each other concerning 14 of the 65 households, although at least one knew of the other's concern in the case of another twelve.

The social and educational background of education department staff and attitudes to work and training

(a) School attendance officers

In Bucks in 1960–61, 13 out of the 14 school attendance officers were men. With two exceptions they were all over 45 years of age and half of them were over 55. Three had joined the service over 30 years ago when they were in their late twenties; but it was more usual to join after the age of 30 or even 40.

With three exceptions, their fathers were manual workers, and with one exception they had all left school at the minimum school leaving age. Half began work in skilled manual trades and half in office or shop work. Five joined the education department directly from the police or armed forces and four from other local or central government employment.

Except for those with police in-service training, none of them had had any full-time further education or training since leaving school. Half had attended non-vocational evening classes at some time in their lives, but not necessarily in subjects directly relevant to their work as school attendance officers. Nine had undertaken some form of voluntary social welfare work. In discussing their careers many emphasised that their entry into the school attendance service had been determined for them by the limitation of available opportunities rather than by a positive choice on their part. They expressed satisfaction with their careers less often than most other social welfare workers. Nine said that, on the whole, they were glad they had come into the work, but only three said they would choose the same job if they were able to start again. Five would have liked to do social welfare work, but in fields like probation or child care where the need for training and a qualification were recognised.

These responses and other comments made by many school attendance officers suggested that they were disappointed with their status rather than with the work itself. Like most other social workers, satisfaction was derived mainly from feeling that the job was a useful one to the community at large and gave them opportunities to help people. On the other hand, there appeared to be dissatisfaction with many aspects of the work. Five men expressed resentment at the pay and consequent low status of the job. But of greater significance was the fact that eleven of the fourteen indicated in one way or another that they felt that the value of their work was not recognised either by their own administrators or by other social welfare workers. For example, one man said, 'We are the very bottom of the ladder with social workers as much as with the general public. Courts place more weight on a probation officer's report made after one visit than they do on the school attendance officer's report based on knowledge of the family over a number of years'.

Those voicing such dissatisfaction often expressed resentment and frustration, mostly directed against the administration which they held responsible for lack of recognition of their abilities and their low status with other services.[1]

The burden of most of the complaints was that they got to know the families who had a long history of truancy, but were not consulted when these families were in trouble for other reasons. They felt that in the course of many years they had acquired an understanding of the way to tackle tough social problems, and were penalised for not having a recognised social worker's training or qualification. One man considered that the appointment of special welfare officers to assess family needs for free meals or help with clothing was tantamount to a vote of no confidence in school attendance officers. If they were considered qualified to investigate school absences and deal with habitual truants, they should be considered competent to assess families in financial need.

Although most of the dissatisfaction expressed was with pay, status or the alleged attitudes of their administrators, nine, or over half, the school attendance officers also expressed some hostility to families who produced persistent school truants or absentees. They felt their own work was made more difficult by a too-lenient attitude towards such families shown by other social service staff as well as by their own superiors.[2]

[1] For example, one said, 'I feel the rot starts at the top and works its way down. There's no recognition of what the job involves and you can't blow your own trumpet. Sitting in Aylesbury they don't understand the value of your work. They think more of the routine clerks who never deal with people, only with forms and bits of paper. There is no excuse for them. They refuse to open their eyes'.

[2] Some of the comments were as follows: 'School attendance is not enforced and truancy is not punished severely enough'. 'The courts don't impose suffi-

They did not all express this kind of uneasiness. Indeed, one or two suggested that school attendance officers should become the all-round social workers of the schools. One of these deplored 'the police method of cross-questioning', which he thought some of his colleagues used when investigating absence, and felt that the service's hope of success rested on building long-term friendly relationships between school attendance officers and families with a long history of truancy.

Five school attendance officers did not feel they were in need of any further training or study. A small nucleus, however, felt their future depended upon being able to learn more of the social work approach. They wanted in-service courses dealing with such subjects as mental health and the administration of the social services. Two officers went even further and said that school attendance officers should be seconded for one or two years and given the opportunity to take a social worker's training similar to that proposed by the Younghusband Working Party for local authority health and welfare staff.[1]

(b) Special welfare section workers

The special welfare section was staffed by four women, two of whom were married. Socially and educationally, they came from diverse backgrounds and took different paths to their present posts. Two of them had university degrees, but no special training in social work. A third had been a mental health nurse, and was currently studying for a university external diploma in Sociology. The fourth had had experience in youth work and had taken a social science course.

All four of them felt that their work was enjoyable and that if

ciently severe penalties. We put in a lot of work for nothing.' 'The school heads are too weak these days. It's do *as* you please and *what* you please.' 'We used to have more authority in the old days', said a third, 'it's a different set-up now. There's too much pandering to parents ... More tightening up is needed. Children are allowed to stay up to all hours and we've no power to intervene'. 'There's not sufficiently stern action taken against particular parents', said another. 'We don't move fast enough'. 'Doctors give medical certificates too easily and probation officers are always prepared to make excuses for their customers.'

[1] One said, however, he would find it difficult to take a course because it would involve his wife and children in too great a sacrifice. However generous the department, it would involve him in extra expense; and he did not want to ask his family to sacrifice so much for him.

they were starting again they would choose a job within the same general field of social welfare. One who would have chosen to be a doctor, wished that the job were less fragmentary and gave greater opportunities for establishing firmer relationships with clients. She imagined that the work of a psychiatric social worker in a child guidance clinic or a probation officer would be more satisfying in this respect.

Although all four workers had had some further education at university level, none had undergone a specific training in any branch of social casework. One, when asked whether she thought such a training might have made a difference to her, said 'I'm bound to have missed something', but added that she was not always impressed with those who had been trained.

In several respects, the comments made by this small group of four workers presented a sharp contrast to those of the school attendance officers. There was, for example, little criticism of the administration of the department or of the policy generally pursued.[1] Again, none of the special welfare workers made hostile comments about clients, although they sometimes felt that their task was a difficult one. 'Rome-making is strenuous', said one, commenting on the difficulty of persuading some families to conform to accepted standards of hygiene and behaviour and of changing attitudes. She concluded, however, that despite difficulties and the mental laziness of some parents who wanted 'peace at any price', she detested the patronising attitude towards such people which she sometimes saw in social workers.

Another contrast was in the interest expressed in the problems of providing social services on both a broad and a narrow front. One member of the section said, for example, 'I believe present services are inadequate in many respects. This is due partly to national policy, but it is also due to working to "the book" '. She believed that regulations were sometimes too rigidly applied.[2]

[1] 'We've a good committee and chairman. They don't begrudge the money spent on this work. We don't have to fight now for every penny', said one. 'We still have to fight for recognition of the job', said another, 'but it's less of a problem than it was'.

[2] The county's provision for camping holidays for handicapped children was criticised. So were arrangements for the care of handicapped children when they had ceased to be the responsibility of the education department. In this connection one worker said, 'Clients resent changing social workers. One of the central issues of social work is how to resolve the question of the need for

Talking about her work, another said, 'For the handicapped there are services, although it's easier for those who know the ropes to get them. There's still too much ignorance and, of course, provision varies from place to place, especially for E.S.N. children. But', she went on to say, 'one of the chief difficulties for the parents of handicapped children today is the amount of advice—often conflicting—they are given from both experts and the public at large'. The parents of deaf children were the most affected. 'They do not know whether to send their children away or not, when to start them at school or what method of communication to build up. The most conscientious suffer most, get the most upset and worried.' The danger of the welfare state as she saw it was that 'it did not so much sap responsibility as fail to foster self-reliance.'

(c) Youth employment officers

None of the four full-time youth employment officers in the county was under 40. One was a widow and the other three married men. They had rather different social and educational backgrounds, but the working experiences of the three men had not been dissimilar, all of them having joined the staff of the local education authority comparatively early in life. The only woman had done clerical and administrative work in commerce before marrying and having children. She went back to work during the war and stayed on afterwards.

None of the officers had had any full-time training in any branch of social work. However, they had all had courses lasting for one or two weeks shortly after taking up their duties as youth employment officers, and had since attended day conferences on particular topics at fairly regular intervals.

When asked whether they would have felt better equipped with a full-time social worker's course, two thought so and two did not. All the officers were agreed, however, on the value of short refresher courses and one-day conferences devoted to particular topics. 'I'm pretty confident I can deal with most cases', said one officer, 'but it's good to revise from time to time and one-day courses are quite sufficient to give you fresh ideas'. He went on to say 'It's good, too, to have personal contact with others doing

some division of specialties between different (administrative) services and the need of individual clients to personalise these services.'

the same kind of work. We should do it more frequently in Bucks than we do. It's a weakness here'.

Like the special welfare section workers, all the youth employment officers were satisfied with their career choices and only one suggested that he would have preferred another type of work. For financial reasons, he had had to go straight to work when he left school in the early 'thirties; given the opportunity then, he would have chosen civil engineering.

With the exception of one man who 'hadn't a clue' why he liked the job,[1] the officers stressed the pleasure they obtained from 'easing other people's minds' or 'making their lives a little happier'. The drawback, stressed by all of them, was the pressure of work. 'The job requires stamina; it is very tiring. Dealing with more than 800 school leavers each year, in my opinion, means that every youth employment officer should have a full-time assistant.' He pointed out that the flood of young people in the post-war 'bulge' was not diminishing and that the work was likely to become even more hectic.

Staff shortages meant, according to one, that vocational guidance work was crowded out by routine national insurance registration work. Another said that if he had an assistant youth employment officer, 'I could devote myself to dealing properly with, first the special cases, second, the handicapped, third, a proper advisory service to industry, fourth, the training of junior staff, and last, the general administration of the service. As it is I don't find time to do any of these effectively'.

Some of the comments were critical of headquarters on the ground of alleged indifference to the need for adequate staffing of the service. One officer, however, felt that his difficulties arose because, although he was an employee of the education department, his work was subject to inspection by the Ministry of Labour.[2] He thought responsibility should not be divided. He also felt that the education department should make radical changes in its attitudes to staff. In particular, he thought headquarters was too remote, 'only notice you to tick you off, never to praise you'.

[1] He decided that it was because he lacked ambition.

[2] 'There are strains of trying to serve two masters. I was once told off by the Ministry of Labour inspector for doing something that I'd been directed to do by my bosses, the local education committee.'

Youth employment officers made some interesting observations on the nature of the problems which faced their service. Three, for example, commented on the way their work was changing as a larger proportion of children stayed on at school beyond 15. One considered that the ending of National Service had contributed to a healthier attitude to work. The youth employment officer covering the north of the county drew attention to special problems for the Londoners who settled in the area. Wages for young people were below those their friends and relatives were getting in London, with the result that many of them 'had a permanent chip on their shoulder'.

(d) Child guidance workers

Both the psychiatric social workers attached to the child guidance clinic had taken a university social science diploma followed by a mental health course. They were both single and under 40. The third social worker, who worked part-time, had not been trained as a psychiatric social worker. She had had a life-time of experience with children, first as a nursery nurse and subsequently as a matron in residential homes for children and as a social worker with the L.C.C.

Both the psychiatric social workers felt their training had given them a good preparation for their work, but that their mental health courses could have been longer. 'Too much was packed into one year. It would have been better spread over 18 months,' both to go into subjects more deeply and to give more time to gaining practical experience. The subjects which were least satisfactorily covered, according to one of the workers were the effects of physical illness on the emotional life of patients and the causes of criminal behaviour. She met many children and families in which either one or both these problems occurred.

Both workers found their work deeply satisfying; but one felt that she wanted to go even more deeply into the causes of mental illness and to take a more active part in treatment. Like those employed in the special welfare section, they seemed confident that those with whom and for whom they worked appreciated their work. Possibly for this reason they did not appear concerned with questions of status. One of the workers said that she did not always agree with the psychiatrist in the child guidance team, either on matters of interpretation or on methods of treatment; but she emphasised that differences of opinion never resulted in personal conflict or loss of mutual respect. Special emphasis was given to the satisfaction derived from teamwork. The sandwich lunches which team members shared almost every day in order to discuss their cases were instanced as evidence of the close working relationship.

Both workers commented upon their work, the social context in which it was done and the limitations of its effectiveness. One suggested that, given more adequate staffing, the first priority would be more home visiting. Both thought their results must often seem disappointing, especially to those who often hoped— unrealistically—for spectacular changes. One said that, in the face of accusations that they rarely had any effect, it was hard not to be able to claim improvements as successes.

Some conclusions and proposals

One of the main questions which needs asking after this review of the work of education department staff is whether the present division of work between sections composed of men and women with very different educational backgrounds and training is an appropriate one. In my view it is not.

In particular, the division of duties between the school attendance officers and social workers in the special welfare section seemed unsatisfactory, and the aims of the department might be better achieved if the two services were brought together in one social welfare division.

When the school attendance system was first established it was assumed that the best way to deal with recalcitrant parents and children was to threaten them with the power of the law. Since that time compulsory education has been accepted unquestioningly by the great majority of parents, and some of the material incentives to absenteeism or early withdrawal of a child from school (for example, poverty and widespread unemployment) have been substantially reduced.

There is an increasing awareness that the threat of penalties is not a particularly effective way of securing conformity to the letter let alone to the spirit of the law by those most likely to break it. On the evidence of this study, the majority of families seen by school attendance officers not only presented problems of truancy and absenteeism for comparatively long periods; they were also families in which these particular forms of nonconformity were only part of a series of manifestations of other equally serious problems of social maladjustment, chronic mental or physical illness or handicap. In many ways, their problems were no less intractable and complicated than those of families visited by the special welfare workers.

Some school attendance officers faced with families with emotional, health and material problems of many kinds were aware of the ineffectiveness of threats of legal action. They tried to establish relationships with parents based not on their legal powers but on their ability to convince parents of their interest in the well-being of their children. In other words, they adopted methods and procedures regarded by social workers as the essential basis for helping individuals to overcome problems of personal relationships, of adjustment to incapacity or handicap and of gross deviance from community norms. On the other hand, some school attendance officers were still authoritarian, not to say punitive, in their outlook and seemed hostile to the more benign policy of persuasion urged on them by their administrative officers.

It is unlikely that the outlook of some of the elderly officers who accentuated the authoritarian aspect of their role will change very much. But it does seem probable that if officers were brought into a division whose aims were avowedly the social welfare of the children, the transformation of the service from one based on the threat of punishment to one based on the broader concept of child welfare, would be more rapid and more consistent.

An additional merit of a social welfare division which included both school attendance and special welfare officers would be to bring to an end an unsatisfactory division between one group composed mainly of male workers with no formal educational qualifications and another group of women with longer schooling and university backgrounds.

There seems to be a good deal of justification for the contention of many school attendance officers that the work they are asked to undertake often requires as much knowledge, insight and responsibility as that which special welfare workers are being asked to do. Better use could be made of the qualities and qualifications of existing staff if no rigid division of work was made into that involving school absence and that involving financial need or special schooling. Those with least training could be given the simpler tasks, such as following up families where there was reason to suppose that a good adjustment had been made to the needs of a handicapped child, and making initial visits to families where there was no evidence of persistent poor school attendance.

The more experienced workers and those with more formal training could carry more of the responsibility for families who needed continual help, encouragement or supervision if they were to maintain reasonable standards for the children's health and education.

In such a division, those with some training could, through informal discussion and more formal in-service training courses, help those without training. On the other hand, those with some training could learn from those with long practical experience.

As far as future recruitment to a social welfare division goes, there seems to be a clear case for recruiting men and women with a two-year social worker qualification for the majority of posts in the service, and for attracting to each division or area one or two persons with a more advanced training in social welfare work. Many of the school attendance officers were profoundly dissatisfied with their status which they attributed to their lack of a recognised qualification. I believe morale in the service as a whole would rise if the men and women coming into it possessed a recognised qualification.

The youth employment service is intended to make the transition from school to work or further education a smooth and well-thought-out process for the whole population of teenagers. It is not principally for those with special problems of physical or mental handicap or of social deviance or deprivation; but when employment and training opportunities for young people are plentiful, much of the work of youth employment officers is inevitably with boys and girls who have special difficulties. If they are to make a significant contribution to these problems youth employment officers need to have some of the skills and insights of the social worker as well as those of the vocational counsellor and administrator.

For this reason, the training of all youth employment officers should continue to include, as it does at present, instruction in some of the subjects which are appropriate to a social worker course. However, youth employment officers should be primarily experts in youth employment generally, and not social workers. They need to determine the appropriateness of jobs for those with certain aptitudes, to assess ability, to inform teachers and employers of changes in education and in employment, and above all, give guidance to school leavers and their parents.

There is, however, a case for attaching trained social workers to youth employment offices to help young people who have special difficulties in securing or keeping jobs. As the social welfare services are at present organised, teenagers are less able to obtain personal guidance and support than parents, elderly people or disabled adults.

There was a contrast between the social class composition of the child guidance workers' clientele and that of school attendance officers and special welfare workers. Child guidance workers saw more middle class families in comfortable circumstances and fewer families where one or other parent was missing.

This contrast raises a number of questions which cannot be satisfactorily answered on the data obtained in the survey. For example, it cannot be inferred that the need for child guidance is greater among the middle class than it is among unskilled manual workers' families because a greater proportion of the former are receiving it. Certainly, the comment of one child guidance worker that if environmental conditions are too bad, families too large and incomes too low, child guidance cannot help parents and children very much, suggests that the criteria used to determine suitability for treatment were likely to favour middle class children rather than children of unskilled labourers, irrespective of the prevalence of emotional disturbance in the two social groups.

There is much to be said for using child guidance facilities to treat those who are most likely to respond to the kind of treatment provided in them. Nevertheless, it must not be forgotten that the system absorbs a considerable proportion of the time of the limited number of trained psychiatric social workers of the country, and may leave virtually untouched and untreated an even greater amount of serious emotional disturbance.

Hitherto, insistence on high standards of qualification for those who work in the psycho-therapeutic team of psychiatrist, psychologist, therapist and psychiatric social worker has helped to set and maintain high professional standards. Nevertheless, these standards may have been won at the expense of children who might have benefited from guidance of a kind. The survey suggested, for example, that the service in Bucks in 1960–61 was meeting only a fraction of the potential demand for child guidance or for work with disturbed family groups in a wider context. It did not cater, except on rare occasions, for children of pre-school age. It was not readily accessible to inhabitants of rural areas nor to children of semi- or unskilled workers.

It is on the assumption that many gross as well as many simple mental health problems in children go untreated that I consider that child guidance clinics should now recruit to their social worker staff men and women who have not had the full qualifications of the trained psychiatric social worker.

There is not likely to be any increase in the number of university-trained psychiatric social workers available to the child guidance clinics in areas like Bucks. On the other hand, there appear to be many suitable applicants for the two-year training courses in social work. If their work were carefully supervised by the psychiatrist and psychiatric social worker, social workers with this training would be able to make a useful contribution to the work of the child guidance teams. In particular, their recruitment might make it possible for the clinic staff to undertake more home visiting. In 1960–61, the value of the psychiatric social workers' efforts was much restricted by their inability to visit homes and see fathers as well as mothers of children they accepted for treatment.

Finally, although there are advantages to be gained from organising child guidance clinics within the education department, on balance I consider it would be better if they formed part of the local authority's health service.

The clinics are a specialist service. They often treat children who may need hospital specialist attention or whose families may need continuous help from welfare officers, home help organisers and health visitors. It was with these services rather than with those run by the education department that the psychiatric social workers were in touch.

F*

Transferring child guidance to the health department might also make it easier to provide treatment for the pre-school child who at present is only rarely accepted by child guidance clinics. Certainly it is widely assumed that many difficulties seen in school-children manifest themselves first before the child goes to school and that earlier treatment might prevent some of the problems encountered later. If there is any substance in this view, which should be properly tested, the shifting of emphasis from the school to the pre-school child might have important consequences for the mental health of the population as a whole.

Some of the contingent changes in social welfare services which would be needed if this recommendation—as well as those relating to the division of work in other branches of the education department—were carried out, are discussed in Chapter XX.

CHAPTER XI

The Work of the Child Care Officers

Children's departments responsible for the care of children deprived of a normal home life were established by the Children Act of 1948. In addition to their duty to take into care children who have no parent or guardian or whose parent or guardian for various reasons may be unable temporarily or permanently to provide them with a home, they are also concerned with children committed to their care by a court under a 'fit person' order.[1] Under the Adoption Act, 1958, they also have a number of different duties in connection with the legal adoption of children.

In Bucks in 1961, the children's department was headed by a newly-appointed children's officer, concerned mainly with policy and administration, who seldom dealt on a casework basis with individual children. When the study period began in October 1960, there were 15 child care officers and during the course of the year one more joined the establishment. Three of the 16 were men.

The child care officers investigated every request for a child or children to be taken into care on a short or long term basis. If there was no better alternative to taking the child into care, the officer had to arrange for the child to go to a foster home, children's home or infant nursery. During the 12 months ended March 1961, 546 children were taken into care or placed under the supervision of the department and 510 were discharged from care. It was not always desirable or necessary, however, to take a child into care, and the child care officers usually dealt with far more enquiries about children than the number taken into care during a 12 month period would indicate. In January 1961, there were 857 children in care,[2] of whom approximately 54 per cent were boarded out with foster parents and about

---

[1] Since this survey, they have acquired further duties and powers under the Children and Young Persons Act, 1963, designed to prevent the break-up of families and the necessity of taking children into care.

[2] In a number of cases Bucks child care officers visited children in voluntary society homes or with foster parents in Bucks, who were the responsibility of other local authorities.

31 per cent in local authority or voluntary society residential nurseries or homes. The remaining 15 per cent were in remand homes, approved schools and special schools, except for a few older boys and girls in civilian jobs who lived in hostels or were in the armed forces.

The increasing emphasis placed on providing the child deprived of his own home with a suitable substitute has made the task of finding good foster parents one of the most important of the child care officer's tasks, and a good deal of the time of the senior officers was devoted to it.

The officers regularly visited all the children in care whether boarded out with foster parents or looked after otherwise. When the child was in a local authority or voluntary society home the child care officer discussed his problems with the staff of the home. When the child was boarded out, the home was visited to give help and support to the foster parents as well as to supervise the welfare of the child.

In addition to these duties, the child care officers in Bucks also had responsibilities in connection with child adoption. Under the Adoption Act the children's department supervised all children placed for adoption on notification by the would-be adopters of their intention to adopt; inspected before the actual placing all adoptive homes for which arrangements were made by a third party, and usually acted as guardian *ad litem* on behalf of the court in connection with the statutory investigations which must be made before children may be legally adopted. In 1961, the Bucks department supervised 142 children placed for adoption and acted as guardian *ad litem* for 28.

An approximate picture can be drawn from diary sheets submitted by 13 of the 16 officers of the comparative time spent weekly with individual clients and in administrative work and travelling. On average, the working week was 47 hours, of which 19 were spent with clients; during that time 23 cases would be seen.

Most of the children and adults concerned were seen in their own homes or in the institutions where they lived. They seldom came to the children's department, and as a result, a considerable proportion of the child care officers' time was spent in travelling, the average being just under 10 hours per week.[1] Administrative

---

[1] 13 per cent of the clients only were seen in the office.

work, including the preparation of case notes, occasional attendance in court and the contacting of other social welfare staff took an average of $17\frac{1}{2}$ hours per week.

The child care officers' clients

For two main reasons, comparisons of the clients of child care officers with those of other social welfare staff must be treated with caution. In the first place, it was not always easy to determine to which household an individual child client belonged. In the case of a child in foster care, for example, should he be described as a member of his foster parents' household or of his natural parents'? Secondly, although identifying a 'main' client in each household did not distort the picture of the work of most social welfare staff, it was often very inappropriate when considering that of the child care officer. Who, for example, should be considered the main client and who subsidiary clients in a household where the child care officer was visiting a foster-mother and several unrelated foster-children in permanent care?

Arbitrary decisions had to be taken in order to press the work of the child care officer into the mould used to describe the work of all social welfare staff.[1] Inevitably, they restrict the value of the analysis of the characteristics of the child care officers' clients. Using the survey's conventions for identifying clients, 36 per cent of the 320 main clients seen by 16 child care officers in the recording period in 1961 were foster children likely to be indefinitely in care. Another 28 per cent, were foster children who were likely to return to their own homes, and 6 per cent were children living with a relative other than their natural parents. Eight per cent were children in residential homes or hostels. Thus, 78 per cent of the clients were children, of whom 30 per cent were under school age, 31 per cent aged 5 to 14 and 17 per cent aged 15 to 18.

The remaining 22 per cent were adults, most of them young. Only 3 per cent were over 45. Some were applying to the children's department to have a child or children taken into care. Others

[1] Where a child was in care, his household was said to be that of his natural parents if he was thought likely to return to it in the foreseeable future, and of his foster parents if he was not. If he was in a residential nursery or home, he was not a member of any household.

were housewives who, usually with their husbands, were in process of adopting a child.[1]

In only 10 per cent of the private households was there a *single* individual who could be described as the client. In 40 per cent at least one other child was an additional client and in 70 per cent one or more adults were also clients. In other words, the child care officer was almost always concerned with many, if not all, members of a family or household, not, like many other social welfare personnel, with one individual.

Largely because child care officers were visiting a number of adoptive homes, they saw a higher proportion of households headed by men in non-manual occupations and a considerably smaller proportion of households headed by semi- or unskilled manual workers than probation officers, school attendance officers and N.S.P.C.C. officers.

Like other social workers whose work was predominantly with children or young persons, child care officers dealt mainly with large households. Only a quarter had less than four people in them, and just over half had four or five. The remaining households had six or more persons, composed mainly of young adults and young children. Only 11 per cent had any members over 60.

Altogether 12 per cent of the households had at least one member with a chronic physical illness or disability and 11 per cent one or more members with mental illness or subnormality. In some instances there was both chronic mental and physical illness or disability. The majority of households where there was some chronic ill-health were those of the natural parents of children in care.

Most households had an adequate number of rooms per person.[2] However, like most of the clientele of social workers dealing with young people, considerable numbers lived at densities of less than one room per person. In addition, 6 per cent were living in houses considered by child care officers to be structurally unsound, and 8 per cent in houses having poor internal decoration.[3]

---

[1] The exact proportion in each of these categories has not been calculated; but the calculation could be made from the collected data.

[2] Thirty-nine per cent were in homes where there was more than one room per person, and 15 per cent in homes where there was one room per person.

[3] Three per cent were described as dirty, a proportion smaller than that mentioned by health visitors (7 per cent), school attendance officers (14 per cent), or N.S.P.C.C. officers (40 per cent).

The relationship between staff and their clients

About a third of the clients had initially approached the department themselves, but the rest had been referred indirectly through another branch of the social welfare services. (See Table 20.)

Table 20

SERVICES REFERRING CLIENTS TO THE CHILDREN'S DEPARTMENT

Service	Percentage of clients referred	Service	Percentage of clients referred
Health Services		Probation and Magistrates	7
Health visitors	8	Police	6
Hospital	7		—
District nurses	2		13
General practitioner	2		
Medical officer of health	2	Housing authorities	2
School health service	2	Education, schools	1
County almoner and		Moral welfare workers	8
welfare officers	2	Voluntary societies	3
	—	Self or relative referral	34
	25	Other children's departments	3
	—	Unknown	11
(continued in next column)		*Total No.* = 320	100

Workers in various branches of the health services, including hospitals, general practitioners and employees of the local health authority followed by law enforcement services referred most cases. Moral welfare workers referred one in 12, usually to arrange for an illegitimate child to be taken into care or when they needed help with the confinement and care of a young unmarried mother.

Usually, the child care officer's task was to arrange for a child's care on a temporary or permanent basis, because of the death, desertion or illness of a natural parent. In 2 per cent of the cases, however, housing difficulties lay behind the request. In 10 per cent, the child had been found to be in need of care and protection by a juvenile court and the child care officer had been named as a 'fit person' to take charge of the child by the magistrates. In 5 per cent of the cases the child care officer was concerned with the care of an unmarried mother and her illegitimate offspring. In only 2 per cent was the initial referral apparently made to try to prevent a family break-up. In one of these instances the child care officer was asked to attempt a marriage reconciliation and in another to persuade the parents of an unmarried mother to provide a home for her and her baby.

Seventeen per cent of the clients seen had first been referred to the children's department within the previous month, including 11 per cent who were being seen for the first time. Exactly half had been known to the department for less than one year, and 31 per cent for from one to five years. One in six, however, had been clients of the children's department for more than five years. These were the children in long term care.

About 15 per cent of the households seemed to the child care officer to present or cause no social problem. Such were those consisting of a married couple and a child placed with them for adoption where, in the opinion of the child care officer, all was going well. There were also households in which a child or children in care had settled down well with foster parents and presented no particular difficulties. In other households the children had been taken into care only while the mother was confined in hospital, and the brief separation was not expected to raise difficulties.

Much more commonly, however, the child care officer was visiting households, or clients in hostels, with a number of more or less serious social problems. According to them, 31 per cent presented one problem and another 25 per cent two or three; while 30 per cent seemed to present or cause four or more separately categorised, even if related, social problems.

The problems resembled most closely those listed by probation officers and N.S.P.C.C. inspectors. Problems affecting the behaviour or care of children were of course common. In a tenth of the households one child or more was the victim of parental neglect or—though much less often—cruelty, and in 28 per cent, children with behaviour disorders. In approximately the same proportion of households, there were disturbed parent-child relationships, and relationships between foster parents and children also were disturbed in approximately 14 per cent of the households. In 16 per cent of the households, the pre-adoptive process was not going smoothly or the household in which the child had been adopted still had difficulties arising from it.

Behind these difficulties directly involving children were often the problems of adults with inadequate or difficult personalities.

Over a third of all the households were considered to have at least one such individual, and marital difficulties were thought to exist in nearly a quarter. Criminal activities of adults and juveniles were known to have been part of the background of at least one person in 5 per cent of the households, and 13 per cent had individuals whose sexual behaviour, promiscuity or extra-marital relationships caused difficulties.

Material difficulties were also relatively common. Sixteen per cent of the households had a housing problem and 5 per cent were known to have rent arrears. Eleven per cent had inadequate means and some were also thought to be mismanaging their means. Seven per cent were living away from relatives and friends and had problems of loneliness, and in 6 per cent of the households one or more individuals had difficulty in finding or keeping suitable employment.

The child care officers' services and contacts with other social welfare staff

The child care officer's reasons for contacting new clients during the recording period reflected the purpose of the initial referral; but many visits were paid to homes where children were already in care, and over three-quarters were, therefore, described as routine checks or friendly visits. Where there were other reasons for visiting it was most often to prepare a report for the court or some other body (13 per cent), or to interview adult relatives of a child in care.

Child care officers classified most of the services they performed as helping to arrange for the adoption or fostering of a child. In only a small proportion of cases did they suggest that they helped with emotional difficulties. Although most social welfare staff without training recorded even less help with clients' emotional problems, most social workers with as much training as child care officers recorded a good deal more.[1]

In the course of the previous 12 months, child care officers had made contacts with at least one other social welfare department

[1] In contrast to the 12 per cent of cases seen by child care officers, psychiatric social workers recorded 64 per cent, hospital almoners 28 per cent, and moral welfare workers 26 per cent. Probation officers and county almoners were only slightly more likely than child care officers to record help with emotional problems.

on behalf of 60 per cent of their clients. Other services were approached for many reasons, for example, for financial assistance, for information about housing or medical care, for help with schooling or employment or advice on many other matters.

Indeed, child care officers were more likely to have contacts with other services than any other group of workers except county almoners, a finding which was specifically supported by the accounts of other workers who happened to have visited the same households as child care officers during the study period.[1]

The social origins, education and training of child care officers

Child care officers as a group were drawn from a less hetero-geneous social class background than the staff of many other services. Twelve of the 16 had fathers in non-manual work, but only one of these—a clergyman—was in an occupation rated among those with the most social standing. The fathers of the other four were skilled craftsmen, two of whom worked inde-pendently.

The educational experience of the children's department's staff was very varied. One left school at 15, did secretarial work in a local authority public assistance department before the war and ultimately became a boarding out officer. In 1948, when the newly-formed children's department took over this work from the defunct public assistance department, she became a child care officer. She was the only member of the Bucks department not to have had a formal training in child care or a course designed for social workers.

Twelve of the 16 officers had taken a full-time University course but only six of them went straight there from school or after national service. These were among the younger officers.[2] On leaving school, five took a full-time training outside the social work field and five went straight into office work. One spent the immediate post-school years in a Japanese internment camp.

---

[1] Of the 36 other staff who reported on households also visited by child care officers, 25 had been in touch with the latter and another 6 knew of each other's concern.

[2] Five had University degrees and seven social science diplomas. Two had external London University degrees and one an external diploma after spare time study.

Those who went straight from school to university took the decision to become child care officers while at the university. Those who entered university as mature students decided before they went to enter a branch of social work.

From a training point of view the staff formed three groups. First, there were five who had taken both a social science degree or diploma and a Home Office sponsored course in child care. Secondly, there were four who had taken the child care certificate but not a degree or diploma, and thirdly, six who had a degree or diploma but not a child care certificate.

There was a contrast between the views on the adequacy of their training of those who had taken a child care course and those who had not. Of the nine who had, only two were generally dissatisfied with it, the majority feeling that, on the whole, it was satisfactory, although there were criticisms of the practical work placements and instruction, and, by those with a social science degree or diploma, of needless repetition of lectures or subjects already covered.[1]

Among the six who had entered child care work without taking the course, but with a university degree or diploma in social science, only one felt that her course had, on the whole, been an adequate preparation for the social work aspects of her work. The major complaint of this group was about the insufficient discussion of cases and the over theoretical approach. Some also complained of inadequate opportunities to learn about child development or mental illness.

A main conclusion must, therefore, be that the special course for child care officers provided those who took it with the feeling that they had a reasonable basis for their work, while those who had only a generalised diploma or university degree in social administration were dissatisfied with it as a basis for the subsequent career.[2]

---

[1] One thought that some of the time spent in lectures could have been more profitably spent elsewhere, and suggested that there should be greater flexibility in arranging the course for graduates in sociology. She also complained that a lot of her time in a children's home had been spent in such chores as counting sheets for the laundry, because there was not sufficient staff to do the routine jobs, let alone instruct trainees.

[2] None of those taking social sciences courses at University had taken the generic casework courses.

Attitudes to the job

Clearly Bucks child care officers were satisfied with their choice of career. All said they were pleased they had become child care officers, and only three said they would choose another career if starting again. One of these latter, but for family considerations, would have become a member of a family service unit, because he considered that it was doing the most valuable work of all in the prevention of family breakdown. As a married man with dependent children, however, he could not accept the drop in salary involved. The second exception would have preferred probation or psychiatric social work, and the third thought she would have been better at scientific work than at dealing with people.

The great attraction of the work, as for most others working in the social welfare field, was that it was socially valuable, gave opportunities to help individual people in distress and at the same time exercise an interest in human beings. One man said, 'I'm interested in sorting out problems for people. I like unravelling string and doing jig-saw puzzles. I don't like a mess. I'm basically shy and don't like performing in public, but I get on well with individuals on their own. So this job suits me'.

The freedom and responsibility of the job also satisfied. One woman said 'I'm my own boss, virtually, and there are not many jobs for women where you can say that', and another said, 'I like working on my own. I've a great deal of freedom and responsibility for organising my day's work and for deciding what policy should be pursued with families'.

There was praise for those in charge of the Bucks department from three child care officers. One said that the children's officer was always available and helpful, and another that 'chief officers are accessible in Bucks as they are not always elsewhere'.

On the other hand, criticisms of the administration were made by five child care officers. One felt that 'where administrative convenience conflicts with casework then the administrative side always weighs heavier'. Another felt that the main difficulty arose from 'working for a local authority. There's a certain priggishness of outlook. Standards are too rigid, too bourgeois'.

Two younger officers regretted the lack of opportunity to learn more about casework techniques, one feeling that she had come across problems the implications of which she would have liked to discuss with a more experienced caseworker. One said she was often emotionally exhausted and got upset when foster home placements broke down. The other said, 'I'm full of self doubt about the rightness of my decisions. How can I be sure I'm making the right ones? It might make a difference if I were religious, but I'm not'. She wished the monthly departmental meetings were devoted to discussing cases rather than administrative details.

One officer suggested that a trained social work supervisor was needed as well as an administrative head, particularly to give more guidance to the housemothers of the county's homes. She was highly critical of some of these and said much of the work which trained child care officers did was useless so long as some children had to be placed in them. 'There is a need in Bucks,' she said, 'for more trained residential staff . . . a need to realise that such staff should be trained. There are homes to which I will not send children as I know the people there are unfitted for the job.'

Poor pay and limited prospects of advancement were mentioned as drawbacks by four of the officers. One suggested that no child care officer could afford to have more than two children! But a complaint made twice as frequently was of heavy caseloads and the lack of time available to undertake serious casework with families on the verge of breakdown. Only one mentioned ingratitude or fecklessness of clients, complaining of 'parents who have no feelings for their children and won't accept their responsibilities'.

Child care officers in their general remarks displayed a more critical and questioning approach to social welfare policies and to the provision of essential facilities than most other groups of social welfare staff. Four workers described housing as 'the greatest unsolved problem of the welfare state and often behind the need to take children into care'. Two considered that housing difficulties were responsible for more family breakdowns in Bucks than in the areas in which they had previously worked. Another suggested that there was also a serious shortage of facilities, such as day nurseries and home helps, which could help to keep children out of care. She deplored the absence of a remand home in Bucks itself where children who had committed an offence or been found by a court to be in need of care and protection could be placed while decisions were taken as to their future, without being sent out of the county.

Three workers described the difficulty of raising money for poor families and one suggested that 'if some money were immediately available I could often give immediate help to tide a family over a lean time'. Another said, 'There's a lack of funds at one's disposal as compared with the voluntary agencies, where funds would be available to be administered largely at one's own discretion'. She suggested that in some cases it would be preferable to pay a mother to keep her children at home, since the alternative of taking children into care would cost the community much more.[1]

Another child care officer said it was a 'matter of regret that the child guidance people would not continue to treat a difficult child while he was in care as they insisted on the child's own mother being present'. She thought the position anomalous since it meant that some of the cases most in need of skilled psychiatric help failed to get it.

Another child care officer complained of a recent move to make child care officers introduce a financial assessment form to their clients—a job previously done from the office. She thought this could 'set the work off on the wrong footing'.

General conclusions

In the course of their work, child care officers dealt with cases differing greatly in kind and complexity. Some households had no problems more serious than the need to make arrangements for the temporary care of older children during the confinement of the mother. In other cases couples adopting a baby who had already been 'vetted' by an adoption society seldom had serious problems: nor did foster homes where children in care had settled down happily. About 15 per cent of the child care officers' contacts seemed to be of this straightforward type.

At the other extreme, about three out of 10 of their week's visits were to households presenting serious difficulties, usually

---

[1] The Children and Young Persons Act 1963 was designed in part to meet this kind of criticism by giving local authorities more power to give material help to prevent family breakdown.

involving several, if not all, members of the household, and which were consequently likely to be visited by workers in other branches of the social welfare services.

The complexity of the problems experienced by some families compared with the simplicity of, or lack of any true, problem in other families needing help seemed to us to pose the same question for the children's department as the Younghusband Working Party faced when considering the work of the local authority health and welfare departments. What kind of staff, with what kind of training, were needed to deal both with straightforward problems and with complex ones? Perhaps the Younghusband solution, that is, a division of work between staff with three levels of training, may also have some application to the work of the children's department.

At the time of the study, the children's department tried to recruit only university trained social workers and there was no room in the establishment for workers with a shorter training, although, as indicated, a good deal of the work was fairly straight-forward, and seemed to be in the compass of men and women of average intelligence and more than average sympathy with a two-year social work training. It did not appear to be essential that those who undertook it should have a full university degree or diploma course.

University trained social worker staff with a more advanced training in social administration and casework would, of course, be needed to support and assist the less highly trained with those families which displayed the most difficult and complex problems, to provide an advisory and in-service training service for more junior staff and to supervise the professional aspects of the work.

The ratio of workers with a university training to those with a two-year non-graduate training would probably have to be higher in the children's department than in the local authority health and welfare services, since child care officers saw a higher proportion of seriously disturbed or inadequate persons needing skilled help.

However, the work undertaken by child care officers in Bucks in 1961 did not seem to justify the department's disproportionate share of the limited number of university trained social workers available to all the social welfare services.

Finally, most of the families presenting the most complex problems were already known to workers from services dealing with other manifestations of family inadequacy, for example, with school truancy, childhood behaviour disorders, delinquency or a threatened eviction order. The children's department was often the last social welfare service to be invited in and this in order to preside at the final break-up of the family unit.

In many instances the staff who were dealing with these incompetent or delinquent families were in touch with each other, passed on information and discussed their mutual problems. Nevertheless, it often seemed that everyone concerned might have been better served if all the services had let one of their number accept total responsibility for the family.

Understandably, departments may feel reluctant to delegate responsibility for some of their cases to workers employed by another department, but it should be easier for them to do so if the worker who is given responsibility has a recognised qualification in social work.

Really, however, I believe that this is not enough and that an even more drastic reorganisation aimed at reducing the numbers of staff who are likely to be visiting such families is indicated. The shape which such a reorganisation might take is discussed in Chapter XX.

CHAPTER XII

The Probation Service

Like so many of the statutory social services the probation service grew from the pioneer endeavours of voluntary workers and charitable societies. The forerunners of today's probation officers were the police court missionaries, the earliest of whom were appointed in 1876 by the Church of England Temperance Society with the specific aim of reclaiming drunkards who came before the courts. Subsequently, it became increasingly common for magistrates to ask the missionaries to supervise offenders likely to respond to a more lenient form of treatment than a prison sentence and who were bound over by the court to be of good behaviour. By 1907, the effectiveness of such work warranted making the service a statutory one, and after 1925 every court had to have the services of a probation officer.

Probation officers, except in London, are appointed by committees of magistrates, and their work is supervised by the Home Office. The expenses of the service are met by the local authorities within whose area the magistrates' courts lie.

The probation service today has been given many more functions to perform than its name implies and it is now essentially a social service of the courts. Its primary duty remains the rehabilitation of an offender while he stays at work or at school. The sentence for some kinds of offence is fixed by law, but when it is not the court may place an offender under the supervision of a probation officer for a period of from one to three years. If the offender is over 14 years old he must agree to abide by the terms of the probation order, which may insist that he live in a hostel or undergo treatment for his mental condition, and always requires that he keep in regular touch with a probation officer.

In addition to supervising offenders, probation officers are often directed to prepare reports on the character and social background of an offender while he is on remand and before sentence is passed. This is most frequently done in the case of juvenile offenders.

Probation officers supervise, as a statutory duty, all those realeased from Borstal, and also play an important part in the after care of prisoners released on licence. Those sentenced to corrective training or preventive detention, if they have been of good behaviour, may be released from prison and put under the supervision of a society or of a named individual, most frequently a probation officer. After care supervision is also provided by probation officers for the majority of juvenile offenders from approved schools.

Probation officers also interview married couples when one spouse has applied for legal separation, and try to effect a reconciliation if they believe it to be in the best interests of the couple and their children. Even if there is no formal application for separation, probation officers are often consulted by married couples in their disputes, and the court itself may direct a probation officer to attempt a reconciliation.

Another duty sometimes given to a probation officer is the supervision of a child or young person found to be in need of care and protection. The courts tend to nominate probation officers as 'fit persons' in those cases where the child who is the subject of the supervision order may also have been delinquent.

In Bucks there were 18 petty sessional courts in the combined probation area. The probation committee, composed of magistrates drawn from these courts, was responsible for appointing probation officers. Every court had access to the services of a male and female probation officer. Some of the officers, especially those working in the north of the county, covered several petty sessional courts, while three men and one woman were attached exclusively to the court at Slough and a second woman spent part of her time there. In all, there were 10 men probation officers, including the principal probation officer, and five women.

In 1959, a Departmental Committee was appointed by the Home Secretary to consider 'all aspects of the Probation Service . . . including recruitment and training for the Service, its organisation and administration, the duties of probation officers, and their pay and conditions of service. . . .'[1] It reported that the organisation of the service was basically sound and that the functions undertaken were both necessary and appropriately performed by

[1] Its Chairman was Mr, now Sir Ronald, Morison, Q.C. *Report of the Departmental Committee on the Probation Service*. H.M.S.O. 1962. Cmnd. 1650.

probation officers. It felt that the methods of selection and training were, in the main, adequate, but made some suggestions for increasing the number of graduates and for modifying training.

Its major recommendations concerned salaries and the machinery for negotiating them as well as conditions of service. It stated the belief that 'current salaries have not enabled the service to be maintained in size or quality at the necessary level of efficiency', and recommended substantial salary increases. It suggested that, although the aim should be to admit only trained persons to the service, it would be unrealistic to forbid the appointment of untrained persons in view of the serious shortage of officers and the pressure of work in the courts.

The nature of the work

The 15 probation officers serving Bucks courts collectively dealt with a rather larger number of supervision cases in 1961 than the average for England and Wales. Bucks male probation officers had an average of 66·4 cases and women 41·8 on their books at the end of the year compared with a national average of 61·1 for men and 40·6 for women.[1] In addition to supervision cases, each Bucks officer had an average of 3·4 matrimonial cases.

Most of those being seen by the probation officers had been known to them for less than a year, and 12 per cent were being seen for the first time. Nevertheless, 42 per cent had first been referred to the probation officer over a year before the recording period and one in 20 had been known to the probation service for more than five years, although the contact might not have been continuous.

Eighty-one per cent of the cases were referred by the courts, most of the individuals being law breakers on probation. In a few instances, the probation officer was merely being asked to report on the social background of the offender before magistrates passed sentence. The 81 per cent also included those released on licence from prison, Borstal or an approved school, who had to report regularly to a probation officer. Seven per cent, however, were individuals not guilty of an offence who had been found by the courts to be in need of care and protection, mainly young girls

[1] Figures from Annual Report of the Principal Probation Officer for the County of Buckinghamshire for the year ended 31st December, 1961.

with unsatisfactory homes who were being supervised by women probation officers.

Most of those not referred to probation officers by the court had been sent to them by the police and a few (6 per cent) had come voluntarily to seek help; such cases were nearly always people wanting help or advice on marital difficulties or family problems.

Probation officers did not interview all their cases as frequently as once a week; but their diary sheets indicated that each was likely to see an average of forty individuals a week, and to spend about half an hour with each. Most of the interviews were with those on probation, the subject of a supervision order or on licence from an approved school, Borstal institution for corrective training or prison. On average, however, probation officers made about two visits a week to obtain information to assist the court in dealing with an individual before sentencing him.

Rather more than half the probation officers' interviews normally were conducted in the homes of the clients, and nearly all the rest took place in the probation officers' own offices. There was, however, a good deal of variation, depending upon the area in which the officer worked. In the north and south-west there was a great preponderance of home interviews. In the Slough and Aylesbury areas, on the other hand, well over half the interviews took place in the probation officer's office. The availability of public transport seemed to be the main consideration.

Although there were considerable differences in the number of cases dealt with by each officer, the differences did not appear to be related to whether or not they interviewed mainly in their offices or mainly by home visiting. Apparently the longer hours needed for travelling by those who conducted a good deal of their work outside their offices came out of the officer's own time.

In 1961, probation officers were expected to have a longer working week than most other social service employees, and their diary sheets indicated that eight of the fifteen worked for forty-eight or more hours in a typical week. Those who thought their work occupied them for at least forty-eight hours a week, with the exception of the principal probation officer and another probation officer at Aylesbury, were men whose home visits considerably exceeded their office interviews. Since no external authority today could compel men and women to work such long hours, the decision to work them must have come from the probation officers themselves, who presumably felt that they could not get through their work satisfactorily without encroaching largely on their own free time for which, of course, they were not paid.

In addition to interviewing and travelling, every probation officer had to spend some part of the working week in court, and administrative work, including correspondence, interviews and telephone contact with other services, relatives and employers, were calculated to take an average of 14 hours a week. For the principal probation officer, whose time was excluded from this calculation, this figure was much greater.

Discussions with the probation officers confirmed the impression given by their written estimates. Although some individuals in other services worked very long hours continuously, probation officers as a group had undoubtedly a longer working week than any other category of social worker in Bucks. They were not alone, of course, in complaining about pressure of work; but they were rather more likely to say that the amount of evening and weekend work involved was a major drawback in their job. Four probation officers said that one of the disadvantages of their work was that they could rarely escape from it.

The probation officers' clients

During the study year the 15 probation officers provided us with information about 390 of their cases.[1] Seven out of 10 of the probation officers' cases were boys and men. They were also mainly young people. One in five was less than 15 years old and nearly two out of every three were under 20. Less than one in twenty was aged 45 or over.

When the probation officers' cases were children of 14 or under, they were most likely to be attending secondary modern schools. Ten per cent, however, were still in primary school and no fewer than 30 per cent attended special schools for handicapped or

[1] Pressure of work prevented some officers from furnishing information about everyone seen during the recording week. When this happened and if the officer had recorded information on less than 25 cases he recorded another uninterrupted series until he completed 25. These adjustments have introduced into the sample an unknown bias, but it is not likely to be large enough seriously to distort the picture provided by the sample.

emotionally maladjusted children or approved schools. Only 4 per cent were in grammar or technical schools.[1]

Ten per cent of those aged 15 years or over were housewives thought not to be working outside their homes. There were also a few women working part-time. Most of those aged 15 and over, however, were men or boys who were either working full-time or out of work. Because so many were aged between 15 and 19, it was not surprising to find that 60 per cent of the adults were single men not themselves the chief economic supporters of the households in which they lived.

About one in six of the probation officers' clients were known to them to have a chronic illness or disability likely to affect their capacity to work or their social functioning. In half these cases the problem was one of mental illness or subnormality. There were other cases where the probation officers knew that other members of the household had some form of disability. In no less than 17 per cent of all the households there was thought to be at least one person suffering from mental illness and in 23 per cent someone with a physical illness.[2]

Two-thirds of the households consisted of a married couple with their unmarried children, and another 7 per cent had two or more such family groups in them. Three per cent of the individuals were not living in a private household at all and another 10 per cent were either living on their own or in households where there were only individuals unrelated to each other by either blood or marriage. Thirteen per cent of the households consisted of a lone parent with unmarried children.[3]

The households were on average larger than those dealt with by other social welfare staff. Thirty-one per cent consisted of six or more people, compared with 12 per cent of the households seen by all social welfare staff. They were also more likely to be households headed by manual workers than were the households of clients of almost every other branch of the social welfare services.[4]

[1] It was not known what schooling those over 15 had had; but nine out of ten were thought to have left school at the minimum school leaving age.

[2] In some instances, of course, both kinds of disability were found in the same household.

[3] In just over half these instances, the lone parent was widowed; but in the remainder he, or more usually she, was divorced or separated.

[4] Only one in 20 of the chief economic supporters in the sample was in a non-manual occupation (Registrar General's Social Classes I or II), and only

The housing conditions of households known to the probation officers were comparable to those of the clients of other social welfare staff predominantly concerned with young married couples and their dependent children: in over a third of the households there was less than one room per person and between five and ten per cent lacked domestic amenities such as baths, running hot water or indoor lavatories, or shared them with other households.

The problems presented and the services rendered

It was not surprising to find that many of their clients' households seemed to probation officers to present multi-faceted problems. In only 2 per cent of the cases seen did the probation officer think that there were no difficulties grave enough to be described as problems. In another 23 per cent the problem seemed to be a single one, usually juvenile delinquency, but in the remaining threequarters there were many problems. Probation officers reported on 390 households or 5·1 per cent of the total reported on by all social welfare personnel in the study year. They saw, however, 1,243 problems or approximately 12 per cent of all those listed. The only social workers as a group reporting more problems in their clients' households than probation officers were the psychiatric social workers attached to child guidance clinics.

The proportions of different kinds of difficulty seen by probation officers compared with other workers are shown in Table 21.

In 86 per cent of the households there was a problem of either juvenile or adult delinquency or both. In nearly half the households the probation officers felt there was a problem stemming from the difficult or inadequate personality of their charge or of someone else in the household; in just under a third they were aware of disturbed parent-child relationships, sometimes involving both parents and more than one child. In a quarter there were marital difficulties and in a fifth problems affecting or arising from sexual behaviour. In 17 per cent of the households the problems seemed to include children's behaviour disorders as well as delinquency.

8 per cent in routine non-manual jobs classified in Social Class III. Among households of manual workers, there was a preponderance of those headed by unskilled or semi-skilled workers (Social Class IV and V) and a relative scarcity of those headed by workers in skilled occupations (Social Class III).

Table 21

PERCENTAGE OF HOUSEHOLDS SEEN BY PROBATION OFFICERS
AND OTHERS WITH DIFFERENT TYPES OF SOCIAL PROBLEM

Type of problem	Percentage of households seen by probation officers	Percentage of households seen by all workers
Criminal activities	45	3
Juvenile delinquency	41	2
Personality difficulties	44	11
Parent-child relationships	31	6
Marital relationships	24	6
Sexual behaviour	20	4
Childhood behaviour disorders	17	5
Keeping jobs suited to skills	15	3
Finding employment	12	6
Mismanagement of means	13	3
Housing	11	8
Inadequate means	9	9
Adjustment to illness or chronic disability	9	14
School truancy	5	2
Loneliness, social isolation	5	6
Rent arrears	3	1
Child neglect or cruelty	3	2

In addition to these difficulties which can be grouped together as problems of forming or maintaining adequate relationships with others or of anti-social behaviour, many of the families faced serious practical difficulties. Eleven per cent of the households had a housing problem. Twelve per cent had problems of finding suitable employment for one or other person in the household and 9 per cent were considered to have inadequate financial resources. The same proportion had to cope with a chronic illness or disability.

A comparison of problem reporting by probation officers and others

The relatively greater frequency with which probation officers reported problems could be a function of both the higher concentration of problems in the households from which their clients came or of a tendency on the part of these officers to be more aware of problems than other social welfare personnel. That both these factors operated is indicated by the evidence from the workers from other branches of the social welfare services who saw 53 of the same households as probation officers during the study year.

In most of these households both workers were aware of many problems. The few exceptions were nearly always health department workers, who had not had any form of social work training, including four district nurses, two welfare officers, two home help organisers and two home teachers to the blind; these reported many fewer problems than the probation officers. For example, in one case the probation officer was supervising a ten-year-old boy on probation. He ascribed the boy's behaviour to 'the break-up of his parent's marriage, his father's desertion, and his mother's depressive illness'. The home help organiser from the health department who visited the home reported only the need for domestic help during the mother's incapacitating illness.

When both workers were aware of many problems in their clients' households, there was naturally a tendency for each to list those problems closest to their own concern. For example, school attendance officers tended to list school truancy or refusal, together with various kinds of problems of family relationships or personality difficulties. They usually did not list delinquency. Probation officers, on the other hand, although noting the same kind of relationship problems, listed juvenile delinquency and normally failed to note school truancy or refusal. Similarly, D.R.O.'s and youth employment officers listed many family difficulties as well as their clients' problems of finding or keeping suitable work, but did not usually indicate problems of delinquency. Probation officers more often than not failed to specify the employment problems with which these workers were attempting to deal.

Contacts with other social welfare workers

In the previous 12 months probation officers had been contacted by at least one other source in connection with half their recorded cases, and in slightly fewer cases (44 per cent) had taken the

G

initiative themselves. Those most likely to contact probation officers were the police, but probation officers themselves were most likely to make contact with the education authorities. They also approached relatively frequently the Ministry of Labour and moral welfare workers.

Although probation officers were in contact with at least one other service about the majority of their cases, there were others where contact had not been established and where it might have been of real value—or so some of the cases reported by another worker as well as a probation officer suggested. No contact had been made between the two workers concerned with five households which both were visiting at the same period of time—it could have been chance that none of the five other workers in these cases had had a social work training; but some of the responsibility for the apparent failure to establish contact may have stemmed from their lack of training. On the other hand, it is also possible that probation officers did not sufficiently appreciate the value of contact with the officers concerned, a D.R.O., a youth employment officer and three school attendance officers.

Social origins, education and experience of probation officers

The social background of the probation officers was mixed. Two men and three women were born into professional families, two of them having fathers who were ministers of religion. Three of the other ten had fathers in skilled manual occupations, one of them working on his own account. The remaining seven were born into families where the father was in either routine clerical work or a black-coated occupation.

Two of the older men left school at the minimum school leaving age without a school leaving qualification and eventually completed technical apprenticeships. Their subsequent careers also had similarities, and both of them found their way into probation through deep religious conviction and personal involvement in voluntary youth work.

Four others also left school without qualifications, took office jobs immediately, but continued to study at evening classes. Three of them were active voluntary workers and said that their religious beliefs had had much to do with their subsequent choice of career. The fourth had had a more academic interest and won scholarships which eventually took her to university. Nine probation officers had school leaving certificates but only one went straight to university and two into vocational training for careers outside social work. The other six took office jobs, and became interested in probation as a result of voluntary social work. Indeed, with two exceptions, deep religious beliefs and experience in voluntary organisations were characteristics which all the probation staff had in common.

Six of the 15 Bucks probation officers were over 50 years old in 1961 and four were in their forties. None were less than 30. Most of the older men had joined the service before or during the war of 1939–45. Seven only had joined since 1945 and only one had less than 5 years experience. The Morison Committee on the probation service did not publish information about the age structure of the service and it is not possible to say whether the comparative absence of young men and women in Bucks and the high proportion over the age of 50 was unusual.

Probation work demands emotional maturity, and, since 1949, the minimum age of recruitment has been fixed at 22. The Morison Committee, while agreeing with the suggestion that 'the ideal age on appointment is probably in the late twenties or early thirties', went on to say that 'it is clear that the service cannot meet its requirements by depending on the recruitment of people who are willing to switch to probation work from other work at such an age; and that recruitment of men and women in their early twenties must not only continue but be encouraged'.

In Bucks only one of the officers had begun a career in or training for probation under the age of 25. Seven had joined the service between the age of 25 and 29, five between 30 and 34, and the other two between 35 and 39. Moreover, there seemed to be no trend towards earlier recruitment. Of the seven probation officers who had joined the service since 1945 none were less than 25 on entry, and three were over 30. However, the views of the principal probation officer about recruitment generally and to Bucks in particular may have had some influence on the selection of officers. He held that recruitment should be from those with a sense of vocation, and the initial consideration should be quality of character, but also that recruits should have had time to rub shoulders with all sorts of people, and this meant earning a living, and not just subsisting on scholarships. He also thought that because probation officers in predominantly rural areas had to work much on their own, they should have had some experience before coming to Bucks and liked new recruits to start in industrial towns where they could work for some years under the guidance of an experienced probation officer. Both the ages of the staff and the fact that almost all had worked in at least one industrial area before coming to Bucks suggest that his views were shared by the committee responsible for appointments.

Attitudes to training

Nine of the 15 staff had taken a Home Office probation officer's training. For three of them this training followed a full-time university degree or social science diploma course. Three had not taken a Home Office course, but had a university social science diploma. Three had had no relevant academic experience or professional training before entering probation work, although all three, since joining, had had at least one refresher course arranged by the Home Office.

The three officers with neither Home Office nor university training agreed that they would have benefited greatly from a full-time course in social work. One said a course 'would give a better grounding for the job'. Another, who had been in the service for many years, doubted whether he could now learn much about his job from a social worker training course, but thought he would still like to take some such course because 'he lacked the theoretical background' and also the status going with a diploma.

One of the three who had taken a university but not a Home Office course had mixed views about the value of his experiences. He said that the university course 'did not help me in my job, but it taught me how to think'. The other two approved of their courses, but criticised the arrangement of practical work. All three had been in probation work for many years and did not now want a full-time course, but each favoured refresher courses on specific aspects of their work or on such subjects as casework. 'I am learning all the time', said one, who wished she had had a recent opportunity to attend a course. Another, although welcoming refresher courses as a way of gathering new information and an opportunity to discuss principles, said that they could not give the young the maturity of the old and the old the enthusiasm of the young.

Only one of the nine officers who had taken a Home Office training course in probation work was, on balance, highly critical of it.[1] The others, though more positive in their appraisal had some criticism of their course. Four mentioned the superficiality of the casework and a too academic approach to psychology. Three mentioned 'almost valueless' practical work placements in a Borstal and an approved school, due to the indifference of the staff to the students' needs. Three believed that attachment to an experienced probation officer for periods of up to a year should automatically follow the completion of the Home Office course. Finally, one said that because the tutors had been Home Office inspectors, 'it tended to inhibit discussion, as people felt that they were being judged'.

All probation officers interviewed said yes to the question 'Do you now feel the need for any further study or training?', and most made specific suggestions as to subjects they would like to see covered in refresher courses, most frequently mentioning mental health, matrimonial work, homosexuality and casework. Several stressed the need for more frequent courses because, as one probation officer put it, 'I work in isolation, and I don't read enough of the literature. You must inter-change opinions if you want to keep alive. I would like more opportunities for discussion and study'.[2]

Satisfactions and dissatisfactions

Every probation officer expressed some dissatisfaction with his work or felt it had some drawback. Nevertheless, when asked whether they were glad that they had made probation work their career, only one voiced regret, as he thought he had 'an essentially practical and technical bent', better used in some other field.

There were four others, however, who, although glad they had

---

[1] He had taken a short course during the war, and thought it was 'completely inadequate', 'too hit and miss, not directed enough' and needed 'much more emphasis on casework'.

[2] Four officers said they would welcome an opportunity for longer release from their job in order to take a full-time course in general casework, or the advanced course for experienced social workers run by the Tavistock Institute of Human Relations.

become probation officers, would go into other work if they were starting again. Three of these would have chosen medicine, which, said one, 'still meant helping people, but is better paid than probation work and so would be easier for the family'. The fourth said she might have preferred almoning or psychiatric social work, where the relationships with clients were not based on legal compulsion. Nine of the 15, however, would not have changed their work at all and spoke of it with unqualified enthusiasm. 'Its practical Christianity appeals to me most', said one, with emphasis on the word 'practical', and he compared it favourably with a vocation in the Church. Another with many years in probation work said he would still choose it 'even if they reduced the salaries by 50 per cent overnight'.

There was almost complete unanimity among the Bucks probation officers about the appeal of the work. They valued it for several reasons: first, because it gave an opportunity, in the words of one of them, 'to help people who are in real trouble'; secondly, because they had 'an overwhelming interest in human nature'; and thirdly, because occasionally they had the satisfaction of seeing an individual who had been delinquent and unhappy find his feet and make a success of his work and his family relations. 'Of course one shouldn't attribute a success to one's own intervention, but you do sometimes feel that you have been instrumental.'

These were the kinds of rewards mentioned by most probation officers when asked about their work. Others said that probation work had helped them to solve personal problems or come to terms with their own personality. One of these said it had taught him humility. Another, a single woman, said she thought it had given her a legitimate outlet for the almost universal desire to 'boss', which she felt most women exercised as mothers. The opportunity for independence and the responsibility for the job too were mentioned by several probation officers.

The general and overwhelming sense of purpose and satisfaction in their work did not prevent most of the probation officers from criticising the way in which the work was organised and from talking about difficulties in the job. Conditions of work were most frequently mentioned. Men in particular complained of the long hours, of evening and weekend work and of the difficulty of finding time for interests outside work. One of the younger officers said it was his wife and children who found this a drawback rather than he himself.

Complaints of the administration of the service usually mentioned excessive 'red tape', lack of support from superiors, colleagues and personnel of other branches of the social welfare services, and the amount of office and clerical work. One spoke of out-dated methods of administration and said succinctly, 'We could do with an O. and M. study'. Another criticised civil servants and local government officers as being concerned only with their own position, not with service. 'They don't want people to have problems between 5 p.m. on Friday and 9 a.m. on Monday morning.'

One or two officers made specific criticisms of magistrates' decisions and the ways in which they used the probation service. One considered that a full-time magistrates' clerk might be the real answer, feeling that a part-time clerk, as in all but one of the courts in Bucks, meant a lack of efficiency and of facilities for the probation officers to do their job. Another criticised the magistrates themselves, as not being sufficiently interested. 'We don't always get the "right type" of magistrate. I would like to see more professional people appointed.'

The other complaints were more difficult to categorise, but some did seem to touch upon the difficulties of achieving the objects of the probation service, whether these were the rehabilitation of an offender or the reconciliation of a married couple. One officer felt that 'regular and fairly formal staff meetings for casework discussions would help the work of individual officers'. One felt there was insufficient consultation and said frankly, 'Some situations are beyond me'. Another confessed to becoming emotionally involved with clients and to feelings of failure when people got into trouble again.

Two emphasised the difficulties of attempting social work in a situation where the probationer was compelled to see them. One said that probation was too closely identified with the police and that 'the public idea of the probation officer was often of the man who waves the big stick'.

Others talked about the difficulties which society itself opposed to their efforts. Thus, one felt that the whole penal system needed radical overhaul, and that prison as a form of punishment 'rarely does anyone any good'. A second mentioned the absence of facilities in places like the Langley estate in Slough as a contributory cause of juvenile delinquency. 'When I think of all the time spent nattering in cafes when I was a student', she said, 'I can't understand why the housing people don't know that young people just want informal places to sit and talk'. A third complained of the inadequacy of national assistance allowances in many instances of ill-health, and thought that poverty was still responsible for too many criminal convictions. Deserted wives and wives of prisoners were particularly vulnerable. They had no insurance rights and great difficulty in making ends meet. Moreover, their youngsters had no father around to provide a good image of what an adult man should be. A fourth thought that 'keeping up with the Jones's improved living standards imposes a great strain' on families where parents were emotionally or intellectually inadequate, and he accused society itself of making the tasks of such families more difficult.

General summary and conclusions

Most social welfare workers were hard pressed at the time of the Bucks enquiry, but it appeared to me that probation officers were working under the greatest pressure of all. Their number had been increased in the last decade with the increase in population, which had helped to keep their formal case loads at a fairly constant level; nevertheless, since probation officers were anxious to develop a close, effective relationship with their clients, they could only carry their caseloads by working very long hours.

Secondly, to a greater extent than all but a few of the other social welfare workers, probation officers were dealing mainly with individuals and households who presented a formidable array of social problems of great complexity, besides that of delinquency. Most other workers had at least a sprinkling of straightforward cases: the probation officers had very few.

Many of the households with which the probation officers dealt were large. Their clients were generally young people—most frequently in their teens—and were less likely than the clients of other social welfare services to present problems of diagnosed chronic illness; but mental disorder or subnormality were not uncommon and childhood behaviour disorders, promiscuity and unsatisfactory relationships proliferated, and were often associated with problems of material hardship and poor housing.

The comparative complexity of the probation officers' work suggests that it can only be done effectively by men and women of emotional maturity and with the ability to achieve some detachment from it. It also seemed to be the field of social service in which it was most essential to provide a pre-service full-time course of training. Those officers in Bucks who had had no training, even after years of experience on the job, felt that they would have benefited greatly from one.

Since many of the probation officers' clients came from households in which there was a wide variety of social, psychological, physiological or economic difficulties, it seems to me that training needs to be as broadly based as possible. Comparison of reports made on households by other workers with those of probation officers indicated that the latter did not always consider the problems of employment, school truancy or housing which were exercising the attention of these other workers.

Probation officers also need to know much about the causes and effects of mental and physical handicap on individuals at different stages of their lives and on their families, and about the causes of deviant behaviour where there is no overt physical or mental disorder. They need to know how handicapped individuals can be helped towards social adjustment, and how far existing social services can provide them with support.

This broadly based knowledge is required not only by probation officers. In the health services for elderly and handicapped people, in work for children with educational difficulties, in services for children deprived of a normal home-life and in the care of unmarried mothers, those who are seeking to meet the social, psychological and economic needs of individuals require the same common core of knowledge about human behaviour and social institutions.

I do not think it is desirable even if it were possible—which it is not—to recruit probation officers in the future exclusively or indeed mainly from university graduates.[1] Nevertheless, every

---

[1] It could be done only if salaries and career opportunities in various branches of social work were raised to the level offered by professions recruiting from

G*

branch of social work, and in particular probation work, needs to attract some of the most able men and women of each generation if it is constantly to review critically its aims and methods and the way in which it should develop to meet changing circumstances. It would be a mistake, of course, to believe that the sole supply of such able men and women is now to be found or in the future will be found exclusively among university graduates, particularly since university places in this country are still so limited. All the same, recruitment to a limited number of posts in social work from those with good university degrees, as the Morison Committee recommended, is clearly desirable, and this can only be achieved if salaries for graduate entrants are at least competitive with salaries in teaching and public administration.

Most probation officers, however, will still be recruited from those without university degrees. Basically, they need the same core of knowledge about the character of human needs and our social services and institutions as do other social welfare workers. There seemed to us, therefore, to be a case for providing entrants to the probation service with the same training course as nongraduates who intend to enter other branches of social work. A two-year social work course at a technical college, followed by a more intensive year of specialised training for probation work, would seem the best way of doing this.

A common basis of training before specialisation might also be expected to improve the liaison between probation officers and other branches of the social welfare services. In Bucks, even where individuals and their families presented a variety of inter-related difficulties which brought them to the attention of staff of several social welfare services, contact between workers in these services was sometimes lacking. A common basic training course is one of the factors which could be expected to lead to improved liaison.

graduates where some altruism in the service of the community is also expected. Moreover, if the proportion of the population receiving a university education remains fairly constant an expansion of the demand for graduates in a single profession can only be met by restricting the supply to others.

CHAPTER XIII

The Welfare Work of the Women Police

The primary duties of the police in Britain are to enforce the law and maintain public order. In carrying out these duties the main work of the policeman or woman has been to patrol the streets, direct traffic, investigate apparent breaches of the law, and apprehend those suspected of having broken it.

In recent years, however, it has been suggested that the police might play a more positive role in crime prevention, similar to that always attributed to the village policeman; that is, that he should be seen as a Dixon of Dock Green, a fatherly, authoritative, reliable, friendly and sympathetic adviser to the individual easily tempted into dishonesty or violence.

The concept of crime prevention also underlies the discretion permitted police officers to give merely a friendly warning to children or adults found committing minor offences. Again, when the police are called in to deal with such incidents as a violent domestic argument, they may act as conciliator or protector of the victim of an assault. Particularly in this last kind of situation the police can play, it is suggested, a similar role to that of the social welfare worker, in addition to performing their primary function of guardians of the law.

In Bucks in 1960–61, the chief constable thought policemen spent little time in tasks which could be considered as social welfare, but that women members of the force were frequently engaged in such duties. The research team therefore explored the extent to which the women in the force, but not the men, were dealing with individuals and families who needed help and advice from the social services as much as they did the protection of the law or the judgment of the courts. Consequently, policewomen were asked to record details of such cases as girls found wandering at night or thought to be in moral danger, women suspected of shop-lifting, complaints that a sexual offence had been committed against a person under age, assault and similar offences.

In 1960–61 in Bucks there were two women sergeants, 12 women constables, two probationers and a woman inspector in the police force. The force was heavily concentrated in the south of the county, eight out of the 14 policewomen and one of the two sergeants having their headquarters in Slough. One woman was stationed in the north of the county and two in Aylesbury. A sergeant and a policewoman covered the High Wycombe division, and two policewomen the Chesham, Amersham, and Chalfonts areas.

During the study period, the two sergeants and nine of the 14 policewomen provided details of 126 cases coming within the scope of the survey.[1] These cases were not, as with most other participants in the enquiry, an uninterrupted unselected series of all cases seen over a definite period of time. They were a selection made by the policewomen themselves based on criteria supplied by the research team. Consequently, they are likely to provide a less reliable account of the work of policewomen in social welfare than were the cases of other staff included in the survey.

The individuals dealt with and their households

Nineteen of every 20 of the individuals dealt with by the policewomen were women or girls. Six out of 10 were children of school age and two out of 10 in their late teens. Only 18 per cent were 20 or more years old and only 2 per cent over 45. One in 10 was a married women; but there were a number of single women living either on their own (6 per cent of the total) or as lodgers in the households of non-relatives.

In the main, the police regarded only one person in any household as their client: in only 10 per cent were they concerned with two or more. Like the child care officers, probation officers and others dealing mainly with young people, their cases were often to be found in households with six or more persons.

The police were unable to provide information about the socio-economic status of a third of their clients' households.

---

[1] The woman inspector of the Bucks force at the time of the survey was wholly engaged on administrative and supervisory work and was not asked to participate in the enquiry. The rest were interviewed but for various reasons five of the women police constables, including the two probationers, did not deal with any cases which came within the definition of relevance in the study period.

Among the remaining two-thirds, there was a preponderance of households headed by semi- or unskilled workers.[1]

Policewomen knew little about the households from which the individuals they were dealing came mainly because 85 per cent of them were being seen for the first time. Only 2 per cent had been known to the police for more than one year and only 13 per cent seen on at least one other occasion during the previous 12 months.

Table 22

CASES HANDLED BY POLICEWOMEN AND RECORDED
DURING THE SURVEY

Total number = 126

Reason for police intervention	*Percentage of cases seen*
Moral danger, cruelty, incest, or in need of care and protection	79
Theft or other felonies	14
Violence or assault (matrimonial cases)	3
Child beyond parental control	2
Emergency mental case	2
Total	100

The comparative frequency with which different kinds of case were handled by policewomen is shown in Table 22. It was not clear from the records how a quarter of these cases came to police attention: but 19 per cent of the individuals regarded by the policewomen as their clients had made the approach themselves. Thirty-nine per cent were referred or brought to the attention of the police by relatives and 3 per cent by friends or neighbours. Only 12 per cent were referred by other branches of the social services. Those referring included a moral welfare worker and a general practitioner, as well as some head teachers, N.A.B. officers, probation officers and child care officers.

An important and almost universal outcome of the contact between police and client was the preparation of a report on the

[1] Over half (53 per cent) were Social Class IV or V, 32 per cent Social Class III, which covers skilled manual and routine black-coated workers, 9 per cent Social Class I and II.

circumstances of the case. In two-thirds of the cases relatives of the individual concerned were interviewed. In a few cases the police went beyond these duties and performed such services as securing financial assistance, hospital admission or medical attention for an individual. In 7 per cent they believed they were assisting with an emotional difficulty as well as, or rather than, in material ways.

Compared with the staff of most welfare services the police made few referrals. Nevertheless, they made at least one contact with social welfare workers in connection with one third of the cases at some time during the previous twelve months or immediately following the study period interview. The officers with which contact had been most frequently established were the children's and probation departments.

The social problems seen by policewomen

In 14 per cent of their recorded cases, the policewomen believed that there were no difficulties serious enough to be considered social problems.[1] The type and frequency of problem seen among the other cases is shown in Table 23.

Table 23

THE TYPE OF SOCIAL PROBLEM DESCRIBED BY POLICEWOMEN
IN THEIR RECORDED CASES

Total number of cases = 126

Type of problem	Percentage of all cases
Childhood behaviour including delinquency	46
Sexual behaviour	37
Parent-child relationships	27
Personality	22
Marital relationships	10
Loneliness or social isolation	8
Employment	7
School truancy	5
Housing	5
Inadequate means	3

[1] Six policewomen recorded at least one case with no problem in the specified categories. Two, however, saw 14 of the 18 cases of 'no problems' recorded.

Although policewomen were aware of many problems beyond the ones with which they were urgently dealing, they were less likely to report difficulties than social welfare staff who also dealt mainly with socially deviant individuals. This conclusion emerges from a comparison of the reports of 27 other workers on 16 of the cases seen by policewomen. Among these 27, only three, two district nurses and a home help organiser, knew less about the households or reported fewer problems in them than the policewomen. In three other instances, there was substantial agreement between the report of the workers concerned. In the majority of instances, however, policewomen specified fewer problems, their average being 2·6 problems per household compared with other workers' 4·2. The discrepancies were on the whole greatest when the other worker was a child care or probation officer.

Educational and social background

In most branches of the social welfare services in Bucks there were few men or women younger than 30 years old, and in many services over half the staff was 45 or over. The women police presented a very different picture. Not one of the 16 officers had reached the age of 45, and nine were under 25 years old.

Seven of the policewomen had left school at the minimum school leaving age. There was, however, a clear trend towards the recruitment of young women with longer schooling and more formal qualifications. Five out of the seven with minimum schooling were over 25. Of the nine under 25, only two left school at 15. Five obtained G.C.E. at 'O' level in at least four subjects, and one had 'A' levels and the necessary entrance requirements for University.

In most branches of the social welfare services in Bucks, a proportion, especially of the women, had come from professional or managerial backgrounds. As far as policewomen were concerned this was not so. One was a farmer's daughter, one had a father in office work, and one a father in the police force. All the others were born into the families of manual workers, most of whom were skilled employees but two of whom worked on their own account.[1]

---

[1] The fathers of two were in H.M. forces when they were born and the father of a third was killed in action.

There was a marked contrast between policewomen and other workers as regards the areas of the country in which they were born and educated. In most other services, the workers had been drawn from many parts of the British Isles, and only one or two had been born and brought up in Bucks. Of the 16 policewomen, however, six had been born in Bucks and one in a neighbouring county. Two had been Londoners, and one had come from Lincolnshire. The six others, including nearly all the new recruits, came from Scotland.

Previous work experience

Policewomen also differed in their work experience from most social welfare workers, many of the latter having come into social welfare work through clerical and administrative work in statutory and voluntary organisations providing social services of one kind or another. Policewomen, on the other hand, had a rather different work experience. One had been a machine operator, then a bus conductor before she joined the force. Two had been shop assistants, one a hotel receptionist, and two laboratory assistants. Six had done clerical work in private industry. Only three had had any work experience with relevance to social welfare work. One had a year of teacher's training, another had nursed, and a third had been a dental receptionist after leaving school.

Social welfare in the training of women police constables

From what the Bucks women police told us about their work experience and career choice, plainly they were not initially attracted to the force because they wanted to undertake social welfare work. Few had had working experience of people in need. Nor had any of them evinced interest by joining an evening class or correspondence course in social affairs or social welfare. Four had worked with girl guides or taught in Sunday school; but this was a smaller proportion of voluntary workers than among the staff of all the other social welfare services except health visitors and district nurses.

Eight policewomen thought their police training had equipped them reasonably well to deal with social problems encountered in the course of their work and none of these considered that a full-time social worker's training would have been helpful. Four did not feel the need for further study or refresher course. The eight who thought their police training had not given an adequate social welfare basis for their work had, usually, been longer in their jobs; but they included four who had joined the police force less than two years previously.

The gist of most of the critical comments was expressed by an officer, who said that the course was 'just a good general education in a policewoman's duties from the legal side. The basic training course is the same as for the men's service. There is little on the social aspects of the work which come to the women to deal with'.

When asked what specifically they would have liked to see in the course, seven out of eight mentioned more information on the causes of social difficulties and on the social services, and several suggested that the full-time course taken by women police probationers at the police college in Warwickshire be extended to give more time to these aspects of their work. One, however, although feeling that her training had not included much social welfare, thought this was as it should be, as she did not believe policewomen should have this approach to their work. She considered that the job should be limited to two duties—helping the normal population in the pursuit of its normal day-to-day business and seeing that the law was observed. 'I don't feel it is part of my job to understand why people behave in certain ways', she said. 'They just do and I have to get on with my job.' These sentiments were not expressed as strongly or as explicitly by anyone else; but there did not seem to be any great enthusiasm for more training in social aspects of the work, even among policewomen who felt that what training they had received had been inadequate.

Attitudes towards the work

The reason most frequently given for liking the work (11 out of the 16 mentioned it) was the variety of duties and surroundings it provided. In joining the force most implied they were looking for some way out of routine jobs where they were always in the same surroundings. Only one regretted her choice of career and thought she might have done better to stick to office work. Most liked active outdoor pursuits, and several indicated that a strong romantic streak had led them into the police force. One said

'Anything in the world can happen. You just don't know what's in store for you. Since the age of 15, police work had a fatal fascination for me. It came from reading detective stories. I always felt this was my line of business'.

Although few expressed special interest in aspects of the work which brought them in touch with inadequate or delinquent people, nine said they enjoyed the opportunity to help people which their work gave them. Some felt there were occasions when their official duties conflicted with their desire to help people. One said, 'I don't like getting people into trouble about petty things', and another, 'I feel sorry for some of these old shoplifters. I don't really want to bring them in'. A third believed that 'Too much fuss is made about the roughs at Langley and Britwell.[1] Of course there are rowdies in every city, but here nothing is provided for the high-spirited youngsters near their homes. There are no cinemas, no dance halls and only one coffee bar at Britwell. No wonder they come into Slough and hang around street corners'.

However, although many said they liked being able to assist people in difficulties, there seemed to be a difference in the way this feeling was expressed compared with workers in the social welfare services. Some of the policewomen's comments showed they liked giving members of the public generally useful information or helping them in accidents. When they mentioned helping people in distress, however, they were more likely than most nurses or social welfare workers to stress their satisfaction at 'being in a position to put people on the right road', as one put it. Only one expressed interest or curiosity about human behaviour. She enjoyed the job because it gave her the opportunity of 'seeing how the other half lives'.

Another attraction of the job for policewomen in the Slough area seemed to be the friendliness of their colleagues. One said, 'There's a grand comradeship among all the staff', and another who had only recently arrived from Scotland said, 'They're a pleasant crowd of fellows. Their wives were very hospitable when I came down here first. The sergeants and all are very helpful. They'll tell you anything you need to know and do it nicely when you've gone wrong'.

Although enthusiasm for the work was general, especially

[1] Langley and Britwell are L.C.C. housing estates near Slough.

among the younger women, some complained about various aspects of their jobs. Not surprisingly, these complaints centred around hours of work and the way in which its organisation limited the scope and character of their domestic lives. Several said they did not mind shift working; but half thought of it as the main drawback of their job. 'Working late shift, social life becomes practically non-existent', said one. Others complained of the short notice that was often given of working duties. 'You can't make any social engagements and be sure of being able to stick to them,' was a comment echoed by a number of them.

One or two of the complaints on the way their jobs affected their lives outside work were of a rather different order. A few agreed that they found it difficult if not impossible to escape from the public image of their profession. They felt restricted in their social relationships by this 'label'. As one officer said, 'When people know you're in the police force they become rather aloof'. 'You never stop being a policewoman', said another. 'If you're on holiday and you tell anyone your job, you have to discuss your work all the time'. She went on to say, 'In desperation I've given up telling people what I do. Not that I'm ashamed of it, but so that I can get away from it sometimes'.

No other drawbacks were mentioned as often as those associated with the hours of work and their effect on social relationships. Despite general satisfaction with the camaraderie within the force, three, however, suggested they were not fully accepted by their male colleagues, one saying that 'some of them (the policemen) treat us with disdain'.

Women police are likely to be more psychologically dependent on the explicit approval and support of their male colleagues than most other women workers. Theirs is a job which, in present circumstances, is most appropriately done by single women, who generally need non-family social contacts more than do married men or women. On the other hand, both shift work and their public image make it more difficult for them than for most women workers to build emotionally satisfactory friendships outside their work. In such circumstances, the individual requires much friendly support from colleagues. In Bucks one of the divisional headquarters seemed less able to create and sustain a supportive atmosphere for policewomen than were the other centres, and

apparent non-acceptance by their male colleagues had made one
or two women unhappy.

General summary and conclusions

Assuming that the 126 individuals for whom records were kept
were reasonably representative of cases in which policewomen
had an opportunity to concern themselves with individuals in
need of social welfare services, then it would seem that policewomen dealt almost exclusively with women and girls. They were
generally called in to deal with an emergency situation only, and
saw them on a single occasion. Most of the cases involved illegal
sexual behaviour; but crisis situations in which family conflict
had resulted were also common.

Usually, the policewomen saw their functions in these cases
as limited. They were there to see that abuses of the law did not
continue and that statements of what had occurred were taken
from women or girls who were victims of the abuse and in need
of care and protection. Nevertheless, because they had incidentally
to deal with individuals who were bewildered or emotionally
upset, they were often able to provide social support.

Compared with nearly all other workers, most policewomen
took a restricted view of their responsibilities to help individuals
in trouble. They believed they had only a limited role to play in
dealing with complicated family relationships, and that they
should not explore more deeply the causes of the events which
brought people into their hands. Half the policewomen were
satisfied, on the whole, with the way in which they had been trained
to deal with this part of their work.

Neither the opportunity to help people in trouble, nor curiosity
about human behaviour had been prime motives in most policewomen's choice of career. It seemed to appeal either to a romantic
streak in them or because it promised adventure, variety and an
active open air life. An added attraction was that it did not require
a high level of educational attainment or an academic bent. The
drawbacks they described were not those which made it difficult
for them to help people in distress. They were predominantly
those which made it difficult for them to participate in the life
of the community outside the police force.

Some of the comments made by policewomen, and especially

by the older ones, showed they had sympathy, compassion and an ability to support the outraged victim of a violent assault or of sexual misconduct. Other comments, however, suggested that insight and understanding were often lacking when policewomen were dealing with such cases as the wilful and apparently ungrateful behaviour of an uncontrolled teenage girl determined to be promiscuous and to rebel against parental discipline. There seemed often too much complacency among policewomen, and especially among the younger ones, about their competence to handle every kind of case including those in which there were problems of sexual misdemeanour.

As long as patrol duties and routine enquiries form the bulk of their work, young, single women attracted by active, outdoor work and the excitement of detective work, and not women who are primarily hoping for opportunities to help unfortunate people, are likely to prove the best recruits. Since policewomen recruits are not 'born' social workers, however, it would be a mistake to try to extend their functions in the social welfare field.

Clearly, all who deal with people in trouble or with ignorant or inadequate people should have some knowledge of the causes of wayward or vicious behaviour and of the ways in which those in a position of trust and authority can and cannot help such people. Without undermining their necessary confidence, it should be possible to persuade policewomen of the value of learning more about human behaviour and the ways to help the inadequate or delinquent. In this connection, the steps already being taken in most parts of Bucks to include policewomen in informal meetings and discussions with other social welfare staff on matters of social policy were to be welcomed.

There is evidence that policewomen are not often well acquainted with the ideas which lie behind the practice of work with delinquents or inadequate people, with recent developments in psychiatric theory concerning family relationships, or with changes in the outlook and practice of the mental health services. If they are drawn into the mainstream of discussion on current social service issues, this will help them to overcome their own sense of isolation from the social welfare services. Policewomen may then also come to see more clearly that their own work is related to that of many branches of these services. Moreover, because they often have vital information about the violent crises which occur in some family relationships, they may make a valuable contribution to the understanding of the social processes which precipitate individual or family breakdown.

At the same time, no attempt should be made to prolong policewomen's contacts with the more complicated cases. As far as possible their efforts should be confined to the emergency situation. Once this has been dealt with, the case should become the responsibility either of the probation officers or child care officers working through the courts, or, on an informal basis, of services like health visiting or moral welfare, which may already be concerned with the welfare of the individual or his household.

CHAPTER XIV

Social Welfare Work by Housing Departments

The housing authorities in Bucks were the councils of four municipal boroughs, eight urban districts and eight rural districts. In 1960–61, they owned and managed about 33,700 houses or flats, some 1,400 of which were purpose-built bungalows or flats for old people.[1] In addition, the London County Council owned and managed two estates in the county with a total of about 8,000 dwellings.

No council built especially for the needs of the physically handicapped other than the elderly, but most altered existing property to increase the comfort or mobility of the physically handicapped. Four set aside some of their older properties to accommodate temporarily evicted families with poor rent records.

The county council's welfare department, in an effort to prevent the break up of families and the taking into care of children, had a guaranteed rent scheme which it operated in conjunction with some councils, the object being to safeguard the tenancy (by paying off arrears and meeting current rents if necessary) while the county welfare officer was trying to rehabilitate the family. In 1960, 11 authorities operated the scheme involving approximately 25 families with over 100 children. In the following year 55 families with more than 200 children were involved for a time.

Staffing

The organisational and staffing arrangements of the councils varied considerably, and it was not always easy to identify the officers responsible for housing 'welfare'.[2] The L.C.C. employed two welfare workers who spent one or two days a week on their Bucks estates. In one borough responsibility was borne by an assistant housing manager who also dealt with the welfare of

[1] Wardens in two areas were employed to look after elderly tenants living in a single building or in the same grounds.

[2] Every authority was asked who dealt with people who got into arrears with rent, failed to take care of their dwellings, took in married sons and daughters and their families, were on bad terms with neighbours, or needed re-housing when they became elderly or infirm.

elderly tenants. In another borough, which had no separate housing department, three wardens were concerned with the accommodation and general welfare of old people, but the housing difficulties of younger tenants were dealt with by the chief housing investigator, who in his turn was responsible to the treasurer. In another borough the work was done by the housing manager and two assistants.

One urban district with two settlements for old people, had two wardens for elderly tenants. The housing manager and his assistant, who were also public health inspectors, dealt between them with any specially difficult problems. A rural district with rapidly expanding population, had four assistants who also dealt with housing welfare.

In the 15 remaining areas a single individual was responsible for housing problems. In nine there was a department dealing almost exclusively with housing, and the man in charge of this dealt with all difficulties arising. In the other six, the man responsible for housing was also responsible for various other aspects of the council's affairs.[1]

Thirty-one of the 34 individuals responsible to their housing authorities for housing welfare were interviewed. Nine of them, although providing information about themselves, did not keep records of cases dealt with, which meant that no information was obtained about the characteristics of the 'problem' households in eight of the 20 local authority areas—three rural districts, three urban districts and two boroughs.[2]

The 22 housing officers who recorded provided information about 406 of their welfare cases, 75 of which were cases seen by the wardens of the old people's settlements in two local authority areas. The remaining 301 were dealt with by housing officers and housing welfare workers.

The characteristics of the households seen

Just under half the recorded cases were of one or two person

[1] Three were clerks of the council and chief finance officers, two chief surveyors, one a public health inspector.

[2] Three who did not record left their posts shortly after the interview, and one said he had not dealt with any welfare problems between the interview and the end of the study year. Five could not find time to record.

households and of these a half were elderly people. One in six had six or more people.[1]

The main clients of housing welfare officers, with few exceptions, were thought to have left school at the minimum school leaving age.[2] Only 12 per cent of the chief economic supporters had non-manual occupations. Among manual workers' families there were roughly equal proportions of skilled and semi-skilled occupations (23 per cent and 22 per cent of the total respectively); unskilled workers' families accounted for 15 per cent of the total. Another 16 per cent were headed by women who were not working and whose past occupations were not known.

Over 70 per cent of the clients seen were already housing authority tenants, mostly living in adequate accommodation, at comparatively low housing densities.[3] A few needed re-housing, either because their dwelling had become overcrowded by an increase in numbers or because it had become under-occupied as children had married and left home.

The conditions of the 29 per cent not living in council-owned property, on the other hand, were poor, and all were on council re-housing lists. The majority occupied property rented from private landlords, but one in 20 was an owner-occupier and 6 per cent occupied tied cottages or dwellings which went with their jobs.[4]

Seven per cent of all the households had at least one member with mental illness and 29 per cent had one with a chronic physical disability. These medical problems were more common or more commonly recognised in the households seen by L.C.C. housing welfare officers and by old people's wardens. Not much overt mental or physical illness was recorded by those dealing with other households.

[1] There was at least one individual of 65 or over in 31 per cent of all the households. 57 per cent of households were headed by married men under 65. There were pre-school children in 30 per cent and school children in 34 per cent. In 5 per cent there were two families.

[2] Only 10 per cent were believed to have had a higher level of education.

[3] Three-quarters of the families were living at densities of one person or less per room.

[4] Only 1 per cent of the dwellings did not have a cold water tap in or attached to the building; but 3 per cent were without a water closet and 8 per cent without a fixed bath. Ten per cent occupied houses in a very poor state of structural repair, and 8 per cent houses in a poor state of internal decoration. Only 3 per cent, however, were considered to be very dirty.

The range of social problems presented was wide. A quarter of the households had no difficulty serious enough to be called a problem. Nearly half presented one problem only and at the other extreme 6 per cent had four or more. Housing was naturally the difficulty most often mentioned (see Table 24). It was the two L.C.C. housing welfare workers, both of whom were trained social workers, who were most likely to report multiple difficulties. Their training is likely to have given them a greater awareness of social problems than the staff of other housing authorities, most of whom had had no social work training. At the same time, since they were dealing with Londoners moved to a new environment, they could have encountered more problems than the staff of other authorities whose clients were mainly local people.

Fifty of the staff from other services reported visiting households which were also seen by housing officers. Twelve of them were district nurses and the households concerned were those of elderly people. In half, the nurses and the housing officers identi-

Table 24

SOCIAL PROBLEMS ENCOUNTERED IN HOUSEHOLDS DEALT WITH BY HOUSING STAFF

Total number = 406

Type of problem	Percentage of all cases seen
Housing conditions	46
Chronic illness or incapacity	13
Loneliness or social isolation	12
Inadequate means	10
Personality difficulties	10
Rent arrears	7
Employment problems	6
Mismanagement of means	5
Marital relationships	5

fied the same problems, usually of loneliness, ill health and inadequate means. In the other six, however, the housing officers saw difficulties where the district nurses did not. There was much greater comparability of reporting when the other worker was a health visitor, county almoner, home teacher of the blind, or on the staff of a service outside the health field.

Contacts between housing officers, clients and the staff of other services

Comparatively few of those seen by the housing officers during the recording period were being seen for the first time. A quarter had been 'on the files' for less than one year, but most had been known to the housing authorities for many years.[1]

In most instances, the client first referred himself or herself to the housing department as an applicant for re-housing. In a few instances, however, he had been referred by the medical officer of health or by a welfare officer. The reasons for the recorded interview were varied. In half the cases the client had initiated the call, in 45 per cent the social worker and in 5 per cent another agency. When the client initiated the contact it was almost always with a housing difficulty of some kind or another. When the housing officer took the initiative, it was often to make a routine check on the client's circumstances or interview the relatives of elderly people; occasionally he visited a tenant to explain his legal obligations or to discuss financial difficulties or problems of securing domestic help.

With the exception of the L.C.C. welfare workers direct contact between housing officers and personnel of other branches of the social welfare service was relatively uncommon.[2] In the cases where it was made a wide range of services was involved. Those most likely to have made an approach to the housing officers were workers from the local health and welfare department (6 per cent of the cases) and the general practitioners (in 3 per cent). Health service workers, in turn, were the most likely to be contacted by housing officers; indeed, apart from the L.C.C. workers, almost no housing officer contacted workers in non-health services. The L.C.C. workers had approached the children's and probation departments and were also in touch with some voluntary societies.

---

[1] Forty-five per cent had been known from a year to five years, and 23 per cent from five to ten years. Five had been known even longer.

[2] In only 14 per cent of the recorded cases had housing officers initiated a contact with another service and in a similar proportion been approached by someone else. This pattern was not so typical of the L.C.C. workers. They had been approached by other services about two-thirds of their cases and had approached others about 30 per cent.

Although it was comparatively rare for housing workers to initiate contacts with other services they knew of the concern of other agencies in a larger proportion of their cases.[1] The National Assistance Board was the service most frequently mentioned as in touch followed by general practitioners. Health visitors and district nurses were often mentioned, especially by the L.C.C. workers.

The fifty cases in which reports were made by other staff as well as housing officers were examined particularly to see whether there was a good reason first for two workers to be visiting, and second for the two workers to be in touch with each other.

Most of the other staff were found to have very specific reasons for visiting the households. Twelve, for example, were district nurses, 10 were N.A.B. officers who were assessing financial needs and resources, and three were probation officers with statutory duties of supervision. Housing officers could not be expected to undertake the duties of any of these workers, nor they, the detailed work of the housing authority. On the other hand, with the possible exception of the district nurses, it seemed that something could be gained if the two workers were in touch with each other, and in a number of instances, profitable contacts had been established.

A single instance of a case seen in north Bucks by a housing officer and a probation officer shows what can be done when the services involved seek a common solution to their different problems. The case concerned a family with eight children from 18 to two years, including a mongol child of six. The probation officer was responsible for a 15-year-old boy on probation for theft. Only after this occurred was it found that the boy was of very low intelligence and could have benefited from special schooling, but he had in fact recently left school almost illiterate, like his father and mother. The father had a poor work record and was frequently unemployed as a result of recurring back injury. The wife was unable to manage adequately on their small and fluctuating income, and had gastric ulcers. They were being helped under the county's guaranteed rent scheme to pay off arrears of rent.

The probation officer reported that although his statutory

[1] L.C.C. workers were also more aware of other visitors to their clients' homes, partly, perhaps, because these homes were more likely to be visited.

responsibility had been to supervise the boy while the latter was on probation, he was trying to tackle the problem more comprehensively. In his own words, 'I have built up a relationship with the father particularly, so that I can now act on behalf of other officers when they cannot get co-operation. For example, I was able to explain the rent scheme to him and get him to pay off some of the arrears, whereas another visitor had been shown the door'. The broad outline of the probation officer's account was confirmed by the housing officer.

Another case involving an elderly man, however, suggested that the goals and methods of two of the workers who were visiting him were so similar that there was some duplication of effort.

The two workers in this case were a housing welfare worker and a health visitor. The old man lived on his own with a large vicious dog to which he was attached. He was receiving national assistance and help with coal bills from the Slough All Good Causes Fund. A sympathetic home-help cleaned his one-room bungalow and he did not have to pay for the service. Despite this help both workers felt that the old man, who was deaf and rather frail, was deteriorating rapidly. He spent much of his small income on feeding his dog and neglected himself.

The L.C.C. housing welfare worker was trying to 'coax the old man into going on holiday' while his bungalow was redecorated and cleaned. Not unnaturally she had to consider the landlord's obligation to maintain housing standards as well as the welfare of the tenant. The health visitor was trying to get him to spend more on himself and less on his dog. Her aim was to slow down the client's physical and mental deterioration and postpone the day when he would need institutional care. In neither the short nor the long term was there any real conflict between the aims of the two services. It might, therefore, have conserved effort if one or other had been asked to accept responsibility and report changes to the worker of the other service.

The housing staff

(a) Old people's wardens

There were five old people's wardens in Bucks, all of whom were married women, and two were in their sixties. Four of the five had had no formal training or education beyond the minimum school leaving age and had spent most of their married lives as housewives and mothers.[1] The fifth had had some experience of nursing before her marriage.

For all of them much of the attraction of the work had been the accommodation that was provided with it. One warden, chosen from 46 applicants, said 'I applied for the job because I liked old people and needed the house'. All were friendly, practical, capable people who dealt calmly with the day-to-day problems they met. Their husbands were willing to lend a hand in repairs and maintenance and to take part in the social activities of the old people. All enjoyed their work and the three oldest ones did not feel they would have benefited from a training in social work. The youngest would have liked, before taking the job, to have worked with someone 'specialised in old people's welfare, either with a warden or in a residential institution'.

Their sympathy with old people was evident in the ways in which they tried to help, however much they might lack the objectivity and detachment of the trained social worker. One of the wardens, for example, made no secret of her strong likes and dislikes for various old people in her settlement. Another identified herself with the old people generally and was excessively hostile to all the other services, accusing them of deliberate neglect, apathy, and failure to provide community services.[2]

(b) Housing officers and assistants

Six of those dealing with housing welfare were women and 20 men, and although the careers of no two of them were exactly alike, there was some similarity in their educational background and working experience.

Nine of the 26 had fathers who were skilled manual workers and another eight fathers in non-manual occupations also in Social Class III. The others had non-manual middle class fathers. Two of the 26 left school at the statutory minimum age. Most of the others stayed on for a year or two longer and left with a school leaving certificate equivalent to at least 4 G.C.E. 'O' level passes. Two went on to qualify for and enter a university, but for

---

[1] Three had been domestic servants.

[2] 'The district nurse and health visitor never visit. The old people have to give themselves their own injections, unless I take pity on them.'

domestic or personal reasons neither had been able to complete their degree course. With one or two exceptions most had joined local government early in their working life.

Among the 26 officers interviewed—20 men and six women—seven men and two women had had no systematic training relevant to their jobs in general housing management. Four of these had, however, taken evening classes in relevant subjects. On the other hand, one woman had taken a university social science course, another an external university diploma in sociology after part-time study, and another a full-time course in housing management.

Eight of the officers had taken courses involving evening and weekend study in housing management or public health inspection, and had passed two qualifying examinations of the professional institutes. Six were taking courses and had still to qualify.

Views on training for housing welfare work

Both the women who had taken university social science diplomas emphasised that their courses were not a training for housing welfare, and realised the gaps in their knowledge. One said, 'It didn't deal with important aspects of housing like structural and architectural problems or with casework. It was definitely not vocational'. But both felt that they had had a valuable preparation for their work.

Those who had completed or were taking courses in housing management or public health inspection had varied views about their usefulness for the social welfare aspects of their work. Nine considered that, on balance, their courses had covered welfare problems adequately and that they did not need any full-time course in social work, two of them saying that they had little social welfare work to do. The others argued that in-service training and experience were the only satisfactory ways of learning about people and how to help them. 'Steady learning of the job on the job is the only satisfactory method', said one, but added that a month's full-time course would have been a useful supplement to his part-time studies and job experience. The other six were more critical of their courses. One said that 'the correspondence course dealt with the administrative and technical aspects and the in-service with the practical. I would have liked more on general sociological aspects and psychology'. Another felt the public health inspector's training he had taken 'would not be an adequate training for those who had to deal with social problems all the time'.

Five of the nine officers with neither training in housing management nor a social science diploma said they would have liked either a full-time course or organised in-service training. One of these felt, however, that although a course in social work would have had general interest it would not have been of particular value in the general work he was doing for his housing department. The other four felt they would not have gained much from either a full-time course or in-service training in social welfare. 'It's a question of common sense', said one. 'Many people with social work training seem to have their heads in the clouds.' 'I have sufficient imagination to realise how the other person is feeling,' said another. 'No course can give me this.' 'You can only learn about people by actually dealing with them,' said a third.

Attitudes to work

The six women interviewed gave the impression of finding greater satisfaction in their work than the men, although like many of the latter, most felt they had come into housing welfare or management by accident rather than design. Only half the men, however, said they were unequivocally pleased to be in their present jobs, and 13, given the chance, would choose some other occupation, frequently, moreover, in technology or craftsmanship, business management or the armed forces rather than in social welfare. Those without formal training were more likely to express dissatisfaction than those with a qualification.

Nevertheless, most housing officers did obtain satisfaction from their jobs, not least from seeing the pleasure and gratitude of those coming from poor housing when they settled into new houses or flats. They also like the variety of their work which did not chain them to an office desk. Some more senior people also mentioned the security of the job and the prospects of promotion.

In describing the drawbacks, on the other hand, nine spontaneously instanced inadequate salaries or other conditions of employment, including opportunities for promotion. One man was critical of the salary scales in local government. 'There's something sadly wrong with the administration of social welfare services when they require people with high qualifications but pay them derisory salaries. I feel strongly on this. Administrators are adequately paid but not those in contact with people, who save the community annually much more than the cost of their salaries.'

Ten individuals, seven men and three women, indicated that they were sometimes in disagreement with the members of their local council on questions of policy. One complained that 'the housing manager is not sufficiently recognised, and his opinions are not always given sufficient weight either by the council or by other departments'. Another said, 'Whatever you do, you must not offend the council'.

One or two of the staff raised wider issues connected with housing policies. One felt his council was not concerned enough to provide suitable housing for ageing people, and one of the L.C.C. housing welfare workers attributed some of the difficulties on new housing estates to lack of foresight on the part of the L.C.C. itself. 'Some of the unhappiness of young mothers moved to Langley was not altogether preventable', she said, 'but the L.C.C. could have done more to provide play and other facilities for children and young mothers'. She thought that particular problems of particular individuals were not examined closely enough, and instanced a family given priority in housing because they had three children with a serious congenital defect. Rehousing them miles away from the hospital which was treating them as out-patients had increased rather than reduced their practical difficulties. People were 'encouraged to think that a move will solve their problems. It doesn't'.

Summary of findings and conclusions

With the exception of the L.C.C. and one borough, the housing authorities did not differentiate housing welfare work from the rest of the work of the department. Housing officers and their assistants saw their work as an all-round administrative job involving the maintenance of property, the collection of rents, the allocation of new tenancies, and any difficult problem arising in the day-to-day work of the department.

In the smaller authorities where housing was only one of the responsibilities of a local government officer who might also be the clerk of the council, rating officer, chief financial officer, surveyor or chief public health inspector, it would have been

H

surprising to have found an individual specialising in social welfare work for the council's tenants. But, apart from two authorities who were employing wardens to supervise the needs of old people in the settlements, only one of the nine authorities with more than 1,000 lettings had made housing welfare work a specialised full-time task for a member of the department.

With the exception of those already specialising in social welfare, housing officers made it clear that they did not consider they needed any specialised training in social work. Most recognised that the correspondence courses for the examinations of the Institute of Housing or of the Society of Housing Managers paid little attention to the problems of difficult tenants, and those who had qualified as public health inspectors had received little or no instruction in psychology or in the causes of social inadequacy. They argued, however, either that the proportion of their time spent on welfare problems was too small to warrant special training for it, or that, given normal sensitivity and sympathy, it could be learned by experience.

Despite this scepticism about training in social welfare work, however, this survey lent support to the view that more of the concepts of social welfare work are needed in the general training of housing managers. This conclusion emerged from the differences between the reports of those fully occupied in social welfare work and those who undertook such work in the general course of duty. The latter were less likely to report the full range of social and economic problems, and they were not as likely to have made contact with the personnel of other social welfare services.

Since small authorities have not the resources to employ specialised welfare officers, those responsible for general housing management should know about the signs and symptoms of family instability and about the social welfare services available to try to prevent trouble from developing.

If training for housing management continues to be through private study based on correspondence courses, with little systematic in-service instruction, it is difficult to see how sufficient understanding of social welfare problems can be developed, although something can be gained by including more applied psychology, social structure and social services in the syllabus.[1]

[1] I am not competent to discuss the more general issues of training for

However, while in-service training remains the main method, much can be said for providing short full-time courses in social welfare of about one month's duration to supplement private study. Such courses might be run on a regional basis by the Institute of Housing Managers.

Local housing authorities might also be encouraged to combine resources in order to provide some *systematic* in-service courses in housing welfare. In the final chapter, it is suggested that a county like Bucks should appoint a social welfare training officer to organise courses for social welfare assistants in many branches of local authority work, and the smaller housing authorities should be encouraged to make use of these facilities.

At the same time, larger housing authorities should consider employing at least one welfare officer with responsibility for assisting council tenants who need help through increasing age, physical or mental disability, fecklessness or misfortune. The volume of work in authorities owning more than 1,000 properties and letting more than 100 of them to old people is likely to warrant the appointment of a full-time welfare officer, who ideally should have some experience and understanding of the general problems of housing management; but, failing this, there is much to be said for appointing individuals with a two-year general training in social work.

Finally, there will be a growing need for wardens of old people's settlements. At present, housing authorities have selected for these posts elderly people who are competent, cheerful, outgoing individuals but who have not had much in the way of formal education so that some of their sterling work may be undone by a limited understanding of the complexity of human needs or awareness of their own prejudices. Given a social welfare worker in the housing department it is not necessary that old people's wardens should themselves be social workers, but the social welfare training officer might lead organised discussions between old people's wardens, with the object of supporting them in their dealings with difficult old people and providing them with an opportunity to gain insight into their own emotions.

housing management which are at present being considered by the responsible professional bodies.

CHAPTER XV

The Relief of Poverty

The work of the National Assistance Board visiting officers

Since 1948, responsibility for giving financial help to those without means or with insufficient resources to meet their needs has rested with the semi-independent central government agency, the National Assistance Board. The Chairman and five members of the Board who are responsible for its affairs are appointed by the Crown on the recommendation of the Prime Minister. They are not members of the Government. The Board is staffed by civil servants, however, and the Minister of Pensions and National Insurance is responsible for answering questions in Parliament about its activities.

The main work of the Board in Bucks is carried out from its four area offices at Aylesbury, High Wycombe, Newport Pagnell and Slough, all of which are under the direction of the London (South) Regional Office of the Board.

In Bucks in 1960–61 applicants for assistance, unless they chose to apply at the area office in person and required only a single payment, were visited by one of the Board's officers in order that means and needs could be assessed. Most of the initial visits in response to such applications were undertaken by executive grade officers; but, because the offices were then often under-staffed and under considerable pressure,[1] clerical grade officers who had less authority and generally less experience undertook some of these visits, in addition to the ordinary review visits to people already receiving grants. At the four offices there was altogether a visiting staff of 20 during the study year 1960–61, of whom nine were executive and eleven clerical officers.

In determining how much an applicant may receive the Board's officers are guided by the National Assistance Act and by regulations approved by Parliament which set a standard of need and

---

[1] Since the present survey was undertaken there has, say the N.A.B., been a considerable reduction in the pressure of work at these offices, since the staff has increased by nearly 12 per cent, whereas the number of weekly allowances dealt with has increased by less than 3 per cent.

indicate the kinds of resources which may be partly or wholly disregarded. The Regulations also provide for additional payments over and above the basic standard of need to meet special circumstances such as the cost of extra heating, an expensive diet, domestic help or laundry. In authorising such additions and in determining such matters as the allowable rent or the contribution to the rent to be expected of other household members, the Board's officers exercise quite wide discretionary powers.

During 1960–61, it was estimated that, on an average, weekly payments from offices in Bucks were being made to approximately 12,500 people. Not all of these would have been residents of Bucks since the four offices were also responsible for assistance to residents in parts of Berkshire, Bedfordshire and Hertfordshire. In these circumstances, it would be misleading to place much reliance on a calculation of the rate per 1,000 of the population receiving assistance. If all the recipients had been Buckinghamshire residents, 27 individuals per 1,000 of the population would have been recipients of weekly grants, a rate which compared with 35 per 1,000 for Great Britain as a whole at the end of 1961.[1] If there were as many dependents per recipient in Buckinghamshire as there were in Great Britain, it would suggest that approximately 38 per 1,000 residents of Bucks were receiving regular help compared with 52 per 1,000 in Great Britain.

Home visiting as part of the officers' work

Most of the officers who recorded for us told us that in a typical week they would visit 40 or 50 applicants in their own homes and have interviews with an additional five or so in the office.[2] In any given year they might, therefore, pay as many as 2,000 visits. Not all of these visits would be to different households. Indeed, the majority said that only 300 to 500 of their annual visits were to completely new applicants. The remainder were paid to those who were already receiving a weekly allowance or to re-applicants who had received such allowances in the past.

The Board's officers gave us some idea of the way in which

[1] Cf. *Report of National Assistance Board for year ending* 1961. H.M.S.O. 1962, Cmnd. 1730, pp. 8, 13, 14.
[2] They gave details of only the first 25 seen in the recording week for the survey.

their typical working week was divided. A few officers spent many more hours than their colleagues with applicants or in travelling and consequently fewer in office work, but the average time with applicants for the whole group was 17 hours. Average travelling time was $4\frac{1}{2}$ hours, while report preparation and assessments averaged 13 hours a week. Time spent on other activities, including contacts with other social services, consultations with colleagues, reading bulletins or journals associated with the work, averaged five hours per week.

The National Assistance Act of 1948 required the Board to carry out its duties 'in such manner as shall best promote the welfare of the persons concerned'. The Board's Annual Report for 1961, commenting on this duty, said: 'even if no such statutory obligation existed, the Board's officers who day-in day-out are visiting the homes of the poorest, and among them the loneliest and least self-reliant members of the community would inevitably come across problems in plenty which cannot be solved simply by the issue of a regular assistance allowance to meet a deficiency in income. Help and advice of all kinds may be needed, and although a great part of what the Board's officers can do in this field must consist of putting the people concerned in touch with some specialist service or organisation, there were also many opportunities for more direct or personal help'.

How frequently, to judge from the description of applicants seen, did the N.A.B. officers in Bucks come up against such people, perceive difficulties other than those of low income and try to assist either by 'direct or personal' help or by 'putting the people concerned in touch with some specialist service'?

Characteristics of those visited by the officers[1]

The information provided by the 20 officers related to 489 households. In 10 of these there were two or more independent applicants for weekly allowances; but in the remainder there was only one applicant with or without adult or child dependents.

Seven out of 10 of the applicants in Bucks were of pensionable age (i.e. 65 for men and 60 for women). This was exactly the

---

[1] Those visited were informed of the enquiry by the Board's officers and told that only if they wished would information be given to the research team. All but one of those seen gave their written consent.

same proportion as in Great Britain as a whole. Six out of 10 of them were women. Nationally there was a rather larger proportion of women—two out of every three applicants.

Just over a third (35 per cent) in Bucks were living on their own—the only person in the household. This was a slightly smaller proportion than the national average of 39·4 per cent. Two out of three applicants were the chief economic supporter of their household, in the sense that they received the major part of any household income. Half of these were men and the other half women. The remaining third, however, were not householders. In these cases they were nearly always lone elderly men or (more frequently) women living in the households of younger people to whom they were almost always related by blood or marriage. In a few instances, they were unmarried mothers not required to register for work, and in a few, disabled persons between the age of 16 and 64. The proportion of applicants in Bucks who were not householders was higher than in the country as a whole where it was 21·7 per cent.

One in five of the applicants was single and one in four widowed. In nearly all these cases the applicant was elderly and was the only person whose needs and resources had to be considered. In the remaining cases, however, the allowance had to provide for one other adult dependent (22 per cent of the households) or for children and possibly other adult dependents of the applicant (17 per cent of the households). In this respect, the Bucks offices seemed to be dealing with a rather larger proportion of married couples than the national average, and with rather more applicants with dependent children.

Social status and housing

It is hard to describe the social class of recipients of National Assistance in occupational terms, since the applicants were not working. Past or usual occupations are likely to be loosely or inaccurately recorded and are, therefore, unreliable indicators of the present social class of households. Moreover, when the householder is a widow, who has never worked or worked only many years earlier and when the last occupation of her late husband is unknown, it is virtually impossible to assign the household to a social class at all.

In these circumstances, the officers assessment of whether the applicant had had any full-time education beyond the minimum school leaving age, although crude and subjective, was likely to give a better indication of the social status of the household. Using this indicator, only one in ten applicants at most were likely to have had a middle-class background. This proportion was a good deal lower than that found among the clients of other services who were also dealing mainly with elderly people. Home help organisers, county almoners and district nurses all had a larger proportion of clients thought to have had more than the minimum schooling.

Although applicants were, expectedly, in receipt of smaller incomes than the clientele of most other social services, there were fewer over-crowded households among them than among the clients of most other branches of social welfare services. In fact, over 70 per cent of the applicants were living in dwellings where there was more than one room per person, and only 11 per cent where there was less than one room per person.

From the point of view of domestic amenities, on the other hand, National Assistance applicants presented a rather less favourable picture than the average of households seen by all social welfare workers. Only one in five of the former lived in an owner-occupied dwelling compared with 34 per cent of all those visited. One in five of National Assistance applicants' dwellings had no fixed bath and no hot water and one in five no lavatory. However, these amenities were lacking in about the same proportion or even more of the homes of those visited by county almoners, home help organisers, welfare officers and district nurses, that is, by workers who, like the National Assistance Board, were dealing predominantly with elderly people.

The housing of National Assistance applicants and elderly clients of other services presents one of the paradoxes of the housing situation. While many of the elderly have too many rooms, younger people with growing families lack space. On the other hand, those who through age and infirmity are likely to find most difficulty in running their homes and keeping them clean, are more often without such basic amenities as a tapped source of hot water or a fixed bath than are younger people who might be considered more capable of overcoming the lack of these facilities.

The applicants' relationships with N.A.B. officers

In most instances (92 per cent of the applicants), as far as the National Assistance Board's own records went, their service began with a request for assistance from the applicant himself or from a relative. It is not essential for the officer dealing with a new request to record the way in which the individual came to apply and it is possible that many applicants were advised by social service personnel to apply to the Board. In the few instances in which it was noted that the request for help came from someone other than the applicant, these were always health service workers, usually a general practitioner. There were also referrals by hospital and county almoners, home help organisers, home teachers and welfare officers; but none were recorded in the series from non-health service workers or from health visitors or district nurses.

Approximately one in eight of the applicants were being visited for the first time. All the rest had been seen before. Indeed, one third had first been known to the Board before 1955, i.e. more than five years before the study period, and 39 per cent had been known to the Board for from one to five years.

Apart from the 12 per cent of applicants who were being visited for the first time, the rest had been visited on at least one other occasion in the preceding twelve months. Sixty per cent of the applicants were receiving either the second or third visit within a year and 28 per cent the fourth or more. Three per cent had been visited on at least ten occasions during the previous year.

Since the officers undertook many more home visits in a typical week than other workers, it was natural to find that their visits tended to be shorter. Only one in four of them lasted more than 25 minutes, and then usually only when the applicant was being visited for the first time, and about the same proportion of visits took only five or ten minutes each.

The problems encountered and the services undertaken

Although the officers described 6 per cent of their calls as 'friendly' ones undertaken as much to keep in touch as to check

H*

financial circumstances, all visits also had this latter purpose. In the event, the officers described 93 per cent of those visited as having inadequate means, which they sought to remedy by ensuring that weekly allowances were paid or that special needs such as a particular diet were met by an increase in allowance. In all these instances, therefore, the service rendered was the provision of basic or additional financial assistance by the Board.

In two out of three of the cases the Board's officers believed inadequate means to be the only problem in the applicant's household, and in 3 per cent did not consider that there was even a problem of insufficient income. In the remaining third, however, the officers considered that there was at least one problem in addition to inadequate means, and in 10 per cent they described two or more additional difficulties.

The problems most frequently described (found in 11 per cent of the households) were those arising from a chronic illness or disability. It was, perhaps, interesting that the officers did not consider that there were more problems of this kind, since they knew that the applicants in 41 per cent of the households had some form of chronic illness or disability and in another 4 per cent there were other sufferers besides the applicant.

Next in order of frequency were problems of finding suitable employment, and housing was listed as a problem in one in 20 of the households visited. Problems of marital relationships and personality inadequacies were also recorded with that frequency. Other problems, including rent arrears, mismanagement of means, loneliness and bereavement, were each described in 2 or 3 per cent of the households and problems of sexual or criminal behaviour in 1 per cent or less.

Seventy-one of the staff from other social services visited and reported on 58 of the households seen by N.A.B. officers. Comparisons of the reports on these households suggest that health visitors and those with social work training were more likely than the N.A.B. officers to see multiple and varied difficulties, whereas those without social work training were no more likely to list difficulties. Indeed, district nurses were less likely to see problems.

The households reported on by other staff were of two main kinds. The first kind was composed of elderly, although not necessarily retired, people, at least one of whom was chronically disabled. These were being seen principally by health service workers and it was noticeable that when it was a district nurse reporting, the N.A.B. officer was likely to report more social problems. When it was a health visitor or county almoner, on the other hand, these workers reported more than the N.A.B. officer.[1]

The second type of household frequently seen by others besides N.A.B. officers was a large one composed mainly of young children and often lacking a male chief economic supporter. Households of this kind were reported on mainly by non-health service workers, although health visitors were occasionally involved. The other worker reporting, especially if he had a social work training, was more likely to record a range of social problems including child neglect, criminal behaviour, disturbed personal relationships, poor work record and mismanagement of means, than the N.A.B. officer.[2]

Two not dissimilar cases can be quoted to illustrate the range of awareness of difficulties found in the reporting by N.A.B. officers. The first was that of a household consisting of a young woman and her three children, the father being in prison. A policewoman visited to investigate the woman's complaint that she had been raped by a neighbour, an allegation which was not substantiated. The health visitor called to help the mother who was given to hysteria and who persistently neglected herself, the children and the house. The N.A.B. officer's report showed an awareness of the household's difficulties and the problems created by the husband's alcoholism and the wife's mental instability.

In the other case, there was a married couple and their 10 children. The man had applied for supplementary assistance while 'temporarily sick' and after a visit—the third to this household—the N.A.B. officer recorded only a problem of inadequate means. However, the family was also being visited by a school attendance officer and a probation officer, and from their accounts it was apparent that there were many problems. The four children above the age of criminal responsibility were all on probation and the eldest was truanting from school. The father was considered a

[1] Comparative frequency of problem reporting in the same households: N.A.B., 22; District nurses, 14; N.A.B., 28; Health visitors and almoners, 36.
[2] N.A.B. 15. Child care and probation officers 41.
    N.A.B. 19. School attendance and police 24.

malingerer, more often out of work than in, the mother neglected the children and was unable to discipline them.

Contacts with other social welfare agencies

It is possible that amongst all the households visited by N.A.B. officers there were many which were not receiving visits from other social service personnel. The officers themselves recorded their knowledge of visits by others to rather more than 50 per cent of all those they were visiting. However, the evidence of the 58 households reported by at least one other worker, suggests that a larger proportion of their households were being visited without the knowledge of the Board's officers, since in a third of these 58, the N.A.B. officers were not aware of the other staff who were visiting.

The social characteristics of N.A.B. officers

Three of the Bucks officers were women, all of them in their late forties or early fifties. Two of them were single and the third was also childless. Six of the 17 men officers were over 50 years old and only four were under 35. This was, therefore, an occupation which in Bucks was filled mostly by men and women in the middle years of working life.

Twelve of the 20 officers had been born into the families of manual workers and four others into families headed by men in routine non-manual work. Only two, both of them women, had fathers in Social Class I professional occupations.

Five of the officers left school at the minimum school leaving age; nine of those who stayed on beyond it obtained school certificates.[1] Seventeen of the 20 took office jobs on leaving school, eight of them in central or local government or in public enterprises.[2] One or two of the older men said that they felt lucky at the time to have found pensionable work. 'Beggars can't be choosers,' said one, commenting on employment opportunities when he started work, 'and we were all beggars then!'

---

[1] The Board's staff in Bucks tended to be older than the average of their colleagues in Great Britain, and at the time of their recruitment to the Board or its predecessors, school leaving certificates or other formal qualifications were not required as a condition of employment.

[2] One of the three other officers started as a blacksmith's apprentice, another as a music teacher, and a third as a regular army officer.

None of the officers had had their first job in the N.A.B. itself. They had joined it either when the Board took over the functions of the department in which the individual had been working, or when the individual was transferred from one department to another or felt that employment in a Government department would offer greater security than employment in private enterprise.[1]

Views of in-service training

With the exception of one clerical officer who had joined the National Assistance Board less than three years earlier, everyone had had some in-service training for their work. No two officers, however, had had quite the same kind. For those who had belonged to one of the services taken over by the National Assistance Board in 1948, there had seldom been any form of introductory course. Most, however, had had a fortnight's intensive full-time course on promotion to executive officer as well as several refresher courses lasting up to a week on special topics. Those who joined the service in more recent years had usually had a week's intensive course within their first year of service, and some had had additional short courses. For everyone, however, training had been mainly on the job, getting to know the regulations which governed their duties and working under the general guidance and supervision of the branch manager.

We did not ask the officers to pass judgment on their training generally, but we did ask for opinions on its adequacy as a preparation for the social work aspects of their present work. Five said the question was meaningless because the social aspects of their work had not been covered at all in their training; eight considered that these aspects had not been adequately covered, and only seven were satisfied.

Eight officers thought that ideally the N.A.B. officer should have a full-time training in social work to be followed by briefer, practical instruction in the Board's own work and the duties of

[1] One said that he hoped for promotion in another Government department and when he was disappointed applied for a transfer. He had no special interest in the Board's activities. Another who came to the Board during the war said, 'I was directed to the Board and, generally speaking, I was not interested in welfare. But I'm always pleased to give assistance to the elderly and to go out of my way if need be to help them'.

the officers. They opted, in the main, for a three months course which is much shorter than the two-year course proposed by the Younghusband Committee for social workers in the local authority health and welfare departments. The same number, although not always the same persons, wanted refresher courses, especially in mental health, the social and psychological effects of ageing and the scope of other branches of the social services.

The overall impression was that as regards training the N.A.B. officers fell into two camps. The first group numbered nine who, by and large, were satisfied with their present training. They did not feel that a full-time course in social work would have been preferable or that they needed any further study or training. They tended to emphasise the importance of experience and the limitation of theoretical learning. Their views were well summed up by one who told us 'The only way to know anything is to do it. You've either a gift for it or you haven't. It's plain common-sense that's needed. Training won't help those with a gift although it could benefit those who lack self-confidence'.

The other camp with 11 in it was not unanimous in its views on the adequacy of past training, on the need for further study or on the desirability of N.A.B. officers having a full-time course in social work. Nevertheless, one or other of their comments indicated that they felt the need to deepen their own under-standing of human behaviour and the ways in which people in need could be helped. The two groups were not distinguishable by any such factor as age, seniority in the service, social class background or the area of the county in which they worked. Nor were they easily distinguishable by the kind of comment they made about their work or the applicants for National Assistance, although there seemed to be a slight tendency for those who expressed the desire for more training to make more critical comments about various aspects of the Board's policy.

Attitudes to work

Fourteen of the 20 officers told us that on the whole they were pleased they had come into their present work; but only nine said they would choose the same career again and this suggested that there was less positive satisfaction with work among N.A.B. officers than among most other groups of welfare staff.

It is hard, however, from the interview records alone to pinpoint the causes of dissatisfaction. Only five officers spontaneously raised the question of their pay or status, and two of these talked favourably about the security of the job and the retirement pensions. The other three comments were unfavourable, complaining either of current pay or promotion prospects. One man, who was anxious about both, told us 'I try not to think about money or material advance, but one is only human and it's bound to make some difference'.

Eleven, however, complained of some aspect of working conditions. For two the problem was the lack of private transport which they found especially trying in bad weather. Another two complained of 'red tape'. One of these said, 'Personally, I find it irksome and frustrating to have to refer some of my assessments to an executive officer for vetting. I have been on the job a long time and should know what I'm about now'. But the most frequent complaint (it was made by nine officers) was of pressure of work, of constant rush and inability to give adequate time or consideration to applicants' cases.[1] 'The work boils down to quantity instead of quality', said one man. 'If we spent the time really required to deal with a case, the work would never be done,' said another. 'If we are meant to be a welfare agency, then we must have the time and staff to do the job properly. At present we scratch the surface of countless problems and don't deal effectively with any of them', said a third, and added, 'We are always falling between two stools'.

Sixteen of the 20 officers suggested that the main reward of their work was the feeling that it helped other people, and several laid special emphasis on the satisfaction of helping the elderly or disabled. This satisfaction, however, was often frustrated by the pressure of work, which, by some officers, was ascribed not so much to their employer's shortcomings as to that of some applicants. Half the officers indeed complained about some applicants with whom they were having to deal. The research workers felt that four of these officers would in any circumstances have had very little understanding of or sympathy for most applicants

---

[1] Cf. footnote, p. 212.

for National Assistance;[1] but the other six who complained about applicants seemed to be expressing frustration with work loads.

It was on the basis of such attitudes that it was possible to distinguish between the majority of N.A.B. officers and the four who seemed to lack understanding or sympathy. The latter expressed punitive attitudes towards some of their cases and were frustrated by situations in which they could not show their feelings. One, for example, told us that the 'more demanding' of the applicants 'were given a certain amount of encouragement from us. We display moral cowardice in dealing with unscrupulous people who are lazy and dishonest. Other applicants criticise us for helping those who won't help themselves and they are right. We do'. Another thought the National Assistance Board was not tough enough when they found they had been 'fiddled'. He complained of 'the Board's unwillingness to prosecute in cases of fraud', and alleged that 'in certain areas the Board is regarded as easy meat'. Another contrasted the way in which he was expected to work with the low standards set for some of the applicants for National Assistance who obtained allowances and whom he variously described as 'loafers', 'work shy', 'lazy ne'er do wells'.

At the other extreme there were two officers in the majority group whose sympathies with those they met often made them experience, as one put, 'a clash of loyalties—between what I feel I should do and what is legally possible'. The other had asked for a transfer to the N.A.B. from another Government department because he wanted to work with the general public, and had found the work rewarding. 'For me, this decentralised department is its chief asset. I didn't like being a cog in a gigantic machine. I find the people here much nicer to work with. There's not so much emphasis on status.' He went on to say, however, that the National Assistance Board was 'the Cinderella' of the social services. He believed that many elderly people felt humiliated by the routine check on their circumstances and that regular supplementation of retirement pensions or long-term sick benefits should be taken over by the Ministry of Pensions and National Insurance, while

---

[1] For example, one N.A.B. officer told us that he was interested in administration not welfare. The drawback to the job as far as he was concerned was 'having to deal with poverty in general, which I dislike, and the work-shy and scroungers in particular'.

those who were unemployed should be dealt with by the Ministry of Labour. The latter, he considered, were in a better position than the National Assistance Board to bring pressure to bear on the work-shy individual to support his family. 'At present', he suggested, 'the man can play the N.A.B. off against the Ministry of Labour and vice versa'.

General conclusions and recommendations

The first and overwhelming impression of the work of the N.A.B. gained from this enquiry was of the tremendous volume of routine visiting work undertaken by its officers.

When each officer was visiting between 40 and 60 people in their own homes each week, the time and attention which could be given to each case could not but be restricted. It was much to the credit of most of the officers that they were able to get to know as much as they did about the difficulties which applicants faced. It was not surprising, however, to find that even when they were aware of difficulties they were seldom in personal touch with other social welfare staff. They simply had not the time. It was also evident that most officers felt themselves to be under considerable pressure of work and that this was the major source of dissatisfaction with work.[1]

The first question which needs asking, therefore, is whether the N.A.B. officers need to pay as many visits to applicants as they did in 1960–61. The Board has a duty to protect the public purse and see that those who are not entitled to assistance do not receive it. Visits to the applicants' homes may be unavoidable when the initial assessments of resources and needs are made; but over 90 per cent of the N.A.B. officers' visits were to applicants who had been seen at least once already and usually more than once in the previous twelve months. Moreover, 72 per cent of the applicants had been known to the Board for over a year, and 33 per cent for over five years. In addition, 70 per cent were over retirement age. The economic circumstances of elderly and disabled people can alter, one would imagine for the worse rather than for the better with the passage of years, but whether the changes are frequent enough to warrant the numbers of visits paid is open to

[1] In this they were not alone. It is unlikely that a situation can ever arise in the social services when staff feel that there is not too much pressure on them.

question. Where the sole purpose of visiting is to check on economic circumstances, could not the number of visits paid be substantially reduced, leaving the officers more time to spend on each essential visit?

The need to check on economic circumstances is not, however, the sole function of a N.A.B. officer's visit. There is a good deal of evidence to show that many old people are lonely and welcome any visitor to their homes.[1] On these grounds alone, the visits of the N.A.B. officers are likely to be socially valuable and should not be reduced in number or frequency if the elderly or disabled have no regular contacts with other branches of the social welfare services.

Since routine visiting of elderly or severely disabled people by N.A.B. officers is undertaken in order to contribute to the general welfare of such people and not merely to check on their financial circumstances, there is a need to consider whether the training which these officers received helped them to make this contribution. The major requirement is that those visiting people in straitened circumstances should have sympathy. In addition, they need to have a good knowledge of the social services and be able to get on well with the staff of other services. Finally, they need to have some understanding of human relationships so that they can appreciate the factors influencing their own relationship with the applicant as well as the applicants' relations with relatives, friends and neighbours.

It would seem that four-fifths of the N.A.B. officers were people who had plenty of sympathy for old or disabled people and that they had given much comfort and practical help to many of those they visited. Not all of them, however, seemed to be well enough equipped with a knowledge of the scope of the social services or of the nature of human relationships to be able to utilise their brief visits to the best advantage. While it may not need a full social work course to acquire this knowledge, steps should surely be taken to increase the N.A.B. officers' knowledge of the social services and to encourage them to make personal contacts with the personnel of other branches of these services?[2] This kind of

---

[1] Cf. Snelgrove. 'The Elderly Housebound.' 1963, and
Arkley, J. 'The Over-sixties.' 1965.

[2] Since this survey was undertaken, the Board has expanded its in-service

knowledge can probably be best acquired by existing staff in the normal course of their work. The personnel of other services could be invited to talk informally about the services for which they were responsible, or to discuss some of the households in which they had a common interest. The usefulness of such sessions would be increased, however, if an experienced tutor directed the session, raised questions which individuals might feel unwilling to voice, and drew the threads of the discussion together. Unless this were done, such sessions could waste time and energy and defeat the purpose for which they were called.

The National Assistance Board might, therefore, consider the training and appointment of in-service tutors who would visit the local offices from time to time to conduct such sessions. They would need to work closely with the branch managers who have responsibility for supervision and whose attitude to continued training as well as to applicants is likely to have a decisive influence on the manner in which the Board's local officers carry out their duties.

A better understanding of human behaviour and relationships would probably be more effectively gained in the well-planned in-service courses at national or regional headquarters, which last one or two weeks and are given by experts. It is already the Board's policy to hold such courses on various aspects of the work which has to be undertaken at local offices, and such subjects as the problem of the ineffectual psychopathic who does not support his wife and family have been covered. A target should, however, be set whereby all N.A.B. visiting officers attend a week's course within a period of two years, in such subjects as the social and psychological problems of ageing and in the comparative value systems of different societies. Only in this way is the task likely to be carried out with sufficient determination and dispatch.

There seems, also, to be a need to review the machinery for selecting officers who will be visiting applicants. One in five of those working from offices in Bucks seemed to lack patience and understanding to such an extent that they were not really capable of providing many individuals with the help and the sympathy they needed. Moreover, the hostility expressed for different

training programme, and special emphasis has been laid on giving officers insight into the nature of their own relationship with clients.

categories of 'awkward' people, gave the impression that these were unhappy individuals whose feelings of frustration and of disappointment with what life had brought them were reflected in their attitudes to others. It is essential that those who visit the elderly, the disabled, the deviant and the ineffectual should be people who are capable of understanding the problems of such people and of insight into their own motivations and their own reactions to the applicants.[1]

Some of the questions raised by the analysis of the visits undertaken by N.A.B. officers, however, do not concern the National Assistance Board alone, but can only be considered across the existing boundaries of the social welfare services. Many of the applicants were known to the officers to be receiving visits from other services, and other households may also have been in touch with other social welfare staff without the knowledge of the National Assistance Board. In these circumstances, it seems worth considering whether a substantial proportion of the man-hours devoted to routine visiting by the Board's officers could not be saved and used in other ways. An alternative deployment of manpower which should be seriously considered, for example, could be achieved by merging the local offices of the Ministry of Pensions and National Insurance and the National Assistance Board and training some of the existing staff to provide a comprehensive service on financial problems. Such a service would be available to all, whether or not they were entitled to benefit under the National Insurance Acts, and might prevent a good deal of effort on the part of those who are in financial need and who at present may have to seek advice about their position at two offices. It could also lessen the feeling of loss of self-respect experienced by many seeking help from the National Assistance Board.

Advice and assistance on other difficulties, e.g. of a social, psychological or material kind and on health matters, however, need to be more readily available than they are now, especially to elderly people, if visiting by N.A.B. officers is to be reduced. Steps should be taken, therefore, to increase the number of social

---

[1] The officers whose attitudes to their clients were considered poor did not come into the Board by what is now the normal machinery of recruitment to the clerical and executive officer grades of the civil service.

workers in the health and welfare services to the extent needed
to give such assistance as is necessary.

Since the more general question of the best deployment of
man-power available to social welfare services affects all the
statutory services in one way or another and not merely the
National Assistance Board, they are considered in the concluding
chapter.

CHAPTER XVI

The Disablement Resettlement Service

Responsibility for helping disabled people between 16 and 65 to find and keep suitable employment is vested in the Ministry of Labour under the Disabled Persons (Employment) Act, 1944. Disabilities may be mental or physical, congenital or acquired through illness or injury.

Disablement resettlement officers (D.R.O.'s) are responsible under the Act for maintaining a register of disabled persons. Registration is voluntary and, with full employment in Bucks, most registered persons were able to find and keep suitable jobs. However, the D.R.O. has to be prepared to give vocational advice to newly registered disabled and to those who need to change their jobs and this means keeping in touch with hospitals and the Ministry's own industrial rehabilitation units where potentialities can be assessed.

The D.R.O. has also to keep in touch with local employers who are required by law to employ a quota of disabled persons if they have more than 20 employees; trying to find a suitable post for an individual while paying due consideration to the employer's own staffing problems calls for tact and an intimate knowledge of local firms and their labour requirements. If someone is too disabled to work in an ordinary workplace, the D.R.O. may obtain employment for him in a 'sheltered' workshop or in his own home, and this means consulting with the local authority welfare department who have general responsibility for the substantially and permanently handicapped.

The service is administered from the Ministry's local offices, the employment exchanges. In Bucks in 1960–61, there were two full-time and two part-time D.R.O.'s at Slough and High Wycombe. At Aylesbury, there was a part-time officer and at the smaller offices in Bletchley, Chesham and Wolverton the work was undertaken by the exchange manager.

Many of the registered disabled were not seen by a D.R.O. in the course of a year's work because they were well settled in permanent employment. Estimates provided by the eight D.R.O.'s indicated that they saw about 3,000 disabled persons during the course of the year, of whom about two-thirds were people registering as disabled for the first time. In a typical week a full-time officer might see about 20 disabled persons and a part-time officer three to six. Most of the contacts took place in the employment exchange, but some were in hospitals or in the medical rehabilitation unit at Farnham Park near Slough. Only in rare instances did the D.R.O. visit people in their own homes.

The eight D.R.O.'s provided information on a total of 87 of their cases. Sixty-six of these cases were seen by full-time D.R.O.'s and the remaining 21 by those whose disablement resettlement work was only a part of their job.[1]

The D.R.O.'s cases

More than nine out of 10 of the individuals seen were men, over three-quarters of whom were the chief economic supporters of their households. Most of the others were young single men still living in their parent's home, but there were a few living alone or in hostels.

Nine out of every 10 persons were believed by the D.R.O.'s to have left school at the minimum school leaving age, which, if the individual had been in need of special schooling as a result of handicap, might have been 16. Nearly all of them were manual workers and lived in households headed by manual workers.

Every individual seen by the D.R.O. had some form of permanent handicap and many had multiple ones. The major categories of handicap are shown in Table 25.

In addition to the disabled person with whom the D.R.O. was dealing there was another mentally disabled person in 3 per cent of the clients' households, and another physically disabled in 13 per cent.

The social problem most commonly listed by D.R.O.'s was that of finding suitable employment (70 of the 87 cases), of keeping suitable jobs (two cases), or of both (15 cases). Closely linked with problems of employment were the difficulties of making personal and social adjustments to chronic illness, which affected a third

---

[1] Pressure of work, particularly in the small exchanges, made it impossible for the D.R.O.'s to provide information on more cases.

Table 25

PERCENTAGE OF CASES SEEN BY DRO'S WITH DIFFERENT KINDS OF
CHRONIC ILLNESS OR DISABILITY

Number of cases = 87

Type of Condition	Percentage of cases	Type of Condition	Percentage of cases
Rheumatic conditions	25	Blind, deaf	11
Heart conditions	21	Digestive	9
Neurological and paralytic		Mental subnormality	1
conditions	20	Diabetes	1
Respiratory	16	All other	3
Mental illness	14		

of the individuals seen. About the same proportion were felt to be without adequate means.

In a few instances, the D.R.O.'s considered there were other difficulties which aggravated the disabled person's problems. The most frequently noted were personality difficulties and inadequacies (13 cases), loneliness (seven cases), and marital relations (five cases). Problems concerning young children were only mentioned in one case.

Twelve households of clients seen by the D.R.O.'s were also reported on by 15 other social welfare staff during the survey, and a comparison of reports showed that 12 of the other workers were visiting to help with a problem arising from the disablement which was also the D.R.O.'s concern. One of these was an occupational therapist, two housing officers, one a psychiatric social worker, four almoners, one a district nurse-health visitor, and three N.A.B. officers. Only three, a probation officer, a child care officer, and a school attendance officer, had reasons which were not directly related to disability for dealing with the household.

On the whole, the accounts of the staff who were concerned with the same individual as the D.R.O. corresponded closely with his; but there were three instances in which they reported more problems than he did. In one of these, the district nurse-health visitor was aware of behaviour difficulties among the children of a paraplegic man which she partly attributed to his disability, and an occupational therapist also visiting this household believed that the wife was neglecting her children for him. In another instance, the psychiatric social worker who was seeing an epileptic man reported that the youngest child was truanting from school.

The services provided

Just over half the clients first came to the notice of the D.R.O. when they went to the employment exchange to seek work. A quarter were first referred by a hospital, in most instances by an almoner or psychiatric social worker. Ten per cent came via the National Assistance Board and 6 per cent through the general practitioner. The remaining cases were referred by workers in the local health and welfare department, by the youth employment service and by a missioner for the deaf.

Rather more than half those seen had been registered as disabled for more than one year and 18 per cent for more than five. Most of those who had been on the register for over a year had been seen fairly frequently, although there was no specified regularity in interviewing. A fifth of the men had been seen at least at fortnightly intervals throughout the year and two had been interviewed even more frequently. One quarter of the disabled persons had been seen for the first time during the recording period and another 20 per cent for the first time within the twelve months preceding it.

In most instances (82 per cent of the cases) the D.R.O. described his service as helping the individual to find suitable employment, and in another 6 per cent making arrangements for training. In 10 cases, the D.R.O. referred the individual to others, e.g. to the N.A.B. for financial assistance or to the county almoner's department for special equipment. In three or four instances, the preparation of a report was the only action taken.

The services with which the D.R.O. was most often in touch were the hospitals and the N.A.B. County almoners were those most frequently singled out by D.R.O.'s when asked to give the research team an example of co-operation. There were, however, instances where the D.R.O. was not in touch with other staff who, like him, were dealing with a disabled person's problem. In only one of the 12 cases seen by the D.R.O. and at least one other worker, for example, was the D.R.O. in touch the other worker, and in only another three recorded that other worker's interest in the household.

The background and training of disablement resettlement officers

Three of the eight D.R.O.'s were over 55 in 1960–61 and none were less than 35. Two were single women. They both began work as clerical assistants in the Ministry of Labour on leaving school at 16 and had had an unbroken career in that department. The careers of the six men were only a little more varied. Two left school rather earlier and only one of the six joined the civil service immediately; but four entered before 25 and the two who joined only in their thirties did so after their earlier civilian employment had been interrupted by war service. Every one of the D.R.O.'s had moved from one part of the country to another in the course of his career in the Ministry and three had had as many as seven moves.

None of the D.R.O.'s had had any full-time course of study since leaving school. Three had taken part-time evening courses and two of these officers had studied subjects such as economics, philosophy and industrial organisation which were likely to be relevant to work in the Ministry of Labour, if not specifically to work as D.R.O.'s.

With one exception, each had had a Ministry of Labour in-service course on the work of the D.R.O. For those who first began to work with the disabled some years before, the course had been a short one of three or four days only. For those whose training had been more recent it had been two or three weeks. One had taken the course more than 10 years before and most had taken it between 1950 and 1955. All had had one or more refresher courses dealing with a particular aspect of employment exchange or disabled persons' work since that time. The aggregate time spent on full-time in-service courses by any one officer did not exceed three months.

With one exception, the D.R.O.'s all felt their in-service courses had given them a good grounding in the social aspects of their job with disabled persons. The exception was one who felt that 'dealing with people is a flair which training cannot give'. He was critical of the course he had taken because he 'could have been given more medical and psychiatric knowledge'. Another said that, when he took the course in 1946, 'there was not much emphasis on psychological misfits', but that the increase in work for the psychologically disabled could not have been predicted.

Nevertheless, although there was general approval of the D.R.O. course, most considered that it should be longer. Only one thought a full social worker course would be useful, but five felt that because existing courses were so concentrated some skimping was inevitable. They opted for longer courses, in order to cover the existing syllabus more satisfactorily.

Only three of the eight felt in need of refresher courses and only one was specific about the subjects he wanted covered, namely, the psychological make-up of those apparent malingerers and inadequate people who constantly failed to keep jobs which seemed suitable.

Attitudes to work

Despite the apparent lack of enthusiasm for further training in the social and psychological aspects of human behaviour, the D.R.O.'s were people who found their work with disabled persons interesting and rewarding, because it gave them many opportunities to help those least able to help themselves. 'I've got a feeling for the underdog', said one, 'and I like working where I can help people directly. This job gives me an opportunity to do that. I know all don't appreciate it and some would prefer to be left in a rut on National Assistance, but it's worth trying'. 'When you succeed, you really succeed', said another. 'There are so many failures that you always have to live in hope. You mustn't give up because you get let down once or twice.' The only man who was not pleased to be working with the disabled thought he had no vocation for it and derived his main satisfactions from administration.

Most of the drawbacks to their work turned out to be grumbles about the inadequacy of facilities and services for disabled people, or the limits to which they could help. One, for example, complained of lack of time. 'You have to be prepared to let people talk', he said. 'The time factor shouldn't enter into it. Until they get it off their chest you can't get anywhere.' Another said he disliked 'having to ask employers to take on someone I know isn't a good employment bet'. Most of his work was now of this kind, since most disabled people could find and keep suitable work. Fifty or 60 on his register, however, were 'from the bottom of the barrel', and constantly out of work. 'Most of them are ageing quickly and have either arthritis, bronchitis or some heart condition. They're worn out and should be taking it easy. Or they're mentally sick or epileptic and are awkward to get on with.'

The problem of dealing with the most difficult disabled persons was a constantly recurring theme. Talking about the work of the D.R.O. in the future, one said he would go to all lengths to persuade employers to give awkward people an opportunity, but that if his efforts were to be successful, 'there would have to be a change in the climate of public and industrial opinion. Most people fear the mentally sick. They don't mind working with physically disabled people or mentally defectives if the latter are cheerful'. Several officers suggested that it was more difficult to find employment for such people in Bucks because the number of employment opportunities in small towns was inevitably limited. Men who couldn't keep a job for long soon ran through the available local opportunities.

Instances of poor relationships with other social welfare staff were also raised on one or two occasions as reasons for finding the work frustrating. One D.R.O. complained that a psychiatrist had not given him a full enough description of a patient's phobia with the result that he had placed the disabled person unsuitably. Another had found a welfare officer unwilling to stretch a point in favour of a disabled person so that an opportunity to obtain suitable work was lost. Another thought too many organisations were involved in work for the disabled. On many occasions he did not know whom to contact and felt it would be easier if he could channel his work through one or two people only, especially where the disabled person's domestic problems were concerned.

General summary and conclusions

The impression gained from the interviews with D.R.O.'s and the reports they submitted suggested that their efforts to settle disabled persons in employment were carried out conscientiously and with tolerance and understanding. They were sensitive to many of the problems for disabled people besides those of securing and retaining suitable employment. Despite the limitations imposed by conducting nearly all their interviews in their offices, in hospitals or in rehabilitation units, they learned a good deal about the domestic circumstances of the disabled.

In a period of full employment most of the registered disabled were able to obtain work. Nevertheless, there were difficulties in settling an increasing number of severely disabled middle-aged people with rheumatic, respiratory and heart conditions, and employment prospects for the 'awkward' people whose temperament made them difficult workmates and employees were not good.

The majority of D.R.O.'s considered that their work did not require a full social worker course if it was to be done well. I felt that, on the whole, the majority were right. Responsibility for the general health and well-being of disabled people should rest with a domiciliary health team (see Chapter XX) which should employ a social worker and be able to call on the D.R.O. when help and advice was needed on employment.

The D.R.O. should, therefore, be considered as a specialist in placing disabled people in remunerative work, and trained as such. Placement work calls for a knowledge of the labour requirements of industry and of ergonomics as well as of ways of determining the capacities of disabled people. It cannot be done without training and there was substance in the suggestion that the Ministry's course was too short to allow the ground to be adequately covered. In my view, it should last at least six weeks. It should include more demonstration of actual cases and ways of handling them, and greater emphasis should be placed on the special problems of those who are disabled in middle age and of those who have inadequate, inconsistent and unreliable personalities. At the same time, the course must aim primarily to equip D.R.O.'s with a wide knowledge of the suitability of different kinds of work for people with varying degrees of mental, physical and emotional disablement.

Although not believing that the D.R.O. should be trained as a social worker, a strong case can be made out for encouraging those who like working with disabled people and show an aptitude for investigating job requirements to make a career in it. At present the D.R.O. is either doing the work temporarily until he is promoted away from it to other work in the Ministry or doing it on a long-term basis because he is not being considered for promotion. There should be opportunities for advancement within the disablement resettlement service.

At the same time, the respective functions of occupational therapists and D.R.O.'s in finding work for the disabled need to be clarified. Occupational therapists from the welfare department in Bucks spent much of their time trying to find work for severely handicapped people to do in their own homes, in sheltered workshops or in training centres. The D.R.O. is also interested in finding work which can be done by individuals with substantial handicaps, although usually he seeks to place the disabled person in a normal work setting. A greater pooling of the efforts of D.R.O.'s and occupational therapists—especially for those below normal pensionable age—would save the time and energy of both and lead to a general improvement in the service for all classes of handicapped people.

Finally, there was less contact between the D.R.O. and other social workers than was desirable. In the households reported on by both D.R.O.'s and other workers, there was no evidence of duplicated or conflicting aims. For example, only the D.R.O. was helping the disabled person to find work; but some of the other workers were concerned with the health or social adjustment of the disabled person and his family, and their mutual tasks might have been easier if they had been in contact with one another. More stress should be laid in D.R.O. training courses on the part which other statutory and voluntary services play in the care of the disabled and the need to co-operate with them.

CHAPTER XVII

The War Pensions Welfare Service

Responsibility for ensuring that no-one need fall below a certain minimum standard of living through lack of financial resources is vested in the Ministry of Pensions and National Insurance and the National Assistance Board. The former is responsible for administering the comprehensive compulsory insurance scheme under the National Insurance Acts. These Acts provide that contributors or their dependents can claim financial benefits either on retirement at or above the age of 65 (60 for women) or in a contingency such as sickness, unemployment, death, widowhood, maternity and so on. The Ministry also administers the Family Allowance Act which gives allowances to parents with two or more dependent children irrespective of their means or their insurance contributions.

Most of the claims for benefits under the Insurance Acts are dealt with by post at the Ministry's branch offices, and payments are made by post or at post offices and Ministry of Labour employment exchanges. Insurance staff seldom visit those who are drawing benefits except to check routinely the validity of a claim or because fraud is suspected. Callers to the branch offices are often new contributors about to obtain work in this country for the first time, or those with queries about entitlement to benefit. The executive and clerical officers who undertake this work are expected to be able to answer questions put to them concerning an individual's rights and duties under the relevant Acts; but they are not generally thought to be confronted with requests for help on a whole range of social or psychological problems which may be associated with financial difficulties. For this reason they are not included in the Bucks enquiry.

On the other hand, the Ministry has accepted responsibility for the welfare of war pensioners and their dependents. This service is administered not from the Ministry's branch offices but from a number of War Pensions offices which generally serve about half the area for which one of the Ministry's regional offices is responsible. The War Pensioners Welfare Service which covered

Buckinghamshire had its headquarters in Reading and its work covered Berkshire, Oxfordshire and parts of Hampshire and Dorset as well.

The staff of the War Pensioners Welfare Service

Two employees at this area office were undertaking welfare work. One was a children's officer responsible for the welfare of dependent war orphans, of whom there were about 15 in Buckinghamshire at the time of our study. During the study year, 1960–61, she visited six of them. The other was a welfare officer. There were some 3,300 disabled war pensioners or war widows in Bucks in 1960–61. The welfare officer was responsible for visiting the severely disabled among them, who numbered about 160. She also visited pensioners or widows at their own request or if asked to do so by a voluntary visitor. Her work took her to Berks, Oxfordshire and Hants as well as to Bucks.

In a typical week the welfare officer would see about 18 people either in their own homes, or at the office or in hospital. Since considerable distances had to be covered, visits to Bucks pensioners tended to be undertaken during particular weeks rather than be spread evenly through the year.

In its welfare work the Ministry relied heavily upon the voluntary members of the Bucks War Pensions Committee set up, like others all over the country, to advise the Minister on problems relating to the welfare of war pensioners locally and to hear complaints.[1] It appointed a panel of visitors to keep in touch with pensioners and widows facing difficulties due to their disabilities or increasing age and heard reports of their visits. The committee meetings, serviced by an officer of the Ministry, were attended by the welfare officer. She was able to indicate which pensioners needed visiting by voluntary workers and arrange to visit herself those whom the voluntary workers considered were experiencing new or special difficulties.

In addition to the two officers working from Reading, the Ministry employed one welfare officer at the National Spinal Injuries Centre at Stoke Mandeville Hospital near Aylesbury. The Centre served the whole country and the Ministry's welfare

---

[1] The voluntary work undertaken by this Committee and its panel of visitors is considered in Chapter XIX.

officer was concerned with the problems of those whose injuries were the result of active service. During the study year, eight of those whom she saw in the course of her work were residents of Bucks.

Training for the work

The Ministry of Pensions and National Insurance did not employ trained social workers as welfare or children's officers. It selected its welfare staff from amongst its executive officers and gave them a specialist short in-service course in children's or general welfare work. These courses were followed by shorter refresher courses in particular problems.

The three workers had stayed at school until 16, and obtained school certificates. Two of the three started their civil service career as clerical assistants and subsequently won promotion to the executive officer grade. The third had first worked in private industry and joined the Ministry as a clerical officer during the war. In their private lives, two of the three had done extensive voluntary work in youth or women's organisations and in societies for the welfare of disabled persons.

Two of the three thought the training they received in the Ministry had given them an adequate preparation for their welfare work. They felt that it was not like that of most social workers and that a generalised course would not have helped. 'I work for an organisation whose rules are there to guide', said one, 'a social work course wouldn't make it easier to conform to the Ministry's policy'. The third felt that when she took her Ministry course in welfare work it had been too theoretical and there had been insufficient opportunity to acquire practical experience. She would have preferred a full-time course of about six months in social work, feeling that this would have equipped her better for her job.

The cases seen by the paid staff

The work of the three officers naturally differed. During the study year, the children's officer saw only six Bucks war orphans in four households, and the welfare officer in the Spinal Injuries Centre at Stoke Mandeville Hospital saw only eight Bucks residents. The welfare officer visiting severely disabled pensioners

I

or elderly widows estimated that about 160 of those in Bucks were seen at least once in the year, and she gave us details of 25 consecutive cases seen over a period of three months.

Two of the four households visited by the children's officer seemed to present no social problems and the same was true of two of the clients seen by the welfare officer in the Spinal Injuries Centre. All those seen by the general welfare officer seemed to her to have at least one kind of problem and six of them had more than one, including one household which seemed to present as many as nine different kinds. This last was a household where a war pensioner had developed a serious nervous complaint. He was able to work as a labourer but was mentally unstable and was unable to keep any job for long. His wife, who had been married before and was of low intelligence, could not understand the nature of his illness or his needs. She was also unable to control the nine-year-old son of her previous marriage. The family had been living in two rooms and, in desperation, had taken a large rented bungalow at £6 6s. od. a week. However, with only a low and irregular wage and a small pension bringing in an average of less than £12 a week, the family soon got into arrears with the rent. It was when they were threatened with eviction that they appealed for help to the Ministry's welfare officer. In short, this was a case where illness, inadequate personality, low intelligence and disturbed personal relationships coupled with the housing shortage and inadequate means, produced an almost insoluble situation.

Most of the clients seen by the Ministry's welfare workers were elderly people and there were few young people in their households. As a consequence, the problems most frequently seen were those caused by the pensioner's disability or by the widow's bereavement or increasing age. In seven out of the 25 cases seen by the welfare officer, for example, she considered that the household was not adequately housed. Over-crowding or poor housing standards were not so much the problem as the unsuitability of the dwelling, given the nature of the patient's disability. In another five cases there were other problems associated with adjustment to chronic disability and in the same number there was difficulty in finding or retaining suitable employment. Despite war pensions, four households were considered to have inadequate means to meet their needs and one, although with apparently adequate means, seemed to mismanage them to such an extent as to give an appearance of dire poverty. These facts are not surprising since 21 of the 37 families seen by all three workers had no current income from wages.

The other problem the welfare worker found among nearly half of the households she visited was that of loneliness. Loneliness was most often mentioned among widows living alone; but it also occurred when pensioners lived with other unrelated persons and in two cases when they shared a house with their own children.

Since the welfare staff were dealing with the disabled and, on the whole, the elderly disabled, it was hardly surprising to find that problems such as school truancy, juvenile delinquency, child neglect and sexual behaviour were not recorded. The children's officer, however, recorded two cases of difficult behaviour among the four families she visited in each of which there were war orphans between the ages of 15 and 19, and she believed that in one there was a problem of parent-child relationships. There were also three households with marital difficulties and eight where someone's aggressive or inadequate personality made for difficulties.

The two welfare workers were seeing a range of problems likely to arise among any group of severely disabled persons and their relatives. However, the visiting welfare officer tended to see and describe problems affecting members of the household other than or in addition to those of the disabled pensioner himself, whereas the welfare worker at Stoke Mandeville Hospital described mainly the patient's own problems. This kind of difference in reporting between hospital-based and domiciliary-based workers was not confined to the Ministry's officers. A similar difference was found between hospital almoners and those whose work for the County health and welfare departments involved them in home visiting.[1]

The reasons for contact and the services rendered

About half those seen by the three workers had been referred to the welfare service by the Ministry headquarters when the right to a war pension had been allowed. Although these cases had all been

[1] See Chapters V and VIII and the discussion in Chapter XX.

'on the books' for many years, they had not necessarily been visited with great regularity. The others, including all those seen by the welfare officer at the Spinal Injuries Centre, had either been referred by the hospital or by a voluntary visitor or were being seen at their own request. In most of these instances the referral had taken place shortly before. Indeed, the welfare staff were seeing one in six of the recorded cases for the first time. When a pensioner or war widow was referred to the welfare service it was almost always with a request to investigate home circumstances, assess the services that might be needed or see whether additional financial assistance could be obtained.

In 14 of the 37 cases the workers either obtained further financial help for the individual from the Ministry or referred the case to the National Assistance Board or a voluntary charity. In eight cases, efforts were made to secure occupational therapy or vocational training to allow the individual to occupy his time more profitably. Other services were given in connection with housing and in three cases the worker felt that she had given an individual some help with emotional difficulties.

Compared with the interviews conducted by many other workers, those made by the Ministry of Pensions officers were fairly long and rarely of less than 25 minutes duration. Most were between 35 minutes and one hour. Record-keeping and making contact with others was, on the other hand, less time-consuming for these workers than for many others—and especially for most trained social workers. While neither the Spinal Injuries Unit welfare officer nor the children's officer spent time travelling to see their cases, the welfare officer spent a considerable part of her working hours reaching the areas of Bucks which she wished to visit from Reading. In some cases it meant travelling 50 miles in a day in both directions.

Contacts with other social services and with voluntary workers

It was not common for staff of other social welfare services to initiate contacts with Ministry staff. Only six had done it in connection with the reported cases. Two of these were N.A.B. officers, two hospital almoners and two county almoners. The Ministry staff initiated many more referrals, in particular to the N.A.B.; but they also made three referrals to housing authorities, two to occupational therapists employed by the county health department, four to voluntary societies with charitable funds, and one to the police.

In general, the three workers felt that workers in other social services were most helpful to them. One singled out the N.A.B. for praise; 'If you put a problem to them, they do all they can', and another spoke highly of the regimental association, of housing authorities and of the D.R.O.'s in Bucks.

The future of the War Pensions Welfare Service

The welfare service for war pensioners and their widowed or orphaned dependents was established in the immediate post-war years. It then dealt mainly with difficulties which severely disabled persons had in finding suitable employment and suitable housing and helped widowed mothers bring up their fatherless children.

At that time, the local authority welfare services had barely begun to develop their domiciliary services for the disabled; the health services had only comparatively limited facilities for hospital treatment of the long-term disabled and only embryonic rehabilitation services. Health visitors were still predominantly occupied in instructing mothers about safeguarding their childrens' physical health and were not trained to help mothers with emotional problems. Moreover, the country at that time felt it owed a particular debt to those who had been severely disabled, had lost husbands or been orphaned as a result of the war.

In those circumstances the nation gave full support to the development of a special service for the war disabled and widowed and for war orphaned children. The question the community must now ask, however, is whether its debt to the victims of the war can finally be discharged by continuing indefinitely to provide this special welfare service for war disabled pensioners, widows and orphans.

There are several arguments for continuing the service as it stands. The needs of war disabled persons are very well known to the staff of the service. The war disabled and war widows might feel abandoned if responsibility for their welfare were transferred to the local authority health and welfare departments. The service has succeeded in attracting and retaining the services of a corps of responsible voluntary workers many of whom now know the pensioners and widows well because they have been visiting them regularly over many years.

There are, however, a number of cogent reasons why it might be better to transfer responsibility for the war pensions welfare service to the local authority's social welfare workers. The first is that the number of war disabled pensioners and war widows is steadily decreasing. In addition, the children orphaned in the war of 1939–45 will all have reached their twenty-first birthday by 1966. Declining numbers will mean that the service will become increasingly attenuated and more and more expensive as it is spread over fewer and fewer individuals. Visiting welfare officers, in particular, who are already spending many hours in travel will be spending an even greater proportion of their working week in this way.

Secondly, there are grounds for believing that welfare officers whose work has to cover several counties cannot know as much about the services available in any locality as do staff whose work is restricted to a single county or part of a county. This might not matter if the services war pensioners required were highly specialised and necessarily restricted to a small group of individuals. The survey information seems to indicate, however, that their difficulties and requirements were comparable to those of elderly and disabled patients receiving help from the county almoners. The latter were able to visit their clients more frequently and were better known personally to their clients' general practitioners and to the personnel of many other branches of the local social services than were the Ministry's welfare officers. The almoners might well be able, therefore, to give a better service than the Ministry's welfare officers, whose opportunities for getting to know about their patients' difficulties or the local services were more restricted.

From the point of view of professional help, therefore, those most deserving of the community's gratitude might obtain a better service if no distinction was made between them and other elderly and disabled persons in the community. On the other hand, disabled war pensioners and elderly widows might feel deprived or neglected if the special responsibilities for friendly visiting and for notifying the authorities of changing circumstances undertaken by volunteers organised by the Bucks War Pensions Committee were to come to an end.

The best solution might, therefore, be for the Ministry of Pensions and National Insurance to ask the local health and welfare authorities to provide the general welfare service for war disabled pensioners, widows and orphans. In Bucks, the duties might well be taken over by the county almoners and social workers.

At the same time, there is a need to continue the friendly visiting of severely disabled pensioners and widows by volunteers organised through the Bucks War Pensions Committee. Since this voluntary body is already organised on a county basis there should be no insuperable difficulties in its continuing to perform its present valuable functions. The social welfare staff of the county health and welfare department could work with the committee in the same way as the Ministry's welfare officers have done hitherto.

Such a reorganisation might have the further advantage of reducing the over-lapping of services of paid staff providing assistance to elderly and disabled persons. It should also economise on the services of social welfare workers by reducing the amount of time travelling from regional offices.

CHAPTER XVIII

The Paid Worker in Voluntary Social Welfare Societies

Most social welfare societies rely entirely upon volunteers, but in 1960–61 there were 29 employees of voluntary organisations who worked partly or entirely in Bucks. Ten of them were moral welfare workers and five N.S.P.C.C. inspectors. The others worked for societies for disabled people, for families of serving men or for general family casework agencies.[1]

Moral welfare work

Eight of the moral welfare workers were employed by the Church of England Oxford Diocesan Council for Moral Welfare and were responsible to six local associations of the Council in Bucks. Two were on the staff of the Northampton Diocesan Catholic Child Protection and Welfare Society. Both the Roman Catholic workers were concerned with both the care of unmarried mothers and child adoption. One of the eight Anglican moral welfare workers acted as principal adoption officer for her Council, and another was in charge of a hostel for girls. Their six colleagues arranged for the care of unmarried mothers. One, in north Bucks, worked part-time for the moral welfare association and part-time as a health visitor in the county's health service.[2]

The individuals served by moral welfare workers

Nearly all those seen by moral welfare workers during the survey were unmarried women and girls.[3] The adoption officer,

[1] The organisations to which those included in the survey belonged are shown in Appendix A, Table 34. A part-time social worker employed by S.S.A.F.A. and the two workers of the Invalid Children's Aid Assn. who had some responsibility for Bucks children were not interviewed.

[2] Only eight of the 10 moral welfare workers participated fully in the enquiry. One was ill during the year and made only a partial record of her work. Another resigned shortly after seeing us and did not provide information on those seen before leaving.

[3] Records from eight workers related to 185 individuals. In the analysis the records of the adoption officer were not separated from those of the moral welfare workers.

however, nearly always identified would-be adopting couples as her clients or occasionally an infant placed with the Society for adoption.

A third of the unmarried mothers were in their teens. In many instances, little was known about the social characteristics of the unmarried mothers' parental homes since they were no longer living in them, and could no longer be regarded as a member of that household. A third were living in hostels at the time of the enquiry and about the same proportion were in lodgings with people to whom they were not related: only a third were living in their parental homes or with other relatives.[1] Some of those in hostels or lodgings were girls whose usual residence was in Bucks and who might return to their home after the birth of their baby: but some were not originally from Bucks and intended leaving the county.[2] All that can be said is that, with few exceptions, the unmarried mothers were manual workers who had left school at the minimum age. The adoption worker's clients, on the other hand, were generally middle class couples and the husband was in a non-manual occupation.

A third of the families had been known to the organisation for over a year. These were usually couples wishing to adopt a second or third child. By contrast, the moral welfare workers had known only 7 per cent of their clients for more than one year. More than 80 per cent had been known for less than six months and 55 per cent were receiving their first visit.

The client nearly always came or was sent to the moral welfare worker so that arrangements could be made for her delivery or for the adoption or fostering of an illegitimate baby or for both. Eleven per cent took the initiative themselves in approaching the moral welfare worker. The clergy or other Church workers were responsible for referring 30 per cent, and secular voluntary organisations 5 per cent. Workers in statutory social services, however, were the most common source of referral, collectively having referred 39 per cent. General practitioners were most likely to refer, followed with almost equal frequency by the

[1] Consequently, analysis of the characteristics of clients' households was not illuminating.

[2] Systematic information was not obtained on the normal area of residence of the unmarried mother in hostels or lodging.

I*

hospital almoner, the health visitor and the district nurse. The children's department referred 7 per cent and the courts, including probation officers, 6 per cent. Cases referred by child care officers were nearly always those where the children's department asked the moral welfare worker to visit and assess the suitability of would-be adopters.

Moral welfare workers usually described their service to the unmarried mother as one of making arrangements for her delivery and for the care of the baby; but, in most instances, they helped with contingent problems. For example, employment was arranged or advice given to 12 per cent. Financial difficulties were sorted out for 14 per cent, and over a quarter of the clients were helped with emotional difficulties.

The moral welfare workers[1]

Two of the moral welfare staff were aged between 35 and 45 and one was nearing 60. Six were in the age group 45 to 54. Seven of the nine were single women, one was widowed and one married. Only one had had children of her own.

Seven of the nine were born into the homes of professional people, no fewer than three being daughters of clergymen. Only one left school at the minimum school leaving age; but two others left without a school certificate. Three were university graduates.

Only one of the staff of nine had started moral welfare work before reaching the age of 30. She had worked for moral welfare organisations in a number of capacities since the nineteen-thirties. Four had had considerable experience in nursing before coming into moral welfare work and two had been school teachers.

Six of the nine moral welfare staff had undertaken the course for moral welfare workers at the Josephine Butler Memorial House in Liverpool, and one had trained as a Methodist deaconess. With one exception, they were generally pleased with the course. The exception had taken it before the war when it was less socially and more religiously oriented and described it as, 'not nearly good enough'. Most who thought the course good made suggestions as to how it could have been improved. Two felt too much

---

[1] One of the 10 staff was not interviewed owing to illness. One of the nine from whom information was obtained was an adoption officer and not a moral welfare worker.

emphasis was given to theology and ethics and too little, in the words of one of them, to 'the everyday family problems'. Another thought there was not enough on legal aspects of the work, or on the psychology of sex. Another had taken an evening extra-mural class in social science after training and thought more of its content should have been included in the moral welfare course.

Five of the staff were pleased to have come into the work and, given a choice, would do the same again. The four others were not sorry to be moral welfare workers, but said they would choose other careers if given a choice again. Two felt they were better suited to nursing, and two would have chosen to be almoners or general social caseworkers. None would have left the social welfare field.

Moral welfare workers expressed the satisfactions they derived from their work in much the same terms as did the staff of other social welfare services, and insight, charity and tolerance were shown by nearly all in discussing their own motivations, their work and their clients.[1] Most stressed the rewards to be had from helping others and five mentioned working independence and variety of experience.

All but one expressed some dissatisfaction or frustration in their work; but there was comparatively little agreement on the causes. Three deplored the fact they had no private life, since their work absorbed so much of their time and energy. 'I've difficulty in finding time for my own pursuits', said one. 'It absorbs me so much, that I've lost my outside interests and contacts', said another.

Problems of pay, status or work organisation were raised by four of the nine workers. One said, bluntly, 'The pay is rotten. If I hadn't a small private income, I couldn't manage at all'.

---

[1] One put her main point in this way. 'I like helping to sort out someone who is at her wit's end.' 'It's the feeling I've comforted someone, not comfort in a sloppy sense, but giving strength', said another, and added 'as a single woman I like the feeling of being needed. A woman's natural outlet for this feeling is in her family. If she hasn't got one she must create an artificial one'. 'It's good to see the girl's appreciation when she finds she's not being judged', said another. Two derived satisfaction from helping young people to face 'their moral responsibilities' or from the opportunities afforded to do 'important missionary work for the Church at home'. 'I run my own life', said one, 'I'm not tied as I was in teaching. I have to discipline myself, but it's worth it'. 'You meet all kinds of people from all walks of life.'

Another stressed 'the lack of recognition of the work done by moral welfare workers'. Two talked about the difficulties of working with the committees of the local association. 'I feel frustrated rather than helped by the Committee', said one of them.

Five workers complained of the inadequacy of some vital services needed for unmarried mothers or of the lack of insight of those in charge of such services. The N.A.B. was the target of two complaints. Another accused health visitors of 'failing to realise the full implications of some of the situations we deal with', and thought there was a lack of co-operative spirit among social workers generally. Two raised questions about the homes for mothers and babies, one considering that staff shortages in these homes were responsible for most of their deficiencies. 'It's getting "living in" staff which causes the greatest difficulty', said one. Another said she 'didn't always see eye to eye with the matrons of mothers and babies homes', implying that they were not always sympathetic to unmarried mothers.

Two workers raised issues concerning the future of their service. One of them said, 'I wish we could drop the word "moral". It sometimes makes it difficult for us to do a job'. The other wondered whether the time was coming when unmarried mothers would be better served by workers from the statutory services. She thought the resources of the Church should be concentrated on spiritual guidance and that the material provision which moral welfare workers now gave should be the responsibility of the community as a whole.

The care of the unmarried mother and her child—summing up

Moral welfare workers were primarily employed in providing young unmarried mothers with shelter and medical care during the latter stages of their pregnancy, delivery and the early months of their child's life. They dealt mainly with individuals during comparatively short periods of crisis. Despite their name, their main concern was to give unmarried mothers immediate material help at what would generally be considered a time of crisis and only indirectly to provide moral guidance.

The maternity services provided under the National Health Services are available to all women irrespective of marital status or age. As society becomes less condemnatory, unmarried women are more likely to use the normal facilities provided by the health services for the care of mothers before, during and after childbirth. Nevertheless, there are many reasons, both medical and social, why the community should concern itself particularly with the welfare of unmarried mothers and illegitimate children. Unmarried mothers are frequently young and socially and intellectually immature. Many come from families which have been unable to provide adequate emotional support, or where there has been conflict between parents and children. They are less likely to be able to rely on support from the putative father of their child and from their own parents and siblings than married mothers who expect a baby.

There is every reason, therefore, to make special provision for unmarried mothers. In particular, there is a need for women who have had at least a general social work training. This is at present provided for moral welfare workers by their own training school; but there seems no fundamental reason why those who have taken a two-year national social work certificate should not, with little further training, go into work with unmarried mothers.

This enquiry suggested that moral welfare workers were trusted by the staff of other services, that they did not force sectarian religious views on those they helped[1] and that co-operation between them and other services was good. Moreover, some sections of the community, including some unmarried mothers, regard pregnancy outside marriage as requiring primarily spiritual guidance rather than material assistance, and look to religious organisations rather than community health services to provide it.

For these reasons there seems little point in suggesting major changes in the present provision of social services for unmarried mothers. Nevertheless, it is time to consider whether the community health services themselves should not take more initiative in developing social welfare services for unmarried mothers. Religious observance and affiliation to religious organisations are confined to a small minority in this country, and the fact that so much of the available help is associated with one or other denomi-

---

[1] The Church of England body assisted women of all denominations and of none.

nation may deter some unmarried mothers from seeking it early enough or at all.

If there is reluctance to seek help from denominational organisations, especially those which have the words 'moral welfare' in their titles, statutory health authorities should consider supplementing the services provided by the religious societies.[1] Above all, there is a need for social workers who are not associated with a particular denomination to provide the same kind of service as moral welfare workers. There is also a need for non-denominational hostels for unmarried mothers.[2]

The work of the N.S.P.C.C. inspectors

The National Society for the Prevention of Cruelty to Children had five inspectors with duties in Bucks as well as in neighbouring counties.[3] The local branches of the Society concerned themselves with winning support for its work and had no responsibility for the investigating work of the inspectors, who reported to the Society's headquarters.

In 39 of the 47 cases seen by the inspectors the household consisted of a married couple and their children. In the eight other instances, there was no adult male, the housewife being either deserted, divorced or unmarried. Although two of the male economic supporters were believed to have non-manual occupations, none of the heads of household were believed to have had an education beyond minimum school leaving age and nearly half were unskilled workers.

The families were usually large ones. A third had only one or

[1] With the encouragement of the Church of England Council for Social Work (the late Moral Welfare Council) more and more local associations are now changing their names to be more in keeping with modern trends.

[2] Local health authorities would require additional statutory powers if they were to provide them, except where they were dealing with unmarried mothers who might be subject to 'fit person' orders.

[3] Together, the five inspectors provided information about 47 cases seen during the study year, but withheld their names and addresses. These included all the Bucks cases seen by the inspectors working from Bedford, Luton and Northampton during the year 1960–61 and all those seen by the inspector from Windsor from April to September 1961. The inspector based on High Wycombe provided information on an unselected series of 25 cases seen over a period of just over a fortnight. Since the total number of cases was small, the picture which they presented of the clientele of the N.S.P.C.C. in 1960–61 was less reliable than the picture of the clientele of many other services.

two children, but 10 had six or more, and four of these had nine or more children living at home. All 47 households were composed of single family groups; there were no two-family or three-generation family units. Forty-two of them lived in rented dwellings, the majority being council tenants. The other five were caravan dwellers, a proportion more than double that found among the households visited by any other social welfare staff. There was also more overcrowding in the houses of those visited by the N.S.P.C.C. inspectors than among those seen by other workers. Twenty-eight were living at densities of over one person per room and nine at densities of three or more persons per room. Between a quarter and a fifth of the dwellings lacked baths or tapped hot water supplies; and N.S.P.C.C. inspectors were much more likely than the workers of any other social welfare service to describe the standard of internal decoration and cleanliness in the households visited as very poor. No fewer than 19 of the 47 homes visited earned this description.

Problems of chronic illness or handicap were not recorded with much frequency. Three households had members with mental disorders and five someone with a physical illness or defect serious enough to impair normal functions.

The N.S.P.C.C. inspectors were usually dealing with households which had two or more different kinds of social problems. Only one case was reported as having no problems. Fourteen were described as having one problem only and 32 two or more. Only probation officers and child guidance workers reported a higher average of problems per household.

In 39 of the 47 cases the N.S.P.C.C. inspectors considered there was child neglect. In only one did an inspector state that there was physical cruelty; but in eight cases, at least one child in the family seemed to be ill-treated by one or both parents rather than simply neglected. The distinction between cruelty and neglect is not, of course, an easy one to make. Ignoring the physical needs of a child beyond a certain point turns the charge of neglect into one of cruelty, and this is equally true when a child's need for love and acceptance is ignored. The eight cases mentioned were those in which the mother or both parents seemed unable to give one child the affection and attention they gave to the others.

In eight of the cases, the inspectors did not feel that the problems were basically those of child neglect or cruelty, but resulted from the general inadequacy of the housewife or the poor work record of the husband. Ten families were described as poor tenants failing to pay the rent or living in squalor; 10 of the families were described as mismanaging their income, and 10, including all those households in which there was no male breadwinner, were described as having insufficient income.

Poor relationships within the family and especially between spouses were listed frequently. There was said to be serious marital discord in 12 and poor parent-child relationships in eight.

Twelve of the cases had been referred to N.S.P.C.C. inspectors first more than 12 months before the study contact, and many had been receiving regular visits for a considerable period. Twenty-four of the sample were being seen for the first time during the study period and another four had not been known to the inspectors at all a month before.

A third of the cases had been referred to the N.S.P.C.C. in the first instance by members of the general public. About the same number came through staff of the local health and welfare department, most frequently the health visitor. No cases were referred by general practitioners or hospital staff. Others were referred by a police officer, a probation officer, a child care officer and a teacher. Nine were cases in which one spouse, with or without justification, accused the other of cruelty or neglect, and approached the N.S.P.C.C. inspector for help. Two of these cases were seen by the inspectors in their own offices. Otherwise contacts took place in the homes of the families.

Inspectors commonly suggested that their functions were of two main kinds. First they investigated family circumstances to report to their own organisation. At the same time, if there was evidence of neglect or cruelty they pointed out to those responsible what their legal responsibilities were and what action could be taken against them.

In a quarter of the cases the N.S.P.C.C. inspectors arranged for the care of a child or children, if only temporarily, outside his or her own home. This action was taken where the inspectors felt that the parents were not able to provide the child with adequate care, and was sometimes taken with the parents' consent rather than against their will.

In the same number of cases the families' difficulties seemed partly financial, and the inspector either gave assistance from N.S.P.C.C. funds or put the individual in touch with the N.A.B. or a voluntary society. Advice or assistance with employment was given in 16 cases, and in the nine cases where poor housing seemed to contribute to the family's difficulties approaches were made to housing authorities.

The inspectors

Four of the five inspectors who served Bucks in 1960–61 were in their forties and one in his early fifties. They were all married men with children of their own.[1]

It was N.S.P.C.C. policy at that time to recruit men with some experience of life and only occasionally were men of less than thirty considered. The inspectors in the Bucks areas had been 34, 38, 39, 41 and 43 years old respectively on joining the society. Two had been recruited within the last two years and were in their first posts. The other three men had joined at various times between 1947 and 1958 and were in their second posts with the society. All these three had worked first in industrial towns.

Three were sons of black-coated workers, one of a skilled manual worker and one of a soldier. One left school at 14 and two at 15: the other two stayed on to 16 and 17. On leaving school they had all gone straight to work, two to retailing, two to clerical work and the fifth to technical work in an expanding industry. For four out of the five this initial experience had been followed sooner or later by regular army or police service. All five spent part of their spare time in voluntary activities and were men with deep religious convictions.

Apart from in-service training as members of the police or armed forces, none had had any formal full-time training before joining the N.S.P.C.C. On joining two had a three-month and three a six-month full-time course which combined theoretical studies at headquarters in London with practical work supervised by the society's inspectors in one or more areas.

All considered that the course was a good preparation for their work and three that it did not need improvement. One thought

[1] Only in special circumstances did the N.S.P.C.C. appoint single men as inspectors, and men with children were preferred.

that more psychology was needed and he and one other worker felt that a one or two years' social science course would give an even better preparation.[1] Three did not feel the need for further study or training.[2]

All the inspectors said they had a great deal of satisfaction from their work and only one, given another opportunity, would have done something different—in his case medicine. The very real sense of satisfaction in the job felt by all the inspectors was expressed in the comments of two. 'I never dreamed I would be so glad about a job—not even when I was in the police force, which I loved', said one. 'I wouldn't change my job for anything', said the second and added, with perhaps a hint of parochialism, 'The N.S.P.C.C. is the only genuine social service. All roads lead back to the N.S.P.C.C'.

Like so many others, inspectors emphasised their working independence as a reason for liking their work—'I'm my own slave-driver'—the variety of jobs and of people helped, the occasional successes and surprises. Two stressed the advantages of working for a voluntary society, claiming that they could be more flexible than if they had been working for a statutory service. Two others said they liked the combination of work for children with an investigating or detective job.

Some drawbacks and difficulties were mentioned; but no two inspectors found exactly the same ones. One could not obtain sufficient material help for some of the families, and thought there was a lack of co-operation from some staff in statutory services. 'It's the other agencies who need me. I don't need them', he said. 'We can get along very well.' Another inspector who found no drawbacks in his work said his wife did not like the area, adding, however, that his army experience had accustomed him to change. 'Home's where you hang up your hat, and we're used to moving.'

Two inspectors talked more generally about their work and the society's place in the community social services. One suggested that their main function should be to keep families together. The

---

[1] One of these was intending to take a part-time course for an external university diploma in social science.

[2] Their attitude was expressed by one who said 'I can't say I feel the need for any further course. We have annual conferences and a chance to discuss new approaches at the annual inspection'.

other was the only one to make suggestions about the organisation of the work. He thought there was room for another inspector in Bucks to cover Aylesbury, Bletchley and the north of the county, since the three inspectors sharing the work in these areas did not have a chance of getting to know the social welfare staff in Bucks well because most of their work was in neighbouring counties.

This officer saw the preventive work of the N.S.P.C.C. continuing to grow. He thought the public more inclined to report cases of neglect which several years ago would not have been considered serious, making it possible to undertake preventive work. Much of his own work was undertaken without threat of legal action; but he could not visualise being able to act effectively without the authority in the last resort to bring offenders to court. He considered, moreover, despite his previous police experience, that this power was rightly vested in a voluntary organisation.

Some general conclusions concerning the work of N.S.P.C.C. inspectors

The N.S.P.C.C. inspectors dealt occasionally with cases of children threatened by physical violence or sadistic brutality. Most of their work, however, was with parents who were liable to endanger their children's health by neglecting their physical and emotional needs. The families were commonly large ones; the mothers were often worn out by child-bearing and by the effort of caring for several small children; the fathers were usually unskilled workers who found it difficult to keep in steady work; household incomes were irregular in amount and often inadequate, and ignorance, limited intelligence or apathy made parents poor managers. Although inspectors sometimes used the threat of legal proceedings, they spent much time persuading parents to make better use of community services which could help them and their children.

Most of the men who did this work came to it after careers in the police or armed forces. On the face of it men with this background might seem better suited to taking disciplinary action than to dealing with situations which call for prolonged support to ineffectual people.

The N.S.P.C.C. seemed, however, aware of changing circumstances, and lectures in the six-month training course were designed to give recruits more insight into the causes of anti-social behaviour and the effectiveness of various ways of seeking to influence it. The annual inspections conducted by senior officers were also used to introduce new ideas to serving inspectors.

Nevertheless, a six-month training which included practice as well as theoretical studies seemed too short to acquire enough knowledge of the social and psychological factors in human behaviour in general and in marital and parent-child relationships in particular, especially when recruits had not had recent experience in studying abstract issues or examining objectively and dispassionately the basis of their own values and beliefs. Nor, given that inspectors need to learn about their own legal powers and methods of work, is six months long enough to learn about the social services available to families.

For this reason, the N.S.P.C.C. should consider first, whether it can lengthen the course for recruits who have no previous background in social work and second, whether it can recruit men and possibly women who have taken courses in child care, probation, or a two-year course in social work.[1] This second proposal seems called for as the work of inspectors becomes more rehabilitative than punitive and thus increasingly resembles the work of social workers in other branches of the social services who are also concerned with family maintenance and the prevention of physical and mental illness and delinquency.

This study suggested that most of the families were referred to the society by members of the general public. Willingness to refer cases of apparent cruelty or neglect to the society does not necessarily imply that there would be less public confidence in a statutory body.[2]

Nevertheless, since wide sections of the public know and respect the society and are willing to ask it to investigate cases of suspected neglect or cruelty, and since social workers from statutory services occasionally find it helpful to ask the N.S.P.C.C. inspector to work with difficult families, there is little point in suggesting that the Society should cease to function. At the same

[1] Since the survey, the Society has begun to take both these recommended courses.

[2] Health visitors, police, probation officers and child care officers were also approached frequently by the general public.

time, new approaches within the N.S.P.C.C. must not be made
an excuse for inaction elsewhere. The problems of effective
utilisation of scarce social work resources is nowhere more acute
than in the area of disturbed and disturbing families which often
come within the province of the N.S.P.C.C. Suggestions for a
re-organisation of these resources so as to conserve and concentrate
resources are considered in Chapter XX.

(a) The work of the missioner for the deaf

The Bucks county welfare department employed the Oxford
Diocesan Council for the Deaf to fulfil its obligations to the deaf
and hard of hearing.[1] The missioner for the deaf was carrying
out, therefore, not only the objects of the Council, which included
guidance and spiritual comfort, but also the duties and powers
of the local welfare department.

The missioner was a middle-aged man who had been handicapped by deafness and early in life had begun to help those
similarly afflicted. With strenuous efforts he educated himself
and worked as a cabinet maker. In his spare time he trained as a
lay reader and finally became a full-time missioner. He provided
us with information concerning 27 households that he had visited
during a week of his work. In over a third of these he was concerned with two deaf persons. These two persons were usually
spouses; but, in a number of instances, the relationship was one
of parent and offspring.

A small majority of those he saw were women (a ratio of 56
women to 44 men). They were widely scattered through age
groups: four were over pensionable age and four still at school.
Apart from deafness, few had handicaps or chronic illnesses, but
two suffered from a mental disorder, one from the effects of a
stroke and one from diabetes. All the households except one were
headed by manual workers or by women with minimal full-time
schooling.

Only one of the 27 cases was a new one. All the others had been
known to him for more than a year and 19 for more than five years.
Most had had regular visits throughout the year. Three had been

---

[1] Under the National Assistance Act 1948, local welfare authorities may
employ voluntary organisations to provide services for the substantially or
permanently handicapped.

seen at weekly intervals and most of the others had been visited
monthly.

Most of the missioner's calls were simply friendly visits to
keep in touch with those on his register and see all was well,
and in some instances to say prayers with the deaf person; but in
six cases problems of employment were discussed, in three money
difficulties and in another two housing difficulties. There were
also problems of loneliness and adjustment to handicap in three
cases and other difficulties in a few. In nine of the 27, however, the
missioner felt there were no problems, the deaf person and his
family having made a successful adjustment.

The missioner had no regrets about his choice of career. His
reward was 'knowing you can help people to be less lonely. The
deaf live in a world of their own, but I can enter it'. He was often
frustrated by the general lack of understanding among hearing
people of the problems of the deaf, and critical of the facilities
placed at his disposal, especially in the way of clerical help. But,
he was dedicated to the work and would not have changed it.

There was little doubt that the missioner provided the deaf
and hard-of-hearing in Bucks with a great deal of social support,
because he could communicate more easily with the deaf than a
hearing person and because he was a dedicated and knowledgeable
person.

It is impossible to say whether or how his work would change
if he were employed not by the Oxford Diocesan Council for the
Deaf but by the welfare section of the local health and welfare
department. On the one hand, his close link with the Church and
with the voluntary society, 'Friends of the Deaf', undoubtedly
gave the missioner personal inspiration and support for his many
attempts to enrich the social life of the deaf. Attachment to the
welfare department might have limited his activities by limiting
his inspiration. On the other hand, there are both handicapped
people and dedicated social workers who lack firm religious
convictions.

The welfare department might, therefore, consider whether it
should not now accept more responsibility for the welfare of the
deaf, as they have for the general classes of the physically handicapped. Indeed, the community has been more neglectful of the
needs of deaf people and is more ignorant of their problems than

it should be. A greater sense of responsibility for their welfare by the staff of the health and welfare services might help to end the unnecessary isolation of the deaf.

(b) The Slough Industrial Health Service almoner's work

The Slough Industrial Health Service was set up in premises adjoining the Slough Community Centre on the Industrial Trading Estate. Staffed by doctors, nurses and an almoner, it provided firms with a casualty service, a treatment and examination centre and advice on preventive measures. Industrial workers receiving medical treatment or advice could be referred by the doctors at the centre to the almoner for help with social difficulties. The firms' personnel officers could also refer workers with socio-medical problems directly to her.

Of the 25 individuals seen by the almoner during the recording period, thirteen were men. The age range was wide: two were under 20 and three over 60, but there was some concentration of 45–59-year olds. Thirteen of the 25 had a chronic disability. Chronic mental illness affected three of them and muscular or rheumatic disorders another three. The seven others included men suffering from respiratory illnesses, neurological and skin disorders and heart conditions.

Three of them were non-manual workers. The others were predominantly semi-skilled factory workers.

In only one case did the almoner feel there were no social problems. Over half (13) had one problem, seven had two, and four at least three different kinds of problem. That most frequently specified was adjusting to a chronic illness or disability.

Four of the almoner's clients had been referred to her more than 12 months before. The referral dates of the others were fairly evenly spread throughout the year. Only four were being seen for the first time. Six cases had been referred for a general exploration of the personal circumstances of the patient; but the rest were referred for specific reasons. In three, the problem was housing, and in two to arrange for transport to work for disabled men. In another two cases, the almoner was asked to arrange convalescence and in two to persuade workers to accept voluntary admission to mental hospital. Marriage problems were the reasons for two other referrals, and, in another, the almoner was asked to arrange ante-natal care and confinement for an unmarried mother. In another, the client had been breaking the law and the almoner was asked by his employer to talk to him.

In 16 of the 25 cases the almoner described her services as helping the patient to deal with emotional problems; but other practical forms of service were frequently given. For example, in four cases she helped with employment, in two with marital difficulties and in two with housing.

Like most of the trained social workers in other branches of the social services, the almoner was usually in touch with at least one other social service on behalf of each patient. These were usually the almoners' departments of hospitals and general practitioners; but staff from many central and local government services had been contacted in addition to personnel officers from clients' employers.

The almoner undertaking this work in 1960–61 had been working in the Industrial Health Service for less than a year. She had previously had a long and varied career in hospital almoning and her experience had included heading the social service department of a unit specialising in plastic surgery. She chose to widen her experience by work outside hospitals. She considered that her almoner's training had been good but that she had been rather too young and immature at the time to gain the maximum benefit from it.

The attachment of a medical social worker to the Industrial Health Service in Slough seemed valuable. Many of the illnesses which incapacitate adult men and women have social components and, in the present organisation of medical care services, these may sometimes best be dealt with by services associated with workplaces rather than homes.

However, if domiciliary medical care was to be re-organised, so that health visitors and social workers were attached to general practice units, a number of problems which are now dealt with at work, if at all, may be more effectively treated in the community. (see Chapter XX).

The work of voluntary casework organisations

Staff of eight voluntary organisations working wholly or partly in Bucks were interviewed and provided information about them-

selves.[1] Seven of them gave details of one or more of the cases
seen during the study year (see Table 26). In addition, the Invalid
Children's Aid Society provided information about the five Bucks
children helped during the year, but not about the staff responsible
for this help. Altogether information was available about 121
cases. The use which can be made of it, however, is limited since
the cases were not a satisfactory sample of the work of the staff of
the organisations.

Table 26

VOLUNTARY ORGANISATIONS PROVIDING INFORMATION ABOUT
BUCKS CASES DEALT WITH BY STAFF IN 1960–61

Organisation	Type	Area covered by social worker	Number of cases seen and recorded during the study period
Slough Council of Social Service and Old People's Welfare Committee	Local	Eton, Slough and district	25
Citizen's Advice Bureau and All Good Causes Fund	Local	Slough and district	25
British Red Cross Society, Bucks branch	National	Bucks	7
Joint Committee of the Order of St. John and British Red Cross, Bucks branch	National	Bucks	25
Church of England Children's Society	National	Bucks, Beds & Herts	25
National Association of Discharged Prisoners Aid Societies	National	Lancaster, Gloucester & Bucks	8
National Spastics Society	National	Northern Home Counties region	1
Invalid Children's Aid Association	National	Countrywide	5

One of the general impressions given by these cases, considered
as a whole, was that nearly half those who were being helped had
approached the agencies themselves. Those referred came more

[1] The secretary of the High Wycombe Central Aid Society did not record
cases.

frequently through statutory services such as the N.A.B., and the health and welfare department staff than they did through other voluntary bodies. Half the individuals had been known to the societies for less than a month but a third had first been referred more than a year earlier.

Most of the general family casework agencies' cases had originally been referred for financial assistance; but the range of problems and the services provided were much wider. Chronic ill-health, in particular, was a common feature of the households. Two-thirds of the cases were again referred to other services for help with housing, medical problems, domestic help and employment.

The only person whose cases were quite different was the Church of England Children's Society officer. He visited those who applied through the society to adopt children or gave their names as willing to act as foster parents. He also visited children at the society's residential home in Bucks and boys and girls who had left school and gone to work, as well as the homes of those who volunteered to take children into their homes during school holidays. In a few instances he called on unmarried mothers who had elected to keep their children and received help from the society in order to do so.

Four of the staff interviewed were men and four women. One was under 30, one over 60, and the others in the forties or fifties. Four, two men and two women, were single.

All the women were daughters of professional or business men and had stayed at school until 16 or 17. Three had taken secretarial training and eventually found paid administrative-cum-secretarial work in a voluntary society. Only one had trained in social work, as a home teacher for the blind, but two of the other three had attended evening classes or week-end conferences in problems of the elderly and other relevant topics.

Two of the men had working class and two middle class origins. One left school at 14 and one had had a university training. They came to voluntary society work in very different ways. One had spent most of his working life in the armed forces. Another had been a successful builder. Another had moved from accountancy to youth work and thence to voluntary society social work. The fourth had been a clerical assistant in a voluntary organisation and taken an external university diploma in social science in his spare time.

Amongst the eight, therefore, three had some training appropriate to social work and all of them felt it had been useful. One, praising the university social science course, said 'Social workers need a liberal education. It's not simply a matter of acquiring social work techniques'. The two who had taken diplomas in their spare time would have preferred a full-time course. The worker who had taken the home teacher's course described it as an 'absolutely superb course for casework'.

Those who had not trained in social work were divided as to the value of a social worker training for the kind of work which they were doing. One felt that, from his point of view, his 'very varied experience in life has been a tremendous help' and that the best training was 'having to look after one's men in the armed forces'. He thought a certain amount of legal training would have been useful, but was not convinced that much else of value could be taught in formal courses. Another suggested that present courses for social workers placed too much emphasis on theory and excluded some of the best potential social workers who were not able to reach the required academic level. Another considered that her work was primarily administrative and that 'the social service aspects come with experience. You learn to sum people up'. Her sentiments were echoed by a worker who doubted the value of a course for the older people who were most suited for the work. Two of the untrained workers, however, gave qualified support to training. One thought in-service training more important than a formal course, since 'a *full* knowledge of all local services and conditions was more important than theory'. She added 'We are surrounded by specialists and therefore don't need to be specialists ourselves'.

Only one of the eight workers felt uncertain as to whether he had chosen the right career. All the others were satisfied with their work, and expressed their satisfaction in much the same way as other social welfare workers. 'I like helping people to gain a sense of security and confidence', said one. Other satisfactions derived from their independence and the variety of work offered.

Some drawbacks were mentioned by all but two of the workers. Three talked of the disappointment they felt when they were not successful. 'I've become case-hardened; but you can't help feeling disappointed when someone lapses back into crime', said one. Two discussed the disadvantages of 'never knowing the end because almost all cases are referred to some specialist agency'. Another disliked the office work involved and the 'form filling'.

Most complaints, however, centred round pay and the difficulties of working for voluntary committees. One of three men who mentioned low salaries said, 'The salary is much too small for a man with a wife and children. You can't do the work well if you're always worrying about your family', and one woman said 'the low salary would be a considerable drawback to someone entirely dependent on it'. Another suggested that the low salary of the voluntary society worker gave him a low status in the eyes of staff from statutory services. She believed that the time was ripe for local authorities to take over most of the work at present done by the paid staff of voluntary organisations, partly at least because the local authority could afford to pay its employees better salaries.

Four of the eight workers mentioned difficulties associated with working for a voluntary organisation. One alleged that the committee members were sometimes guilty of 'promising the client the earth, and then expecting us to get it for them'. Another complained that 'voluntary workers gossip about clients', and made the work more difficult. A third suggested that 'the society has an axe to grind and must always come first', and implied that this order of priority sometimes conflicted with the interests of the client. He added, 'Voluntary workers are often unreliable and undependable, and no pressure can be brought to bear because they *are* voluntary'.[1]

Some general conclusions concerning the work of voluntary organisations

Most of the work undertaken by paid workers employed by the C.A.B. and Old People's Welfare Committee in Slough, and by the British Red Cross and Joint Committee was for elderly and disabled people and their relatives. It consisted largely in obtaining

---

[1] 'Many middle-aged women join the society to take up good works and are more of a nuisance than a help. They join it for personal gain or prestige. Their help is too amateurish. In particular, office conditions tend to get chaotic.'

financial help to meet special needs for food, clothing, medical or domestic equipment or in referring patients to appropriate health and welfare services. Contacts with individuals tended to be of limited duration and there seemed little opportunity to form a long-term supporting relationship.

There seemed some administrative advantages in this work being undertaken by the employees of voluntary organisations. In the case of the C.A.B., for example, it would not be easy to decide to which local authority department a social service information centre should belong. The absence of departmental affiliations is here a positive advantage. Another advantage, if the staff are trained social workers, is that they can direct the efforts of voluntary workers into the most useful channels. For example, trained social workers can see that available financial resources are distributed wisely.

A further advantage of trained social workers on the staff of voluntary organisations is that they can help to bridge the gap between the work of social welfare workers attached to statutory services and the unpaid work of volunteers. The understanding of social problems, their causes and effective treatment, which has been acquired by trained workers, must be transmitted to voluntary workers. At the same time, it is likely that the social workers' own understanding will increase if their decisions are being critically examined by an informed and interested public. Involvement of trained workers in the affairs of voluntary societies helps to ensure a close link.

On the other hand, there were several disadvantages in voluntary society employment for the trained worker. First, salaries were low and had not risen to the same extent as those of employees of local or central government. Too low a salary structure must limit unduly the size of the pool from which recruits to social work can be drawn. Secondly, relationships between the paid staff and the voluntary committee members, to whom the former were responsible, were not in the nature of things easy. Some workers felt that they were subjected to too much control, and that some of the decisions reached were arbitrary and based on the personal prejudices of forceful committee members. On the other hand, friction of this kind was not confined to voluntary societies. The staff of statutory social services also felt frustrated by apparent indifference to their problems on the part of elected Council members or administrative superiors.

The final verdict, therefore, must be inconclusive. The paid staff of voluntary societies were helping to meet needs which were not being met adequately by statutory services. They were also helping volunteers to deepen and extend their knowledge of social problems and the possible solutions to them. Against these advantages must be set the disadvantages of low salary scales, and the possibility that decisions reached by voluntary committees are more arbitrary and less likely to reflect community interest as a whole than decisions reached by elected representatives in local government.

CHAPTER XIX

The Contribution of the Voluntary Worker to Social Welfare

The primary object of the survey was to describe the work and clientele of the staff of statutory and voluntary bodies. However, many organisations promote social welfare by the voluntary efforts of their members, and their existence and activities influence the work of paid social welfare workers.

This chapter presents a general picture of the scope of organised voluntary social welfare work in Bucks. It is based on information provided by bodies which considered their main function the well-being of those in need.[1]

There were, broadly, four types of society. First there were those who could help anyone in trouble or need as a result of illness, frailty, bereavement or poverty. Secondly, there were societies who helped people with particular disabilities. Thirdly, there were welfare organisations for service and ex-servicemen and their families. Fourthly, there were societies which pursued definite objectives such as marriage guidance or Family Planning. The work of voluntary associations of each of these four kinds is considered separately.

1. *The work of voluntary organisations concerned with general welfare*

The societies with general welfare aims which provided information about their work in 1961 are shown in Table 27, together with the type of activity they undertook.

A number of organisations were still concerned with the alleviation of poverty or hardship caused by the death or incapacity of a breadwinner or the dwindling income of an elderly person. In Slough, voluntary organisations had over the years agreed that, as far as possible, this kind of assistance should be centralised and assessment of needs made by a paid social worker. Voluntary workers in the various organisations represented on the

---

[1] Appendix D contains an account of the methods and criteria used to approach voluntary organisations.

Table 27

SOCIETIES PROMOTING GENERAL WELFARE AND THE SCOPE OF
THEIR ACTIVITIES

Name of organisation	Number of local branches in Bucks	Religious or Secular	Type of Assistance organised (see Key)
All Good Causes Fund, Slough	1	S	A.
British Red Cross Society	11	S	B.C.E.H.
Catholic Women's League	1	R	D.E.F.G.H.
*County Care Committee	3	S	A.
Citizen's Advice Bureau	3	S	J.
League of Hospital Friends	3	S	E.F.
Mothers' Union	45	R	D.E.F.G.H.
†Old People's Welfare Committees	12	S	E.F.G.H.
Rotary Club and Inner Wheel	8	S	E.A.H.
St. John's Ambulance Brigade	4	S	C.E.
Slough Nursing Fund	1	S	A.E.
Toc H & Toc H Women's Association	10	R	A.D.E.F.G.H.
Women's Voluntary Services	22	S	A.D.E.F.H.

Key to type of assistance provided:

A. Financial help/coal, clothing, etc.
B. Medical equipment/supplies.
C. Nursing instruction/first aid.
D. Meals on wheels/domestic help.
E. Car transport.
F. Sick visiting.
G. General visiting/vigilance.
H. Recreational.
J. Personal advice.

* County Care Committees also included representatives of the staff of the county health department and county councillors.

† Old People's Welfare Committees were co-ordinating bodies to encourage organisations to undertake work for the elderly and to prevent overlapping.

Committee of the All Good Causes Fund had, however, the responsibility for suggesting those who should be beneficiaries. Much of the help dispensed was in the form of goods rather than cash and this was also true of other societies which made gifts to those in need.[1]

The county care committees also dispensed financial assistance and material help. They had originally been tuberculosis after-care committees; but as the number of T.B. cases declined during the fifties, they began to help those with other kinds of chronic illness or disability who were in need of special diets, prolonged convalescence, alterations to their dwellings or rehabilitation courses. During the financial year ending March, 1961, 86 persons were so assisted. Most of the cases were referred to the committees by the county's medical social workers; but some came from voluntary workers.[2]

The primary purpose of the old people's welfare committees established in the main towns was to co-ordinate the work of statutory and voluntary agencies helping old people.[3] They considered gaps in the provision for elderly people and how best to fill them. The service most often initiated and paid for by the old people's welfare committees themselves was chiropody. In two areas a 'good neighbour' scheme had been initiated by the committees. Elderly people could place a 'good neighbour' card in their window to show that they wanted somebody to call.[4] The secretaries of the committees were members of the county welfare service.

Most branches of the Mothers' Union did not organise welfare work. In the words of one of them, 'Personal help is sometimes, indeed quite frequently, given, but not by the Mothers' Union

[1] Coal and clothing were frequently specified as gifts. Mothers' Union branches most frequently gave food and flowers to elderly people. The League of Hospital Friends spent money mainly on equipment which would benefit patients or staff generally (e.g., television). Money raised by the Slough Nursing Fund, on the other hand, went to individuals, usually on the recommendation of the county medical social worker.

[2] Altogether, the Committees' expenditure amounted to about £3,500 of which roughly 40 per cent came from funds raised by the Committee through flag days, special appeals and collections taken up in other organisations. The county council provided the balance.

[3] In Slough, the committee employed a social worker to visit and assess the social and economic needs of elderly people and to advise those needing help. She also kept in touch with social clubs for elderly persons run by various organisations.

[4] These schemes were not the same as the 'good neighbour' service which some local health authorities have instituted on a regular basis to supplement the home help service.

K

as an organisation. We urge members to help neighbours or relatives on an individual basis and encourage neighbourliness and concern for others'. Many of their most active members were members of old people's welfare committees, the British Legion or the British Red Cross and undertook much voluntary social service in these capacities. Some branches, however, arranged a rota of members to help at infant welfare clinics or old people's club meetings and to visit elderly people in hospital or at home.

Commenting on the kind of service which their branches could give, some secretaries drew attention to the difficulties arising from the increasing age of their own members. One said that over half her members were over 65, many of them in need of help themselves. Others suggested that although neighbourliness was still much in evidence, especially in rural parishes, lack of transport made it difficult for those who were elderly themselves to visit any but near neighbours. Several pointed out that younger women tended to be tied by family or working commitments and could not contribute much to the welfare of others.

The Toc H branches in Bucks had usually a small number of active members who dedicated themselves to serving unfortunate people in the community. They aimed less at raising money or making gifts than at providing elderly, sick or disabled people with personal services or friendly support. Most of the branches, for example, arranged special entertainments for hospital patients or those living in residential institutions for mentally or physically handicapped adults or children and where possible invited them to social events in the community or to their homes.

Most Toc H secretaries drew attention to human needs which they felt no statutory service could meet. In the words of one of them, 'the vast army of the uncommitted seem to be under the impression that "the state" should fill all needs and do not understand that the greatest need today is for friendship, love and a genuine desire to befriend and help those less fortunate than ourselves'. They felt there were no limits to the scope of voluntary work, but only a shortage of men and women willing to do it. Some attributed the shortage of voluntary workers to apathy, 'particularly among the younger folk', others to the counterattraction of television and others again to the heavy commitments of men resident in the area who travelled to work in London and only returned late in the evening.

The St. John's Ambulance Brigade in Bucks provided a voluntary corps of nursing members and first-aiders who attended public gatherings of many kinds. In a few instances, members undertook night nursing for elderly bed-ridden patients whose relatives were unable to provide continuous care. Commenting on their work, the secretary believed that 'the taking over of all ambulance transport by the County lessened the interest of members'. Ambulance work had had a wide appeal for recruiting purposes. The Brigade was now attempting to build up a nursing reserve, an activity which had brought them more closely in touch with local hospitals.

The Brigade's county secretary felt there was difficulty in finding people for their work with the result that the most ambitious training projects had to be restricted and a few willing people were over-worked. She attributed the shortage to the work requiring a preliminary training, to people having many other interests and to a lack of good leaders to direct the work and inspire the members.

Much of the effort of the Women's Voluntary Services in Bucks was devoted to running a 'Meals on Wheels' service for the home-bound. Altogether, some 3,500 Bucks residents were served on at least one occasion during 1961. The service was confined to the main towns in the county, that is, to Aylesbury, Slough and High Wycombe. In a normal week approximately 550 meals were delivered by about 165 members.

About the same number of members did voluntary work in hospitals and a similar number helped to distribute welfare foods at infant welfare clinics. Even more members were regular helpers at old people's clubs and provided cars to take housebound people out. The W.V.S. also ran clothing depots, where members sorted worn clothes which were given to local families or sent to other parts of the country or the world. A few members took part in rather more specialised work. Several, for example, acted as receptionists at blood transfusion centres, two were active in prison welfare, fourteen helped in the home care of disabled people, and four ran the Citizen's Advice Bureau in the Aylesbury area.

The divisions of the Bucks branch of the British Red Cross Society ran a medical equipment loan system which was extensively used in the home care of elderly patients referred by district nurses, county almoners and general practitioners. The division also recruited V.A.D.'s and by evening and special courses kept them up-to-date with first aid and simple nursing techniques, and some members undertook voluntary nursing of elderly patients or helped in local hospitals. Every division arranged car transport for patients who needed to attend hospital for treatment. In several areas members regularly visited old people's homes and sometimes took the residents out. They also read to the blind. In some places, members undertook the distribution of welfare foods at infant welfare clinics, and in some ran clubs for elderly people.

Commenting on their work and its relationship to statutory services, several secretaries pointed out that they 'have been requested to do more welfare work over the last ten years than ever before'. Most gave the impression, too, that relations with the personnel of the statutory services had improved.[1]

Most felt there was a shortage of voluntary workers, the only two exceptions being in the Amersham and Chalfont areas, where there were relatively more middle class households. In north Bucks emphasis was given to the lack of people to lead activities rather than to a shortage of volunteers. Where there were shortages, lack of time and family responsibilities were held responsible. In the Slough division, however, the Secretary felt that difficulties were exacerbated by competition from other welfare organisations also searching for suitable recruits.

The problem of finding enough volunteers was not the only difficulty. Some secretaries drew attention to the lack of suitable accommodation for meetings and/or old people's clubs, and most felt that, given more transport for elderly or disabled people, the range of their activities could be widened.

Some branches of the Rotary Club and Inner Wheel provided gifts of coal and food for elderly people, took otherwise house-

---

[1] 'There's more liaison now between our members and statutory social welfare services', said one. Another said, 'there is a closer link with the W.V.S. and the county health department in getting to know where there are elderly people who can be brought into the old people's clubs and also in arranging for them to have the benefit of "Meals on Wheels".'

bound people out in cars, and arranged social outings. Other branches, however, did not undertake such activities as a branch, but encouraged 'the practice of service by its members in their personal, business and community life'.

Organisations were asked whether their voluntary workers gave advice or guidance about such matters as employment, housing, marital relationships, illegitimacy or mental health. Only the Citizen's Advice Bureaux indicated that they were systematically asked for help on such matters and they almost always referred enquirers to statutory or voluntary social services where expert advice was available. So did other societies when they were asked for advice.[1]

2. The work of voluntary societies for severely handicapped people

The voluntary organisations helping those with specific disabilities which had at least one locally based branch or group in Bucks and provided information about their work are listed in Table 28.

Before 1948, the Bucks Association for the Blind had employed home teachers of the blind and provided whatever services were at that time available to blind persons in their own homes. The National Assistance Act of 1948 gave the local authority welfare departments statutory responsibility for the welfare of permanently or substantially handicapped people including the blind, but allowed them to employ voluntary organisations to discharge this responsibility. In Bucks, the welfare authority employed home teachers, but asked the six local divisions of the county association to work with them to provide as full a service as possible. The divisional committees of the association, composed of voluntary workers, met regularly, therefore, to hear reports from the home teachers, to arrange for friendly visiting and for social events of different kinds, and to raise funds in order to

---

[1] In a few instances, voluntary workers with nursing training were recorded as giving advice on care of the elderly. Some members of the Mothers' Union and Toc H were asked for guidance on family relationships, teenage difficulties and employment. Some of those who gave advice had appropriate qualifications, for example, they were employers, lawyers or social workers. Generally speaking no special expertise was claimed for those who gave advice.

Table 28

SOCIETIES HELPING THOSE WITH SPECIFIC DISABILITIES AND THE
SCOPE OF THEIR ACTIVITIES

Name of Organisation	Number of local branches	Type of Assistance (see Key)
British Council for the Welfare of Spastics and Friends of Ponds	1	A.H.
Bucks Association for the Blind	6	A.B.D.E.F.G.H.
Bucks Centre Committee for the Deaf and Friends of the Deaf Association (Oxford Diocesan Council for the Deaf)	2	A. + Technical help
Deaf Social Clubs	3	H.
Infantile Paralysis Fellowship	1	A.B.D.E.F.G.H.
Multiple Sclerosis Society	1	A.E.F.G.
Muscular Dystrophy Group	1	A.G.
National Spastics Society	2	A.H.J.E.

Key to type of assistance provided:

A. Financial help/coal, clothing, etc.
B. Medical equipment/supplies.
C. Nursing instruction/first aid.
D. Meals on Wheels/domestic help.
E. Car transport.
F. Sick visiting.
G. General visiting/vigilance.
H. Recreational.
J. Personal advice.

provide blind people with equipment for easier living and with a wider choice of reading and other leisure activities.[1]

Commenting on their work, one divisional secretary suggested that the work of volunteers had declined with the increase in the number of workers employed by statutory services. Two others, however, thought that although the expansion of statutory services had led to better facilities for the blind, the need for voluntary workers had increased. An increasing proportion of the blind only became blind or partially sighted in old age, and voluntary workers could do much to alleviate the loneliness which blindness could bring in its train.

[1] The secretary to the Bucks Association for the Blind was a member of the staff of the county health and welfare department.

Two divisional secretaries did not feel that they lacked suitable volunteers, but one in the south of the county considered that it was more difficult to obtain voluntary workers from among manual workers and their wives and that recent immigrants to the county had less feeling than longer established residents of social obligation to the county. One secretary felt that once individuals had committed themselves to voluntary service there was little likelihood of their giving it up. The problem was to find recruits. Two secretaries felt their work was limited by lack of funds. Some regular sources of income, for example, the Sunday Cinema Fund, had diminished, while the numbers of registered blind and partially sighted had increased.

The Bucks Centre Committee of the Oxford Diocesan Council for the Deaf supervised the work of the deaf missioner,[1] and organised two societies called 'The Friends of the Deaf Association', one in Aylesbury and one in Slough. Although membership was open to anyone, most of the active members were parents or relatives of deaf people.

The Friends gave practical help to deaf people, including much financial and practical help to the three clubs for the deaf in Aylesbury, High Wycombe and Slough which were run entirely by deaf persons. The secretaries were not worried about the number of voluntary workers coming forward to help. However, they stressed that they could always do with more funds and capital to improve the clubs and other recreational facilities for the deaf. The Friends did not visit deaf people or give advice on problems arising from deafness.

Societies helping the blind and deaf in Bucks had a comparatively long history. Voluntary societies for other severely handicapped people in Bucks had all been formed since 1948, the initiative having been taken by the severely handicapped themselves or their relatives.

These societies were usually formed because those concerned felt strongly that too little was being done for people with the specific disability. By forming a society they hoped first to raise funds for research by arousing public interest in the problems of the handicapped; secondly, to stress the needs of the handicapped to the welfare authority and in this way improve the services they

[1] The work of the missioner to the deaf is considered in Chapter XVIII.

received; thirdly, to help those who could not afford special equipment or holidays, and for whom the welfare authority could not make adequate provision; fourthly, to provide training and educational and social facilities for their members, and lastly, to improve and maintain the morale of handicapped people and their relatives by widening their social horizons, giving opportunities for discussing mutual problems and encouraging self help.

The British Council for the Welfare of Spastics ran a home for young adult spastics at Ponds in Seer Green near Beaconsfield. Eight groups, known as Friends of Ponds, had been formed throughout the county to support the Home and improve its amenities. Group members in Seer Green itself and elsewhere entertained some of the young people from Ponds in their own homes or visited them at Ponds. Voluntary members did not give advice or guidance to the spastics or their relatives.

Voluntary helpers of the Slough and District Spastics Welfare Society, affiliated to the National Spastics Society, devoted much time to fund raising intended to provide and improve day and residential centres for spastic children and adults. During 1961, however, direct financial assistance was given to 12 families, usually to enable parents to give the spastic member of the family a holiday or to take one themselves. The Society's voluntary helpers sometimes gave advice on the treatment of the condition, on employment and on matters of mental health. The secretary felt that parents of spastics were 'more readily inclined to come forward to the group or the National Spastics Society for advice', and that co-operation between the county and local voluntary organisations was improving. He thought there was a shortage of people prepared to give voluntary service to the society.

The one branch of the Muscular Dystrophy Group in Bucks confined its activities almost entirely to fund raising for medical research, but helped parents of children with muscular dystrophy who lived in the area, the emphasis being on mutual support rather than financial assistance.

The Multiple Sclerosis Society branch in Slough had only been in existence for two years. Its members were nearly all sufferers from multiple sclerosis or their relatives. They did not seek to do the work of the county almoner; but felt that sufferers from multiple sclerosis would benefit from the additional and special interest which the society showed in their welfare. The committee's main tasks were fund raising and visiting, and the secretary felt more people were needed to share the work. Longer stablished voluntary organisations recruited most of those prepared to do voluntary work in the community, but she was hopeful that the Multiple Sclerosis Society's recruiting problems would be eased as its activities became better known.

The Infantile Paralysis Fellowship had one branch in Bucks, in the High Wycombe area. As its name implies, it was intended to bring together the victims of poliomyelitis. The dramatic decline in the incidence of this disease from the middle of the 1950's had mercifully reduced the number of people with residual paralysis, and, shortly before our survey took place, the Fellowship had decided to open its doors to all those who had been permanently handicapped by illness or injury.[1]

The Fellowship undertook a wide range of services for the severely disabled. About 70 people were taken out regularly in cars and approximately the same number driven regularly to social clubs. Financial help and help in kind was given, and six members helped with nursing or domestic chores to relieve relatives from time to time. The secretary and another member with legal qualifications frequently gave advice to members on matters arising from their handicaps, and in particular on employment or the management of the handicap itself.[2]

The Fellowship worked closely with the county medical social worker, who was described as 'the mainstay of these disabled people'; but believed that 'there is still a very great need for the voluntary worker'. It was not too difficult to find people willing to help, but a sacrifice was demanded. People had to be 'prepared to give up a great deal of time to visiting, writing and phoning'.

3. *The work of welfare organisations for service and ex-service personnel and their families*

Six voluntary organisations concerned with the health or welfare

[1] Since the survey the Fellowship has changed its name to the British Polio Fellowship.

[2] The problem which seemed most urgent to the Fellowship was that of residential care of young severely disabled people. The shortage of suitable institutions meant that many young people had to go to homes for elderly people which were not at all suitable for them.

K*

of service or ex-servicemen and their dependents had one or more branches in Bucks and provided some information about the scope of their activities. (See Table 29.)

Table 29

SOCIETIES FOR THE WELFARE OF SERVICE OR EX-SERVICE PERSONNEL
AND THEIR FAMILIES AND THE SCOPE OF THEIR ACTIVITIES

Name of organisation	Number of local branches	Type of service provided by voluntary workers (see Key)
British Legion (+ Women's Sections)	88	A.E.F.G.H.
British Limbless Ex-Service Men's Association	3	A.E.F.G.H.J.
Buckinghamshire War Pensions Committee	1	F.G.
Forces Help Society & Lord Roberts' Workshops	14	A.G.
Joint Committee of St. John & British Red Cross Society—War disabled department	1	A.F.
Soldiers', Sailors' & Airmen's Families Association	12	A.G.

Key to type of assistance provided:
A. Financial help/coal, clothing, etc.
B. Medical equipment/supplies.
C. Nursing instruction/first aid.
D. Meals on Wheels/domestic help.
E. Car transport.
F. Sick visiting.
G. General visiting/vigilance.
H. Recreational.
J. Personal advice.

The Buckinghamshire War Pensions Committee existed to advise the Ministry of Pensions and National Insurance on the welfare of war pensioners. The chairman was appointed by the Minister and the committee members were chosen either as representatives of local voluntary organisations or for the personal contribution they could make to the work. They undertook to visit severely disabled war pensioners and elderly war widows and appointed other voluntary workers to do the same. In 1961, there were 43 volunteers visiting about 225 pensioners or their widows.

In most instances, the voluntary workers' visits were undertaken merely to keep in touch with the housebound and see that all was well; but, in ten cases, severely disabled housebound individuals were regularly taken out by car. In six instances, voluntary workers considered that a housing problem needed consideration and referred the cases to the Reading office, and four cases of marital difficulties and 12 problems arising from the pensioners' physical disabilities were referred in the same way. The War Pensions Committee itself had no funds but voluntary workers took up 50 cases of particular financial hardship during the year.

The committee did not feel that it had been difficult to recruit sufficient voluntary workers. Since its members included representatives of voluntary societies, it worked closely with other local organisations, and its members were often active in such organisations as the British Red Cross Society, the W.V.S. and the Women's Section of the British Legion. The relationship of the voluntary workers to the staff of local authority social services or to the hospitals was indirect and more remote, since they did not refer cases of hardship or difficulty to them but to the Ministry of Pensions War Pensioners' Welfare Service in Reading.

The Bucks Association of the Forces Help Society had 14 divisions in the county, each of which appointed local 'friends' who did not visit regularly but reported cases of financial need among the families of servicemen in this area. Heads of divisions were authorised to make payments of up to £5 to individual families without reference to the Bucks secretary.

The society had no paid social worker in the county; but the social worker who worked part-time for S.S.A.F.A. was available to assist in special cases if required, for which she received from the society a small honorarium and part of her out-of-pocket expenses.

There was no clear demarcation between the cases helped by the Forces Help Society and those helped by other organisations for service or ex-servicemen. The society usually gave help in emergencies only, or when there was illness in a family. The number of applicants received by the society had steadily declined due not only to decreasing need but to the growth of alternative forms of help. Twenty-five families were given money during 1961, an average of £5 each, and some others received gifts of clothing. Many of the applicants were described as of limited intelligence and incapable of helping themselves, though a few were old soldiers whose age and pride prevented their asking for assistance from statutory or other civilian bodies. No referrals were made to any statutory social services during 1961, but some were referred to the appropriate regimental association and a few were personally advised by the secretary on employment problems and legal rights.

The society's 'friends' were recruited only by personal recommendations and the Bucks association had always had some difficulty in finding suitable people. It was not unduly worried about recruiting difficulties, however, since the needs which it had been formed to meet had begun to taper off.

S.S.A.F.A. had a rather more extensive organisation in Bucks than the Forces Help Society. There were 12 divisional secretaries and 60 village representatives, all volunteers. The one paid worker worked part-time for the association in the south of the county. Most of the village representatives were women, many of them over sixty. It was not easy to find suitable younger women.

During 1960, S.S.A.F.A. had helped about 130 people in Bucks, the majority of whom lived in the Slough area. It made gifts both from its own funds and also from money raised from other organisations, particularly from regimental associations. In addition, it ensured that families were receiving any help to which they were entitled from the National Assistance Board or other statutory service. It also made enquiries on behalf of units of the armed forces when serving men asked for compassionate leave. For example, its representative would check that a soldier's request for compassionate leave on the grounds that his father had died and his widowed mother needed help was genuine.

S.S.A.F.A. representatives did not often deal with enquiries about housing or employment, though they were sometimes asked to provide legal advice and representation in a court of law. When representatives came across difficult situations, such as problems of serious marital discord, they referred them to the secretary of the Bucks association, who in turn would ask for the help of a trained social worker from the national headquarters of the association.

The British Legion had 88 branches in Bucks during 1961 with rather more than 11,000 members. Their activities were co-ordinated by a Bucks county committee. There were also 67 women's sections. Although there were fewer women members, they were more active in the field of voluntary service than men. Voluntary service was organised locally by an elected service committee, and all ex-servicemen were eligible for assistance whether or not they were members of the British Legion.[1]

Much of the help given was on an informal and unrecorded basis. Financial assistance was frequently given to elderly ex-servicemen, to the sick and to widows. Loans were also made to help ex-servicemen establish themselves in business. Where necessary, too, service committees approached other voluntary organisations for funds, and ascertained whether further assistance could be obtained from the N.A.B. Sometimes the service committees found that N.A.B. rules frustrated the Legion's efforts to provide financial help.[2]

The secretary of the Bucks County Committee emphasised that the Legion's welfare work was more and more concentrated upon the elderly and ageing. The great need was for volunteers to lighten the lives of the elderly by offering friendship and evidence of concern. The secretary believed it was becoming more difficult to find 'willing horses' to provide this kind of service.

After the second world war, the Order of St. John and the British Red Cross Society established a Joint Committee to co-ordinate their work for the war disabled. The secretary of the Joint Committee of the Bucks branch was a paid worker;[3] but during 1960–61, about 200 war disabled pensioners were visited at least once, the work being shared by about 40 volunteers. When those visited were found to need a particular service or a holiday or convalescent care, the secretary referred the case to an almoner or to a statutory or voluntary organisation which could help. The Joint Committee made gifts, averaging £7 or £8 each, to about 80 individuals during the year, in many instances to cover hire purchase commitments. Cases of financial need, how-

---

[1] Ex-officers in need and their widows and dependents were dealt with, however, by the associated Officers' Association.

[2] In one case the Legion decided to make a weekly allowance of 10/- to an ex-serviceman of the first world war. As a result, the N.A.B. reduced its weekly allowance by 7/6 a week, leaving the man better off by only 2/6 a week.

[3] See Chapter XVIII for an account of her work.

ever, were usually referred both to the Ministry of Pensions and to other ex-servicemen's organisations. Voluntary workers did not themselves give help or advice; but if it was needed they referred the case to the branch secretary.

The secretary of the Joint Committee thought that the development of statutory social services had 'taken away the need for voluntary help to a great extent', and instanced the expansion of occupational therapy facilities in hospitals and local authority welfare departments. Calls for financial help had also declined with the reduction in the number of survivors among the war disabled. For this reason, the committee did not view with undue alarm the problem of finding voluntary workers to undertake the work.

There were three branches of the British Limbless Ex-Service Men's Association covering different parts of Bucks in 1960–61. The help given by voluntary members of the association was mainly restricted to visiting. The secretary of one branch reiterated the point made by others dealing with ex-servicemen and their dependents, namely, that the problems were increasingly those of the elderly disabled.

4. Societies with specific objects
Voluntary work with prisoners and their families

There were several voluntary societies concerned with the welfare of prisoners or their families. None was organised on an exclusively Bucks basis, however, and consequently did not deal only with prisoners who came from the county. The Berks, Bucks and Oxon Discharged Prisoners Aid Society had headquarters in Oxford, and in 1961 gave money to 29 discharged prisoners from Bucks. The sums given were small, averaging less than £1 per man. Some assistance with clothing was also given to 14 men. Voluntary workers did not participate directly in visiting or other services for this Society.[1]

The National Police Court Mission was an Anglican organisation centred on London. It had a Good Samaritan Fund from which grants could be made by probation officers. The Mission also ran a number of approved probation hostels, and two boys

---

[1] A description of the work of the paid worker employed by the Society is included in Chapter XVIII.

from Bucks had been placed in them during the year. The general secretary did not feel there was difficulty in recruiting lay members to service on the diocesan committees which organised the mission's activities on a regional basis. Fund raising was difficult due to 'the popular idea that in the welfare state all human needs are taken care of by statutory officers and statutory funds'.

The National Association of Prison Visitors was a voluntary organisation which, with the approval of the Prison Commissioners appointed visitors to H.M. prisons. There were four men who held appointments to the two prisons in Bucks at Aylesbury and Grendon Hall (Spring Hall). Comparatively few of the prisoners were from Bucks since the prisons were not primarily local ones.

The Family Planning Association

There were two branches of the Family Planning Association in Bucks during the year 1960–61. One, in the Slough area, had been in existence for more than ten years and served people from neighbouring Berks as well as those in south Bucks. The other, the Amersham, Chesham and District branch, had been started only in 1959. There was no branch in Aylesbury, High Wycombe or the towns in the north of the county.

The main task undertaken by the branches was the organisation of a family planning clinic, from which married people could obtain advice on methods of contraception and purchase suitable contraceptive devices. An additional function of the clinics was to give advice in cases of sterility or sub-fertility. These functions were carried out on a sessional basis by medical officers assisted by trained nurses. Voluntary members of the F.P.A. carried out the administrative tasks. Volunteer workers also dispensed contraceptives and sterilised instruments used during the examination of clients. Outside clinic sessions, volunteers arranged meetings to publicise the work of the clinics and obtained financial support for the association's educational and charitable aims.

An organisation providing advice on family limitation, sterility and sub-fertility is likely to receive requests for help on many aspects of marital adjustment. The voluntary members of the association did not deal, however, with these requests or act in any way as social workers. They only drew the attention of the doctors to the problem.

During 1960, rather more than 1,500 people visited the Slough clinic. The Amersham/Chesham Clinic had about 550 clients in 1960–61. During the year a special note was made of the source from which new patients came. Table 30, presenting the results of this special recording, indicates that the overwhelming majority of clinic users learned about its services either from personal acquaintances who had used it or through the statutory health services.

Table 30

SERVICES OR PERSONS REFERRING NEW PATIENTS TO THE AMERSHAM BRANCH FAMILY PLANNING CLINIC IN 1960-61

Sources of referral	Number	Per cent
Friend or previous clinic user	80	31
Family doctor	76	29
Hospital (doctor, nurse, almoner)	44	17
Local authority health worker (health visitor, district nurse)	23	9
Family Planning Association Head-quarters	20	8
Press Advertisement	14	5
Marriage Guidance Council	2	1
Total	259	100

The Amersham/Chesham and district branch also made an analysis of some of the personal and family circumstances of 368 of the clients who visited the clinic for advice or fitting between October, 1960 and September, 1961. (See Table 31.) It shows that the clinic was used most by women of 26 to 35 and by roughly even proportions of women with no children, one child, two children, and three or more children. It helped only a few with small incomes;[1] two out of three had family incomes averaging over £20 a week, suggesting that, on the whole, it met a demand from the more well-to-do.

6. *The work of marriage guidance counsellors*

There were two marriage guidance district councils in Bucks,

[1] The average weekly earnings of male manual workers in a selected group of industries was assessed at £15 3s. 0d. or £788 p.a. in April 1961, the mid-point of the study year. Source: *Ministry of Labour Gazette*, August 1961.

Table 31

AGE, NUMBER OF CHILDREN AND FAMILY INCOME OF THOSE USING
THE AMERSHAM/CHESHAM FAMILY PLANNING ASSOCIATION CLINIC
DURING 1960-61

Clients' Age	Num-ber	Per cent	Clients' living children	Num-ber	Per cent	Clients' family income	Num-ber	Per cent
Under 21	30	8	None	85	23	Under £500	5	1
21–25	123	33	One	89	24	£500–£749	46	12
26–35	173	47	Two	95	26	£750–£999	66	18
36 or more	42	11	Three	48	13	£1000 or more	251	68
			Four	11	3			
			Five or more	6	1			
			Un-recorded	34	9			
Total	368	99	Total	368	99	Total	368	99

one centred on Slough and the other on Aylesbury.[1] The Slough
council had seven counsellors recognised by the National
Marriage Guidance Council and the Aylesbury council two.
Most other parts of the county were without counsellors; but
some cases were referred to the district councils based on towns
in neighbouring counties.[2]

All the marriage guidance counsellors gave their services
voluntarily. In order to become counsellors, however, they had
to be approved by a selection committee and receive specialised
instruction from staff at the national or regional headquarters
of the Council. Nine of the 11 counsellors provided information
about themselves and 89 of their Bucks clients.[3]

[1] During the study year, the Northampton Diocese of the Roman Catholic
church was establishing a council to advise Roman Catholic couples and had
begun to train counsellors. Their work had not started, however, by October
1961.

[2] Two counsellors from one of these neighbouring district councils were
known to have a few Bucks cases during the study year.

[3] Names and addresses and any information which might identify a client
were withheld.

Three-quarters of the marriage guidance counsellors' 89 clients were wives and a quarter husbands. Four out of five were between 20 and 44, approximately one in eight was over 45 but not yet 60, and two were not yet 20.

Fifteen of the couples were childless. Large families were unusual: only four couples had four or more children. Three-quarters of the counsellors' clients were living with their spouses when they were seen by the counsellors. Nine were living alone, with unrelated adults or with their own parents, and nine were lone parents living with dependent children. Most of the counsellors' clients were skilled manual workers or their wives, but they had rather more middle class clients than most social welfare staff.[1]

Four-fifths of the clients were being seen for the first time. Only three had been known to the counsellors for more than a year. The fifth who were not being seen for the first time, had been seen comparatively frequently in the previous year.

Half the clients took the initiative themselves in seeking help from the marriage guidance counsellors. The others were referred from a wide variety of different sources. Friends or neighbours of the clients referred eight and the same number came through voluntary bodies. Probation officers referred six and general practitioners five. Others referring one or two each included health visitors, welfare officers, police, and child care officers.

In 75 per cent of the cases, the counsellors believed that the marital difficulty was not the only one. One or two other difficulties were usually listed, and 15 households were considered to present four or more distinct problems. Apart from marital difficulties, the problems most frequently noted were sexual relations outside marriage, sexual perversion and problems of inadequate or aggressive personalities. Poor parent-child relationships in ten families were less often an additional problem than might have been expected. Child neglect, arising frequently as a result of marital estrangement, was mentioned in seven cases. Housing difficulties and mismanagement of means were both listed in eleven households.

---

[1] Twenty-five per cent were classified as Social Class I or II compared with an overall average for all service personnel of 16 per cent. Conversely there were fewer Social Class IV or V households (24 per cent against 38 per cent).

In most instances the counsellors described their work as an attempt to help individuals with their personal relationships. In only a few instances did they give advice on other matters or refer clients to another service for help.

The marriage guidance counsellors

Five of the marriage guidance counsellors were women and four men.[1] Six were between 35 and 44, one between 45 and 54, and two between 55 and 64. One of the women was widowed; but the rest were married, two being man and wife. At the time of the survey, all had dependent children, with the exception of the married couple whose children were older and had left home.

All the counsellors had middle class backgrounds themselves and all of them had been residents for many years in the towns or villages where they were living in 1960-61. Two of the men were company directors, a third a master tradesman and the fourth a headmaster. The women were all housewives without paid work at the time of the enquiry. Two were married to ministers, and the other three had middle class husbands.

Two of the counsellors had not done any voluntary social work before becoming marriage guidance counsellors. The others had been involved in voluntary service of various kinds including F.P.A. work, prison visiting, youth work, and visiting for the Mothers' Union. The ministers' wives had been active participants in various parish activities.

Counsellors were not asked what had prompted them to take up marriage guidance work; but several spoke spontaneously of the circumstances in which they had begun. One had seen the marriage of personal friends break up and felt that it and many others might be saved if the partners had more insight and more understanding of the adjustments needed on both sides. Another had been impressed by the advice given to her by a gynaecologist, who was also a marriage guidance counsellor, and decided to try to help other people in the same way. Another who recognised that her own marriage had not been fully satisfactory wanted to help others with theirs.

None of the counsellors had been doing marriage guidance for more than five years. Their length of service as counsellors

[1] One of those not seen was a man and the other a woman.

reflected the comparative youthfulness of the service in the county and, indeed, in the country as a whole.

None of the counsellors had had a training in social work. One had a university arts degree. Two had teachers' diplomas and another was a state registered nurse and trained midwife. One was a trained secretary and one had taken a course in industrial design. The other three had had no further formal education or training after leaving school.

The short course in marriage guidance taken by those selected as counsellors consisted of four concentrated two-day study periods spread over a number of week-ends. After completing the course, counsellors were encouraged and expected to attend one or two day refresher courses also held at week-ends. Case discussion meetings were also held regularly by the district councils, and some of these were attended by a psychiatrist.

The counsellors all praised the courses arranged for recruits and the case discussions which provided the basis for continued study. Three said the introductory course was particularly helpful in teaching them how to listen, which they considered to be their most essential function. They were not asked specifically about the length of the course and only one suggested spontaneously that it should have been longer.

Five felt that the subject matter covered in the course was just right. Four made suggestions which they thought would improve it. Two considered that more was needed on legal aspects of marriage and the family, two that more emphasis should have been given to psychiatric problems and one that the psychological teaching was too abstruse. Two suggested that in a short course less time should be given to factual description of the social services, much of which was available in written guides and the time saved used to discuss issues which were not so thoroughly documented.

In discussing the satisfaction derived from their work, the majority of counsellors tended to emphasise the gain in their own insight resulting from the training and the work, and like the staff of most social welfare services they talked about the pleasure of helping people.[1] On the other hand, there were frustrations. Some

---

[1] 'To see the strain and pain slide off a person's face. It sounds awfully pi but you know what I mean', said one. 'I've always found that people like to

felt sad when little could be done to save a marriage—'just bolting the stable door after the horse'—or when clients' expectations were unrealistic. 'Expecting a magic wand waved', as one counsellor put it. Feelings of inadequacy were frankly acknowledged. Two felt depressed when confronted with the selfishness and bitterness which underlay some intimate human relationships. Two talked of the apprehension they still felt about their ability to help. One said that she still longed to tell people categorically that they were doing wrong, but knew that this was useless and that she must resist the temptation. Others, and the men who had full-time paid work and whose counselling had to be done in limited free time, complained about the difficulty of devoting sufficient time to the work. Others suggested that in the future much greater emphasis should be given to and time expended on pre- and early marriage counselling as a means of improving adjustment in marriage and of preventing breakdown.

Summary of main conclusions

The problems arising in the wide range of social welfare activities in which voluntary workers participated are many and varied and cannot be summed up adequately in a few paragraphs. Nevertheless, the survey, however superficial, leaves a number of strong impressions.

First, most voluntary workers in 1960–61 were helping people who were also the main concern of the statutory services, that is, the elderly and the chronically sick or disabled, many of whom had slender means.

Second, the dividing line between the work of paid and voluntary workers was by no means clear cut. It is widely believed that workers from statutory services are primarily providing essential *material* supports, such as financial assistance, housing, nursing care, medical advice and domestic help. Voluntary workers, on the other hand, are pictured as providing the human contacts, the day's outings, the flowers, the Christmas gifts, in short, the 'frills'. In practice, however, the lines were blurred. Much of the effort of voluntary workers went into improving the material living

confide in me. I like being able to use this quality to help people bring into the open something that's been making them feel unhappy', said another.

standards of the elderly and the chronically disabled.[1] This was particularly true of organisations for the welfare of servicemen or ex-servicemen and their families; but it also applied to other societies. Moreover, for certain important material facilities, staff from statutory services had to refer patients or clients to voluntary societies. For example, those requiring medical and nursing equipment in the home had to be referred to the British Red Cross Society. Those needing clothes or household equipment would usually be referred to a voluntary society and not to the N.A.B., and those needing extra nourishment to the W.V.S. for Meals on Wheels.

Nor were paid staff always pre-occupied with meeting material requirements while voluntary workers provided intangible services such as friendship. Paid staff regarded it as their function to provide non-specific, general friendly support as well as specific professional services. Most voluntary workers, on the other hand, gave specific help when they visited elderly or disabled people, as well as evidence of friendly interest. They read to the blind, took the handicapped out in cars, served meals on wheels or teas in old people's clubs, did the shopping or small domestic chores and dug the gardens.

The main difference between the social welfare work of paid and voluntary workers seemed to us to lie not in the character or immediacy of the needs they met, but in the extent to which they took the initiative in diagnosing the extent and character of the needs to be met and the responsibility they assumed for instituting or changing a service. In only a few instances did voluntary workers give advice to people on their personal problems. Most secretaries of voluntary societies went out of their way to point out that voluntary workers were asked to report apparent difficulties to the paid staff of the organisation and not to initiate action or give advice themselves. Paid workers employed by either statutory or voluntary bodies, on the other hand, were usually entrusted with responsibility for diagnosing the character of the need and for suggesting the service which should be provided.

A third conclusion was that there was at local level a proliferation of societies with similar or almost similar objectives. Some had been established to serve specific categories of people, for

---

[1] Paradoxically, some voluntary effort of this kind was frustrated by the reduction in help from the N.A.B. which sometimes followed.

example, ex-servicemen or their widows; others served those with specific disabilities; some served all those who held a particular religious faith when they were ill; others helped hospital patients or sick people irrespective of their age, diagnosis, occupation or religious affiliations. Consequently, those eligible for help from one society on account of their past occupation were often eligible for help from another society on account of their age and so on. This inevitably meant that a good deal of the time and energy of voluntary workers was used up in administering the separate organisations and co-ordinating their activities with others in order to avoid confusion or overlap. Since the supply of voluntary workers was limited, there was less time to devote to serving individuals in need than there would have been had there been fewer societies to run, fewer committee meetings to hold and less need to establish co-ordinating committees.

The proliferation of societies aggravated other difficulties. Although some secretaries claimed they had no difficulty in finding suitable voluntary helpers, most suggested that volunteers were not forthcoming in sufficient numbers and that there was a particular shortage of people prepared to undertake administrative duties or act as leaders. Active members were frequently elderly retired people who had devoted many years of their life to voluntary services, and who, when they dropped out, were not being replaced. Younger middle class women who used to form the mainstay of the voluntary movement were either absorbed by family commitments or in paid work outside their homes.[1]

A reduction in the number of voluntary societies at local level, other things being equal, could be expected to reduce the need for leaders and administrators and limit unproductive competition between societies for active recruits. It could also simplify liaison between staff of the statutory bodies and voluntary workers. Moreover, since there was evidence that many individuals were active members of more than one society, it would help reduce the burden of organisational work imposed on those described by secretaries as 'the few willing horses'.

[1] Changes in the marital status of adult women, in family size, in opportunities for employment and in the supply of domestic servants have all played a part in changing the contribution which women make to both voluntary and statutory organisations.

There is a possibility, however, that a reduction in the number of organisations would affect adversely the supply of voluntary workers. Part of the attraction of voluntary work may be that it provides opportunities to undertake *organisational* work outside the home. If opportunities were more restricted there might be fewer volunteers for social welfare activities. Again, there are grounds for thinking that many people like to belong to small groups and may not be so willing to serve if organisations were larger. Yet again, no one is equally concerned for *all* those who need the services of voluntary workers. Experience and predilection lead to orders of priority. The society which helps one category of person, for example, sufferers from multiple sclerosis, or ex-servicemen, may succeed in arousing the compassion of some who would not be moved to help others whose needs were roughly similar but who were not victims of this particular disease or had not served in the armed forces.

Categorical answers cannot be given to such problems; but it appeared that the moves towards co-ordination of voluntary special services in the Slough area and on a more limited basis elsewhere had not restricted the overall voluntary effort. Indeed, observers from both statutory and voluntary bodies felt that it had led to a more effective contribution from volunteers. There were still complaints in Slough, however, of competition between societies for active voluntary workers, and it is probable that such competition can only be avoided altogether if separate organisations agree to form a single unit at local level. Such a move seemed worth exploring particularly for voluntary societies concerned with the welfare of ex-servicemen and their dependents. It also seemed desirable that the respective activities of the Women's Voluntary Services and British Red Cross Society in the county might well be reconsidered. The responsibility of each of these organisations for *some* services was clearly differentiated; but in some spheres, and particularly in services to the elderly, there seemed considerable duplication of effort.

The work of the voluntary workers of the Family Planning Association and the Marriage Guidance Council was altogether different from that of other volunteers. The Family Planning Association workers were helping to facilitate a community service which was mainly used by people who were not psychologically, physically or socially handicapped. If, in providing this service, voluntary workers became aware of clients with serious difficulties, they simply drew them to the attention of their professional staff. This was as it should be, and it did not seem necessary or desirable to staff family planning clinics with trained social workers.

An important question about the family planning service, however, was whether it was right to depend upon volunteers to take the initiative in establishing clinics and to administer them. The considerable numbers using the Amersham clinic from its inception suggested that there was a large latent demand for advice on contraception. This is consequently a service for which the local health services should accept responsibility, and they should not wait upon the initiative and voluntary efforts of public-spirited local women. There is no doubt that, if clinics were established in High Wycombe, Aylesbury and Bletchley, they would be fully used. Moreover, wives of manual workers might be more prepared to use the clinics than they do at present if these were staffed by employees of the local health authority and not by volunteers. In the prevailing climate of opinion, latent demand from working class wives is not likely to find open expression, so that the initiative should come from the local health authority.[1]

Unlike voluntary workers of the Family Planning Association, marriage guidance counsellors were providing a service primarily for people with serious social difficulties. Little of their time was devoted to pre-marital counselling. Most of it was spent in attempting to save marriages already in jeopardy. In Bucks, at least, they served men and women of all social classes, of all ages and of varying family responsibilities. They seldom dealt with people who had serious chronic illnesses or disabilities and whose marital difficulties for this reason might be known to personnel of various branches of the health service.

Marriage guidance counsellors were not, however, the only workers who were trying to prevent marriage breakdown. The survey indicated that many social welfare workers were aware of marriage difficulties and tried to help clients cope with them. This was particularly true of probation officers and child care officers, but it was also common for health visitors, welfare officers, school

---

[1] In my view, a family planning clinic should be a community rather than a hospital service.

attendance officers, psychiatric social workers and others to encounter people who were experiencing difficulties in their marriages.

If there were no marriage guidance counsellors, therefore, this would not mean no marriage guidance; but, in my view, there is room for an organisation whose workers are primarily concerned with marriage guidance. Many people needing this kind of help are not in touch with any other social welfare staff who might provide them with it. Many general practitioners who are asked for help by their patients have not the time nor the competence to give it. There is, without doubt, a need for those whose marriages are going through a period of crisis to have a detached person listen to their problems, help clarify the underlying issues and give evidence of sympathetic understanding.

Although many marriage difficulties are closely associated with mental or physical ill-health, many are not. It does not, therefore, seem necessary or, considering the shortage of medical personnel, desirable for a specialist marriage guidance service to be part of the health service. It would also be difficult to make such a service the responsibility of either the children's or the probation depart-ment, since attachment to either one would have the effect of limiting the potential clientele. In a reconstituted social service framework, such as that outlined in Chapter XX, marriage guidance could form part of a general family welfare service. Until that time, however, there is little to be gained by providing a statutory rather than a voluntary service.

Finally, marriage guidance counsellors should be trained social workers, or, in exceptional circumstances, professional people with at least a three month's course in counselling. In my view, they should be paid for their work, which could be done on a regular part-time or sessional basis. This would end their amateur status, which was certainly a factor in making many doctors and social workers reluctant to refer people to them.

Voluntary workers in other branches of the social services have largely ceased to give advice or prescribe treatment or action to those who use them. Marriage guidance is in this respect anachron-istic, and its potential value to the community ultimately depends upon it being provided by men and women who have recognised qualifications for the work and are paid to do it.

CHAPTER XX

Social Welfare Services today and tomorrow

Some General Conclusions and Recommendations.

Since the inception of this survey in 1960 there have been many signs that those responsible for social welfare services of all kinds throughout Britain have been considering the future of their work. Prompted by recruitment difficulties, by the demands of staff for training, recognised qualifications, higher pay and status, by an increase in some forms of social problems and by new ideas of how to tackle such problems, social workers, planners, politicians and educators have begun to ask how far social welfare services are achieving their purposes and whether radical changes are needed in them.[1]

The Bucks survey was carried out in a single administrative area of England and Wales. No other county quite resembles it in population, in the nature of its economic life, in its social problems and in the organisation of its social welfare services. Yet, to a greater or lesser extent, every area of Britain is wrestling with similar problems and is having to determine how best it can develop its services to meet changing needs. Bucks, in a sense, can be taken as a microcosm of the whole, and the analysis of the work of its social welfare services, therefore, has a relevance beyond the confines of the county itself.

In the chapters dealing with particular services attention has been drawn to features of their work which seemed to need reconsideration and possibly modification or more radical change. Some of the recommendations with which each chapter concludes could be undertaken piecemeal by individual services without

[1] See particularly: *The Ingleby Report: Three Critical Essays*, David Donnison, Peggy Jay, Mary Stewart. Fabian Research Series 231. December 1962.

Personal communication from David Jones of the National Institute for Social Work Training and his paper, '*Child Guidance and the Social Services: An outsider's view*' to the 21st Child Guidance Inter-Clinic conference, N.A.M.H London 1965 (to be published).

'The Family and the Social Services', Somerville Hastings and Peggy Jay, Fabian Tract 359. February 1965.

Professor R. M. Titmuss, 1965 Talk to the Royal Society of Health, reported in *Guardian*, 29.4.1965.

affecting materially their relationships with other social welfare organisations. But many of the problems were shared by most services and solutions to them cannot be found by unilateral action. They require common consideration and co-ordinated action.

Five major issues were, in my view, highlighted by the enquiry as needing such comprehensive consideration. The first four are the inter-related issues of staff recruitment, training, deployment and co-ordination, and the fifth, the place of the voluntary worker in social welfare. Before considering each, however, brief reference must be made to the other part of the equation, that is, to clients of the services and their social welfare needs.

Society is irrevocably committed to trying to prevent illness and mitigate the effects of physical or mental handicap among people of all ages and economic circumstances. It recognises that this can only be done by bringing a variety of medical and social skills to the aid of the afflicted and those who care for them. It is committed to the rehabilitation of offenders as well as to the protection of society from them, and it has also an interest in the quality and stability of family units because marital and parent-child relationships help to determine the actual dependence of children and adults on the state. These commitments and interests are so broad, and becoming broader, that no absolute limits can be set to the needs which welfare services *could* meet.

Certain assumptions have to be made, therefore, about the needs which social welfare services will be asked to identify and meet. Some of these can be predicted with some confidence. For example, given current mortality rates, it is clear that domiciliary health and welfare services and voluntary organisations will have to devote increasing resources to the care of the elderly and to those disabled by chronic illness in middle and old age.

The second major concern of the social welfare services will be with the health and social development of young children and adolescents and of their families. Genetic counselling, higher standards of ante-natal care and obstetrics may continue to reduce the comparative numbers of children born with severe physical or mental handicaps or acquiring them early in life. But the survival rates of the handicapped may continue to improve. Special educational and employment problems of the handicapped and difficulties which their relatives face in caring for them will still challenge the health, education and employment services and call for their close collaboration.

Nor, on present showing, is there likely to be any reduction in the number of children, young persons and parents needing either help and guidance in maintaining reasonably satisfactory inter-family relationships or supervision when they break the law. Among the current trends which prompt such a conclusion are the increasing number of illegitimate births, especially to young people, of early marriages and of early divorces, of children reared in fatherless families, and of juveniles convicted of various offences.

In 1960–61, nearly every service in Bucks[1] had vacancies for staff which had been unfilled for some months, and workers complained of their inability to give sufficient time to individual clients. Society, in short, was unable to mobilise resources to meet its recognised commitments. Since needs are limitless, the problems are those of determining priorities, and the factors which will restrict the growth of the social welfare services are those associated with staffing. How many workers of what calibre is it possible to recruit to the services, how should they be trained and deployed and how should their work be co-ordinated to ensure the best utilisation of resources? These are the questions to which I now return.

Recruitment

In 1960–61, approximately three-quarters of the social welfare staff, including district nurses and health visitors, were women, and 80 per cent of these women were single. Some of the unmarried women were in their twenties and early thirties, but the majority were older. In other words, about 60 per cent of the staff were single women likely to have an uninterrupted career in social welfare services.

In the next few decades, the number of women remaining single throughout their potential years of working life will diminish even more rapidly than it is doing at present. The ratio of married to single in every ten-year age group from 15 to 65 increased between 1951 and 1961, and high marriage rates since 1961 suggest

[1] The staff situation in Bucks was probably typical of the non-metropolitan south of England, but was likely to be better than that of counties further north.

that the trend continues. Moreover, marriage besides being more popular is occurring earlier for both sexes, and the time interval between women's marriages and the birth of their first children is not lengthening.

Since it is no longer possible to depend upon lifelong spinsters to staff the social welfare services, the recruitment of married women and of men will need to be seriously considered.

There is little doubt that much of the work of the social welfare services would appeal to mature women who have experienced the difficulties of child-rearing and learned the necessity of tolerance, sympathy and understanding. When their own family commitments become less binding, many seek work beyond their homes and could be attracted by social welfare work. Since other employers, and especially the schools, are also making efforts to tap this source of labour, social welfare services will have to offer working mothers hours and conditions which compare favourably with those offered by others. This should not be difficult.

Some social welfare work is emergency work and needs staff available at all times to tackle it. But most of the work is not of this kind and could be undertaken by women working on a regular sessional basis or during school hours only. The employment of part-time staff is becoming a common feature of both public and private enterprises: if the absorption of such labour is to be speeded up, full-time staff will have to show flexibility and tolerance. They will be helped to do this if they can be convinced that their own salaries and career prospects are not jeopardised by the employment of part-time workers.

While some social welfare services, particularly those associated with the treatment of offenders and the mentally ill or defective, have employed men, social work from its inception has been predominantly undertaken by women. Able men attracted to work which involves giving personal services to people in need have chosen professions such as medicine, the law, teaching and the Church, rather than the social work professions.

There is no intrinsic reason, however, why men should not make a substantial contribution to the social work field.[1] In the

---

[1] Just as there are few intrinsic reasons why women should not contribute to professions consisting mainly of men, for example, medicine, law and the Church.

care of the physically and mentally handicapped, and the counselling of young people whose behaviour gives cause for concern, men are needed as much as women. The only substantial reasons why they have not taken up the work are that it has not had sufficiently attractive financial rewards or ultimate opportunities for planning and administration. Once again, it is work that is likely to make the most appeal to men with some maturity and experience, who may have become dissatisfied with their careers chosen early in life. However, most men would hesitate to change their career in their thirties or forties when their commitments to their families are likely to be greatest, if by doing so they face substantial reductions in income.

Up to the present, the social welfare services have recruited a small number of university trained women, but have relied for most of their social welfare staff and particularly for the men on those with good secondary schooling but no further full-time education. Although strenuous efforts will be made to expand university education in the next decade in line with the recommendations of the Robbins Committee,[1] the supply of university students will fall far short of the demand, and it is unlikely that social welfare services will be able to employ a much larger proportionate share of the graduate population. The competing demands from industry and commerce and, within the social service sector, from educational institutions are likely to be even more compelling. The social welfare services will have to reconcile themselves to recruiting most of their staff in the future as they have in the past from those with good secondary level schooling who are not selected for the restricted number of university places, but who will be able to profit from a broadly based professional training at a college of technology or further education. But even this will prove difficult unless the welfare services can offer career prospects and salary scales equivalent to those which men and women expect in branches of teaching or administration which also call for a good secondary schooling.

The problems of securing adequate numbers of suitable recruits to the social welfare services will not be easy to solve in the present state of the employment market and they will not be

[1] Report of the Committee on Higher Education 1963 (Cmnd. 2154) H.M.S.O.

solved if sectional rather than comprehensive solutions are sought. This is one area, therefore, in which collaboration at both central and local level is essential.

Training

The Bucks survey results suggested that training for work in the social welfare field should also be considered on a comprehensive scale.

In 1960–61, comparatively few of those working in social welfare had had a systematic full-time training for social work, although some during their training for occupations other than social work had had some incidental instruction in subjects such as psychology and social administration. Others had had only a few days' instruction on social factors affecting their work in pre-entry or in-service training courses. A few had had no formal instruction of any kind.

Some of those whose work forms an integral part of the social welfare services do not, in my view, need a full-time academic course in social work. For example, it would be a mistake to think of women police constables, disablement resettlement officers, N.A.B. officers, occupational therapists, youth employment officers, housing managers and district nurses as social workers in the sense of social counsellors. Their tasks are essentially technical, educative, protective or managerial. It is true that, like doctors, lawyers and others whose work involves giving people advice or assisting them, they would benefit from learning more about human relationships and the availability of services; but given the need to establish priorities and concentrate upon the essentials in training, most of their time must be spent acquiring the specialised knowledge needed to help their clients.

The essence of the work carried out by most social welfare staff, however, was social counselling. Some workers only helped those with an identifiable handicap or a particular social problem. Home teachers of the blind, welfare officers, psychiatric social workers and the deaf missioner, for example, all dealt with individuals with a particular physical handicap or with mental disorder; home help organisers were only concerned with those needing domestic help; and child care officers, probation officers, school attendance officers, moral welfare workers and housing welfare workers were usually alerted by a single manifestation of a social difficulty. Almoners and social workers attached to casework agencies were likely to give help and advice on many personal problems arising from illness or social incompetence and health visitors covered, if anything, a wider range of people, counselling them on aspects of domestic life which might threaten the mental or physical health of the children or the cohesion of the family unit, as well as advising on infant feeding and the management of minor ailments. However different the functions of these workers appeared to be, they all needed a common core of basic knowledge about the determinants of normal and abnormal human behaviour and relationships and about the social services.

In 1959, the Younghusband Working Party recommended that local health and welfare service staff should have a two-year general theoretical and practical training leading to a nationally recognised certificate in social work.[1] It considered that the amount of specialist knowledge required to work with specific disabilities was comparatively small and could be learned mainly on the job provided the course in social work had laid the general foundations of approach. It believed that a general training would have three incidental but substantial advantages. It would conserve and concentrate the limited facilities for training which could be made available both in institutes of further education and in the practical work setting. It would create a wider range of career patterns from which those who entered the field could choose, and it would improve working relations between social workers in different parts of the service.

I believe the findings of the Bucks survey support the Younghusband recommendations concerning training. Moreover, they indicate that grounds for advocating a common basic training in social work regardless of specialities extend beyond the local authority health and welfare staff. In my view, the social needs which the hospitals are trying to meet could largely be provided by a generally trained social worker. So too could much of the counselling work undertaken in the education, children's and

[1] Ministry of Health and Department of Health for Scotland. '*Report of the Working Party on Social Workers in the Local Authority Health and Welfare Services.*' H.M.S.O. 1959.

L

probation services and in various branches of the voluntary services.[1]

The information collected in the Bucks survey about actual counselling work undertaken was too superficial to permit detailed recommendations about training. The main body of knowledge which should form part of the common training for all social workers seems, however, reasonably clear.

First, the social worker must have some knowledge of human growth and development in both its physiological and psychological aspects throughout the chief phases of the life cycle from birth to old age and death. He must be aware of the basic human drives and of the significance of the social relationships into which individuals enter especially in their family unit. He must 'know sufficient about health and disease to recognise, and have some understanding of, variations within the normal as well as deviations, particularly as manifested in mental and physical handicaps, mental illness, "problem" family living and unmarried parenthood.'[2]

Secondly, all social workers should be knowledgeable about the social and economic circumstances in which people live. They must appreciate the influence of kin, neighbourhood, school, religion, the work unit and other formal and informal groups in the formation and maintenance of community and group norms and values, and in the attitudes displayed towards those who deviate from these norms.[3]

Thirdly, social work training must give students a knowledge of the scope and character of the statutory and voluntary social services. It should deal with forms of social care and the circumstances in which they need to be used. The social worker should be made

[1] The Council for Training in Social Work, established by legislation in 1963 on the recommendation of the Younghusband Working Party, has already begun to devise syllabuses for General Social Work training. There are now two-year courses in General Social Work in a variety of institutions for further education which are attracting suitable applicants who want to choose social work as a career as well as those who have been seconded by local authorities. Courses are also being arranged at such colleges in child care for non-graduates. These courses can share much of the basic theoretical teaching.

[2] Ibid: p. 253.

[3] Ideally, theoretical knowledge of this kind should have been reinforced by personal experience of work in a manual occupation and residence in a working class area particularly if the trainee comes from a middle class background.

aware of the problems of administering the social care services, of mobilising resources for them and of determining priorities. In addition, he must become conscious of the need for continuous critical scrutiny of the work of the services.[1]

While the majority of entrants to social welfare services in the future should have a general training in social work, provision will also be needed for more advanced training for filling administrative, supervisory and training posts, and for some specialist training for those electing to work in certain of the services. In my view, the universities should accept responsibility for advanced courses. The present courses in social studies should be modified to meet the needs of mature students with experience in the social services who need to extend their understanding of the underlying principles of social work, of administration and of planning and evaluation. They should also institute graduate studies leading to higher degrees in social work and cognate fields.

Although the *common* features of social work and the interchangeability of staff between different social welfare fields need emphasis at present, some aspects of social welfare work will require special training. For example, those working with the blind or the deaf will need additional skills and insights to help such people. Probation officers, too, will need more knowledge of criminal behaviour and the law than can be covered in a general social work course.

Some of the needs for special training can be met in the final stages of the two-year course, when students can be encouraged to concentrate on the social work field which most excites their interest. But provision should also be made for continued theoretical study as well as supervised probationary work for those entering most branches of the services from the general training courses. This task should be shared between the employing services and the training schools.

Basic training and advanced courses must be supplemented by systematic and sustained in-service training, which can be most effectively planned and organised on an inter-service basis. Every

[1] Scrutiny depends often on conscientious record-keeping. The Bucks survey showed that many workers disliked record-keeping, considered it a waste of time and did it poorly. The record-keeping demanded was not always essential; but some recording is inescapable and it is important that an understanding of its value should be part of the basic training of a social worker.

major local authority should appoint a social welfare training officer to organise continued professional social work education for all the departments employing such workers and to keep closely in touch with training establishments. There is no reason, moreover, why housing authorities in county areas, central government departments and voluntary organisations should not utilise such a service. Co-ordination of this kind would not merely have the advantage of economising efforts: it should also lead to greater inter-departmental co-operation.[1]

Deployment of social workers and co-ordination of social welfare services

The common consideration by social welfare services of the problems of recruitment and training would go a long way to improving relationships between workers in different sections of the services. In particular, it should go some way to dispel much of the insecurity and concern with status which was characteristic of the staff of a number of social welfare services in Bucks.

In some ways, however, it seemed difficulties encountered by staff in carrying out their functions and their consequent dissatisfactions were due to their misplacement in the framework of social service organisation. For example, hospital almoners were sometimes trying to take measures which they would have been better placed to do if they had been working in a domiciliary based service, and health visitors were working in contexts which made it difficult for them to build close relationships with their clients' general practitioners.

I believe also that the piecemeal development of social welfare services had led inevitably to some incongruities which can be eliminated. For example, some workers with no formal education after the age of 16 and little in-service training were accepting responsibility for the support of individuals and families with a formidable array of complicated psychological and social problems. By contrast, university trained social workers were, in some instances, working intensively with small numbers of people whose behaviour was much less disturbed.

---

[1] A social welfare training officer should preferably be directly responsible to the Clerk of the Council and not to one of the chief officers whose department employs social workers.

These and other anomalies seemed to arise from the division of tasks between different branches of the services, and it seemed increasingly clear to me that they could not be satisfactorily solved unless there was a fairly radical re-deployment of staff between services.

I have, therefore, concluded this report on the social services by making some general proposals for their future organisation. They are given in outline only because to do more would require another substantial treatise; but it is hoped that the arguments in support of them are implicit in the findings reported in earlier chapters.

The proposals are based on the assumption that the domiciliary health services will employ social welfare and nursing staff at least equivalent in numbers to the total of health visitors, home nurses and social workers proposed by the Bucks county health and welfare department for 1972.[1] Secondly, it has been assumed that there will be a proportionate increase in the number of social workers in other branches of social services, and that these workers will be available to staff the re-organised services, and thirdly that the ratio of general practitioners to the population of the county, which was approximately one to 2,200 in 1960–61, will be maintained.

These assumptions are conservative rather than radical. They suggest that a county of about half a million inhabitants will have about 670 workers in its social welfare services of whom approximately 250 will be medically qualified men and women in general practice and local government, 170 will be people with a basic training in nursing, (that is, district nurses and health visitors) and 250 will be those with either a general social worker's certificate or specific pre-entry training for their work. The present and suggested distributions of manpower between services are shown in the two tables which follow.

[1] In the ten-year plan which the Bucks county health and welfare department presented to the Ministry of Health in 1962 the authority aimed to increase its health visiting, district nursing and social worker staff both to meet an estimated increase in population and to increase the ratio of these workers per thousand of the population. Nevertheless, the Bucks plan provided for a smaller ratio of nurses, health visitors and social workers to population in 1972 than the average planned by all local authorities in England and Wales.

Cf. 'Health and Welfare. The Development of Community Care.' Cmnd. 1973. H.M.S.O. 1963.

In place of the present deployment of staff in statutory and voluntary services, I propose that three major services should employ most of the social workers needed. These services should be:

(1) A health and welfare service.

(2) A school and youth welfare advisory service.

(3) A family welfare service.

Table 32

THE APPROXIMATE NUMBER OF SOCIAL WELFARE STAFF (FULL-TIME EQUIVALENTS) IN BUCKS IN 1960–61†

Division of the social services	Number of staff	Number per 100,000 population	Division of the social services	Number of staff	Number per 100,000 population
Local authority health and welfare services			Employment services	12	2
District nursing-midwifery	120	24	Financial assistance	20	4
Health visiting	47	9	Housing welfare	8	2
Other health and welfare workers	38	8	Moral welfare	8	2
Hospital social workers	17	4	N.S.P.C.C.	3	1
General practitioners	225	46	Voluntary casework agencies	8	2
Education and youth service	30	6			
Child care service	16	3			
Probation service	15	3			

† Excluding home helps, staff of residential institutions, hospital workers (other than social welfare staff), midwives.

In addition, some trained social workers would be needed in an advisory capacity or to organise and conduct training in services dealing with employment, housing and financial assistance. They would also play an important part in the treatment of offenders in prison. Social workers are also needed in voluntary social welfare services to strengthen and lead the work of volunteers.

Table 33

SUGGESTED NUMBER AND DEPLOYMENT OF SOCIAL WELFARE STAFF FOR A RE-ORGANISED SOCIAL SERVICE SYSTEM IN BUCKS

Main social counsellor services			Other social services requiring social workers		
Division of the social services	Number of staff*	Number per 100,000 population	Division of the social services	Number of staff*	Number per 100,000 population
Health & Welfare Service Health units			Financial Assistance Assessment officers	44	9
General practitioners	230	46	Social workers	1	—
Health visitor/nurses	80	16			
Assistant nurses	80	16	Employment		
Social workers	40	8	Disablement resettlement officers	8	2
Local Authority Advisory & Ancillary			Housing		
Medically qualified	12	2	Special groups housing welfare	8	2
Others: nursing, health visitors and social workers	15	3	Treatment of Offenders Domiciliary based probation and aftercare officers	18	4
Hospital social workers	20	4			
School & Youth Welfare Advisory Services			Voluntary Organisations Family caseworkers, moral welfare and adoption staff, C.A.B., marriage guidance counsellors	20	4
Medically qualified	12	2			
Health visitors—school counsellors	30	6			
Youth counsellors	15	3			
Family Welfare Services Social workers ⎱ Health visitors ⎰	50	10			

*Full-time equivalent.

The health and welfare services

(*a*) *In the community*

In Bucks, the community health and welfare services were organised in a single department of the local authority, and in my view this is as it should be. The elderly infirm and the physically handicapped who are the main clients of the welfare services are frequently in need of medical advice and treatment, domestic help and nursing attendance, that is, of services which are at present the responsibility of the local authority health department. Socio-medical needs can best be met by considering that the domiciliary services especially for old people and for younger disabled men and women are indivisible.

The combination of domiciliary health and welfare functions in one local authority department in Bucks did not, however, automatically bring in its train a satisfactory deployment of staff. The role of the health visitor, in particular, seemed an anomalous and unsatisfactory one in 1960–61, and G.P.'s were often unaware of the range of social services which could assist their patients.

These unsatisfactory aspects of the health services could, I believe, be overcome if general practitioners worked together with health visitors and social workers in a *home based health unit.*

The smallest health unit should consist of three general practitioners, one health visitor, one state enrolled nurse, and a part-time social worker. Larger practices would be able to command more health visiting, nursing and social worker help. The unit collectively would be responsible for the prevention of illness among those registered with the G.P.'s, for the care of patients during illness, and for advice to the mentally and physically handicapped and their relatives, and it would mobilise community resources when these were needed.

Within each health unit, the G.P. would have clinical responsibility for his patients. The health visitor would still be mainly concerned with primary prevention; but she would give more advice than she was doing in 1960–61 on the treatment of illness and the management of chronic conditions and severe physical handicaps. When necessary she would also undertake those home nursing tasks which call for the skills and experience of a highly qualified nurse. In these ways she would be making more use of the knowledge she acquired at all stages of her training. The bulk of home nursing, however, does not require a high degree of nursing skill, and would be carried out by the state enrolled nurse working if necessary under the health visitor's direction.

The social worker would concern him or herself with individuals and families who needed long term intensive social support and particularly with the mentally disordered and the severely disabled. When needed he would mobilise support from other branches of the services and at all times would work closely with the health visitor.

The work of all the health units in a local authority area would be supplemented by services organised by the local authority itself. These would consist of ancillary socio-medical services on the one hand, and of advisory services and training facilities on the other.

The most important of the *ancillary* services would be child guidance, domestic help including meals on wheels, occupational therapy provided in day centres and on a domiciliary basis, home teaching for the blind and deaf and hostel and sheltered residential accommodation for the elderly, physically and mentally handicapped, mentally ill and homeless. These services would call both for staff with recognised qualifications in teaching, handicrafts, nursing, occupational therapy, physiotherapy and domestic work, and for a limited number of social workers to help in the administration and to determine priorities.

Where *advisory* services are concerned, the medical officer of health and his medically qualified staff would be available to advise health units on community health problems, on the control of infectious disease and on new methods of disease prevention by mass or selective screening techniques. They would also provide advice on methods of organising medical care, immunisation or screening procedures, would disseminate new information to health units and help to stimulate research in these units.

At local authority headquarters, there would also be small teams of senior health visitors, nurses and social workers who could be consulted on problems arising in the day-to-day work of the health units and, if called upon, help to handle difficult cases. These senior staff would also arrange for the continuous education of their own professional colleagues working in the health units. They could also contribute on a reciprocal basis to the in-service training of workers in other branches of the social welfare services. As far as possible the staff at local authority headquarters should be chosen from those with advanced training in health visiting, nursing or social work.[1]

(b) In the hospital

In Bucks in 1960–61, the hospitals employed the majority of medical social workers with university qualifications. The need for highly trained social workers in both general and psychiatric hospitals is, however, less urgent than the need for such workers in domiciliary services. The opportunities for intensive family casework and for long term support of the chronically ill were more limited in the hospital than in the domiciliary setting. Hospital staff were not well placed to get to know about the problems of the households to which the patients would return. They were less frequently faced than those working in the domiciliary field with the need to take independent decisions as to the best course for the patient,[2] since they worked closely with consultant psychiatrists and other specialists.

For these reasons, the social and medical rehabilitation of hospital patients, wherever possible, should be the responsibility of the home based health units. The health visitor and social worker attached to these units should be encouraged to continue to serve patients and their families during periods of hospital-isation.

---

[1] In my view, the domiciliary midwifery service should be organised by hospitals and not by local authorities. General practitioners who wished to deliver their own patients in hospital or home should for this purpose be considered clinical assistants to the consultant obstetrician. They could, if they and their patients wished, provide some or all the necessary ante-natal supervision. Such an arrangement would have considerable advantages over the present system where responsibility for the care of the mother during pregnancy and childbirth may be divided between two or more of the arms of the health service. It would also help to ensure that mothers were delivered in the place best suited to their needs.

[2] The findings of this survey tend to confirm the results of the study made by G. F. Rehin, H. Houghton and F. M. Martin of the work of personnel of the mental health services. See: Nuffield Provincial Hospital Trust, 1964. *Problems and Progress in Medical Care.*

Relieved of some responsibilities, hospital social service departments would have a more circumscribed role than they have at present and should consider employing those with a two-year general social work training. Their first responsibility would be to see that patients' problems are known to their domiciliary health units, and that the latter are provided with specialist advice about problems arising from the patients' illnesses. In hospital it would help medical and nursing staff alleviate patients' anxieties or morbid fears and support the dying and their relatives.

A school and youth welfare advisory service

In Bucks in 1960–61, the education department was responsible for the health and welfare of school children and for the youth services. As well as the school health service, for which the County Medical Officer of Health was responsible, the education department had a number of services for the welfare of school children and young persons, including child guidance clinics, special welfare arrangements for handicapped children, a school attendance service, a youth service for teenagers and a youth employment service for school leavers and young persons.

In my view, this organisation of services had a number of unsatisfactory features. Health visitors attended routine school medical examinations but felt that this work could be done by those with less training. School attendance officers who had no social work training felt that the value of their work with difficult parents and disturbed children was not recognised by their superiors and resented it when special welfare workers dealing with handicapped children and their parents were also asked to assess families thought to be in need of free meals or assistance with clothing.

If health units comprising G.P.'s, health visitors and social workers were established, the school health service could concentrate on the kind of functions which a well-ordered occupational health service performs for an industrial unit. That is to say, it could search for and eliminate or reduce the environmental health hazards which may exist in schools. Together with teachers it should consider the factors in the school environment which reduce children's capacity to learn or affect their physical and mental growth, and it should be concerned with health education in both its narrow and its widest sense.

In carrying out these duties, it would need to examine new school entrants and follow up children whose previous medical and family history suggests they may experience particular difficulties in learning. In considering both the general school environment and the health needs of particular children, the medical staff should work more closely than they have done in the past with teachers and with the school heads. They would also need to consult with the children's G.P.'s.

While health problems underlie many educational difficulties, particularly where children have been ascertained as needing special schooling, there is a need for a more general school welfare advisory service able to advise parents and adolescents about emotional problems encountered in the process of development from child to adulthood. Such a service might be staffed by social workers or health visitors who could be called school counsellors. They would also perform the functions which in 1960–61 were undertaken by school attendance officers and special welfare workers.

In primary schools, social counsellors would investigate absences from school and act as a link between the domiciliary health unit, the family and the school. They might well be health visitors with additional training in educational psychology or generally trained social workers with additional training in human physiology and disease processes. In the secondary schools, social counsellors should have had a general social work training. They would also investigate school absences and any disquieting changes in the pupil's educational progress or social behaviour. They should also help boys and girls make wise choices about further education, training or employment on leaving school, consulting youth employment officers in this work as well as the children's teachers.

Another section of the school and youth welfare advisory service would also be responsible for the provision of youth clubs and other leisure facilities for young people. Youth leaders should be trained for this work and the training should be such as to qualify them for a branch of social work at a later stage of their working lives when they no longer wished to work exclusively among young people.

Family welfare service

It is both inevitable and proper that health services and a school welfare service should be concerned with families. The community's interest in families, however, extends beyond its concern for health and education, because the extent to which the social services rather than private citizens cope with dependency in childhood and old age and social deviance at all ages depends largely on the quality of family life.

In Bucks in 1960–61, many services were dealing with problems in families where there were young children. The children's department concerned itself with children needing care, temporarily or permanently, from people other than their natural parents. The health and welfare department through health visiting and rent maintenance schemes provided support for families which might otherwise have broken up, and its mental welfare officers often shored up families whose stability was threatened by mental disorder. General practitioners gave advice on sexual relations in marriage and tried to help couples with family management problems. The education department's special welfare section arranged financial and social assistance for the families of handicapped children or for those with low incomes. Probation officers dealt with matrimonial dissension in families where there were young children and supervised young people who were often the products of unsatisfactory home conditions. Moral welfare workers helped unmarried mothers to make arrangements for their own and their children's future.

I would like to see a bringing together of the services most concerned with various aspects of child and family welfare into a single unified department within the local authority framework which might be called the family welfare service.

A family welfare service would perform eight main functions. It would:

(*a*) advise and help parents, and especially lone parents, who are experiencing difficulties in bringing up their children;

(*b*) advise and assist married couples whose relationships with each other and with the outside world are unsatisfactory and whose ability to provide adequately for their children is consequently in jeopardy;

(c) help parents who are feckless, inadequate or disturbed to maintain minimum standards in their children's interests;

(d) help to re-settle and supervise children whose own homes have been non-existent or broken;

(e) protect children who have been neglected or cruelly treated or are in moral danger in their own homes;

(f) supervise and rehabilitate those under 17 years old who have been found guilty of offences against the law;

(g) help unmarried mothers to make the best arrangements for their own future and for their illegitimate children;

(h) advise and assist those who want to adopt children.

The family welfare service would thus take over the work of the children's department and part of the work at present undertaken by the probation service. It would also extend into the field at present catered for largely by voluntary organisations such as the moral welfare councils, the National Society for the Prevention of Cruelty to Children, and some casework agencies.

It would be staffed primarily by social workers with a two-year training; but there would also be a need for men and women with advanced training to supervise the work of junior staff, to organise in-service training and refresher courses and to help in the introduction of new methods of work for family maintenance. Health visitors who develop particular interests in work with 'problem' families could also play a useful part in this service. Initially the service would rely for leadership on child care officers and on some family caseworkers, probation officers and health visitors coming into it from other social services. There would be some need for specialisation of function within the service; but as far as possible the staff would be encouraged to learn about and gain experience of the wide range of problems which the family welfare service would have to handle.

Additional social welfare provision

Most of the needs for counselling would be met by social workers in the three major services whose functions and staffing have been outlined. Social workers and others, however, should be able to summon three types of additional provision for their clients, namely, financial support, employment, and housing, and special provision needs to be made for law enforcement and the treatment of offenders.

(i) *Financial support*

The present situation in regard to the provision of financial assistance to individuals and families with insufficient income derives from the historical development of the social security services and now has many anomalies. In particular, the existence of two central government departments each with local offices and each supporting people who are unable to earn has disadvantages.

Those who need help from the National Assistance Board are often entitled to benefits from the Ministry of Pensions and National Insurance. If there was a common administration of pensions and assistance, the cost of the service to the country might be reduced. It might also be easier for individuals to apply for and accept the financial help they need in sickness, unemployment or old age. I would like, therefore, to see the Ministry of Pensions and National Insurance and the National Assistance Board amalgamated to form a single department.

Those who work in such a department need not, in my view, be fully trained social workers; but they do need to gain in their pre-entry and in-service training a considerable grasp of the circumstances through which people come to need financial assistance from the state. They also need to understand their own prejudices and how these are likely to affect their feelings towards their clients, and they must have a good knowledge of the framework of the social services so that they can refer clients for other kinds of help.

The department should, however, consider employing a limited number of trained social workers. They would advise at national and regional level on the way in which developments in social therapy or in other branches of the social services were likely to affect the work of the department, and would play an important part in pre-entry and in-service training.

(ii) *Employment advice*

The Ministry of Labour at present provides services for the

disabled worker and has a number of training centres where men whose skills are not needed can be trained or re-trained for jobs where workers are much in demand. It also supervises the work of youth employment officers in areas where it does not provide the service itself.

If social workers are attached to domiciliary health units and school counsellors to schools, some of the work which disablement resettlement and youth employment officers now try to do could be better performed in these services. These officers in future would become more expert advisers on employment opportunities offered by local employers and on the skills and abilities needed for work of various kinds. The D.R.O.'s, in particular, would spend time finding out what local jobs could be done by people with particular disabilities and persuading employers and employees to give the disabled opportunities for creative work either in normal workplaces or, if this was difficult, in sheltered workshops or in their own homes.

The D.R.O.'s and youth employment officers should not be trained social workers. They must have a sound knowledge of industrial organisation, on the one hand, and some knowledge of ergonomics and occupational therapy on the other. Some training must also be given on the nature of the problems which disability can create for disabled people and their relatives, in order to encourage them to contact domiciliary health unit social workers. The D.R.O. and youth employment officer, however, should become experts on industrial organisation and on the suitability and availability of work open to the young and the disabled.

The work seems to me to be specialised and best done by those who have had some training for it. It should, therefore, be an occupation with career prospects and not merely, as it tends to be at present, a job done for a limited number of years by those at a certain stage in their careers in the Ministry of Labour.

(iii) *Housing*

Housing and the improvement and maintenance of the standards of domestic amenities are tasks which local authorities will have to meet for many years to come. Earlier marriage, the rising cost of building, the higher standards of domestic amenity expected, and the competing demands of industry, transport, agriculture and open spaces for scarce land will combine to ensure that housing need is not satisfied.

In particular, housing authorities will have the task of making more adequate provision for people whose needs cannot be met in the open market, i.e. the elderly, the handicapped, the large family with many dependent children and the family whose income is small or erratic.

Small rural and urban authorities cannot afford to employ specialised officers in the housing department. Indeed, the housing officer may combine his functions with those of public health inspector, finance or valuation officer or clerk of the council. Nevertheless, in their training, those concerned with housing management should learn more systematically than they do at present about people who need special consideration for housing or special help in maintaining adequate domestic standards.

In larger authorities there can be some differentiation of function within housing departments and a social worker who would consider particularly the housing of the elderly, the handicapped and the large family should be employed. To avoid duplication, however, his function would be to refer cases with complex problems to health visitors and social workers in the family welfare service or domiciliary health units, concentrating himself on interpreting their needs to his own authority and on securing environmental improvements for them.

(iv) *Law enforcement and the treatment of offenders*

In the last decade, the probation service has been asked to take on more and more functions associated with the treatment of offenders and with matrimonial reconciliation. The report of the Advisory Council on the Treatment of Offenders on the organisation of after-care[1] believed probation officers were the most suitable people to undertake both the compulsory supervision of those released on licence from prison or from borstal institutions and the rehabilitation on a voluntary basis of all prisoners after the completion of their sentences. It suggested, however, that social workers be appointed in increasing numbers to prisons to participate in the treatment of offenders and begin the process of rehabilitation.

[1] Home Office, 1963. *The organisation of After-care.* H.M.S.O.

I believe that some of the work at present carried out by the probation department could best be done under the auspices of a family welfare service rather than directly under a service whose orientation is necessarily formal and legalistic. In particular, those under 17 who commit offences should be treated as socially maladjusted rather than as criminals.[1] Similarly, the matrimonial reconciliation work of the probation service, although usually initiated by a magistrate, should be conducted at least in its initial stages by the family welfare service. Many probation officers would need to transfer, therefore, to that service.

In this event the social work of the courts would be devoted primarily to the treatment of adult offenders both in and outside prison, and a considerable expansion of the probation and after-care service would be needed for it.

Policemen and women, except in rare circumstances, cannot usefully be considered as social workers. The greater part of the time of the women police in Bucks in 1960–61 was taken up with law enforcement, the detection of crime, the control of traffic and answering general enquiries from the public.[2] Both men and women are recruited for these duties at an age when they are unlikely to have much interest in the underlying social and psychological difficulties of those with whom they come in contact.

Nevertheless, because they are inevitably dealing with many complex, unstable and deviant people and with the distress which such people give to relatives and neighbours, their initial training should include some teaching in psychology and sociology and in the causes of individual or social pathology. They also need to have a good working knowledge of the social services available to help the victims and the perpetrators of crime.

The probation service would be, as it was in 1960–61, the social work service of the courts, but with its work confined to the adult population. They would still make social enquiries designed to help magistrates in sentencing, supervise offenders put on probation and those released from prison and help plan the rehabilitation of the prisoner in his family and neighbourhood and

---

[1] Such a course does not necessarily mean a 'tender' or 'soft' treatment in place of a 'firm' or 'tough' one.

[2] The work of men in the force was not studied; but the team was given to understand by the Chief Constable that policemen had even less time for preventive or rehabilitative work than policewomen.

at work after his release. In this, they would collaborate with social workers attached to prisons and to the family welfare service.

In Bucks, probation work seemed to be the most exacting form of social work and it is essential that those who undertake it should be trained. Most probation officers in Bucks had had a Home Office training and half had been to a university. A two-year social worker's course would form a good preliminary basis for the majority of probation officers, if it were followed by a short Home Office course and a year's probationary service working under supervision. The probation service should, in my view, have a considerable proportion of university trained social workers, who should be expected to make a substantial contribution to our understanding of social deviance and ways of coping with it.

The voluntary social welfare services

Before this enquiry, I believed voluntary societies should confine their activities to work which could be undertaken by unpaid amateurs, that is, by citizens with a social conscience who wanted to help others but had no special training for doing so. Work best done by trained social workers working in a paid capacity should be a responsibility of the statutory social services. Examination of the work of voluntary societies and their relationships with statutory services in Bucks convinced me, however, that this concept of the respective roles of the statutory and voluntary services, although substantially correct, needed some modification.

First, trained social workers in voluntary organisations were clearly in a position to deepen the public's understanding of social problems, i.e. to educate, inform and enlist positive community help for the under-privileged. In practice, therefore, although I would like to see the establishment or expansion of statutory social services to provide for those whose needs were being met mainly by the paid staff of voluntary associations, for example, for the unmarried mother, I also feel that voluntary associations have still a valuable part to play.

Secondly, voluntary work was fragmented by the proliferation of voluntary societies which had the effect of multiplying the amount of organisational and committee work done by volunteers and reducing the time available for voluntary social service to the elderly and the handicapped. As a result voluntary service was less effective than it might have been. I believe, therefore, that voluntary societies need to forego some of their independence, encourage their members through lectures and seminars to learn more of the multiplicity of needs and the contribution which voluntary workers can and cannot make to meet them, and work more closely with social workers from the statutory health and family welfare services. Such a relationship would strengthen both parties and improve the service they gave to the elderly and the handicapped.

In conclusion

Since the inception of this survey there has been a growing appreciation of the need to evaluate the activities of the social welfare services, to ask what purposes they serve, how effectively they do it and whether the same objectives could be obtained with the expenditure of less time and effort.

The Bucks survey was an attempt to examine critically the work of different statutory and voluntary organisations in social welfare, and no punches have been pulled in presenting the strengths and weaknesses which the research revealed.

I hope that the use to which the information provided by the social welfare workers of Bucks has been put in this report has convinced them that the arduous exercise in which they partook has helped to clarify issues and will ultimately improve both the satisfactions which they derive from their work and the services which they offer to those in need.

Finally, it is now possible to do what, as a nation, we were not able or willing to do immediately after the war, namely, to introduce new methods of working and new forms of administrative structure in such a way as to be able to measure their effects. In other words, planned experiments are now both socially and politically expedient and should be the basis upon which changes in the services are initiated in the future. I hope, therefore, that some of the recommendations for the recruitment, training and re-deployment of social welfare staff with which the report has concluded will be the subject of planned experiments.

Methods and Questions used in the Survey of the Clients of Social Welfare Staff

In order to obtain an unselected sample of cases seen by social welfare staff, each worker was asked to provide information on all the cases seen during a week of the year starting 1st October 1960. If this number did not reach 25, the worker was asked to continue to record details of consecutive cases seen until information had been obtained on 25. Collectively the cases seen during the recording weeks of every worker present a picture of the clientele of the social welfare services in a typical working week. The total cases seen in the consecutive series represent samples of the caseloads of each social welfare service. The comparisons drawn between the work of different branches of the services are based upon the information obtained about the consecutive series of cases whether or not they were seen within the recording week.

To avoid seasonal and geographical bias in recording and to make the survey less burdensome for the services themselves, each worker included in the enquiry was allocated a recording week during the year starting 1st October 1960, in such a way as to spread recording by workers in the same agency and part of the county throughout the year. Workers replacing others who had already recorded were not included but workers appointed to new posts before August 1961 were. Those transferring from one area of the county to another were not asked to record cases again.

Workers were usually seen a day or two prior to the start of their recording week; the enquiry was explained and verbal instructions given on how to complete the forms. Where a worker was known to have very few clients in Bucks, he was interviewed early in the study year and asked to start recording the unselected series of Bucks cases at once. At the end of the year, the worker was allocated to a recording week at random and only cases seen during that week were included in the analysis of the typical week's work in Bucks.

Information was recorded only about individuals 'on the files' of the service who were actually seen during the recording period, excluding those seen only in the street, at church, during welfare clinic sessions, at social gatherings, or in other public places (unless a meeting had been deliberately arranged); tenants of or applicants for local authority housing unless they presented social difficulties; young people receiving routine information or vocational guidance only from youth employment officers; individuals seen by policewomen in connection with traffic offences, licences and matters relating to aliens.

Information was recorded by social welfare workers on a standard form which provided many answers in pre-coded form. To ensure

Table 35

THE SEASONAL SPREAD OF INTERVIEWS WITH SOCIAL WELFARE STAFF

Agencies	Number interviewed in the quarter year ending:				Total
	Dec. 31 1960	March 31 1961	June 30 1961	Sept. 30 1961	
National Assistance Board	5	6	5	4	20
Ministry of Labour	1	1	5	1	8
Ministry of Pensions and National Insurance	2	—	1	—	3
Hospital Almoner and allied Social Worker	6	6	4	3	19
Hospital Psychiatric Social Worker and allied Social Worker	1	—	—	1	2
County Education Department:					
Educational Special Welfare	1	—	1	2	4
Child Guidance	1	1	1	—	3
Youth Employment Service	1	2	—	1	4
Youth Service	3	2	1	3	9
School Attendance Service	4	4	3	3	14
Children's Department	4	4	3	5	16
Probation Service	4	3	5	3	15
Women Constabulary	3	3	5	5	16
County Health Department:					
District Nursing Service (inc. joint appointments as DN/MW and Health Visitors)	26	33	32	28	119
Health Visitors	11	14	13	9	47
Almoners and Social Workers	2	1	3	2	8
Home Teachers for the Blind	1	1	3	1	6
Home Help Service	1	3	1	3	8
Occupational Therapy Service	1	2	2	—	5
Welfare Officers	3	2	2	4	11
L.C.C. Housing	1	—	1	—	2
Housing Authorities	15	8	5	3	31
Voluntary Services	12	10	5	1	28
Total	109	106	101	82	398

Table 36

THE GEOGRAPHICAL SPREAD OF INTERVIEWS WITH STAFF

Agencies	Number interviewed who worked in the					Total
	North	Centre	South West	South	Whole County and/or outside	
National Assistance Board	3	3	7	7	—	20
Ministry of Labour	2	2	3	1	—	8
Ministry of Pensions and National Insurance	—	—	—	—	3	3
Hospital Almoner and allied Social Worker	4	4	3	8	—	19
Hospital Psychiatric Social Worker and allied Social Worker	—	1	—	—	1	2
County Education Department:						
Education Special Welfare	—	—	—	1	3	4
Child Guidance	—	—	—	2	1	3
Youth Employment Service	1	1	1	1	—	4
Youth Service	1	1	4	3	—	9
School Attendance Service	2	2	5	5	—	14
Children's Department	3	3	5	5	—	16
Probation Service	2	3	4	6	—	15
Women Constabulary	1	2	4	9	—	16
County Health Department:						
District Nursing Service (inc. joint appointments as DN/MW and Health Visitors)	27	21	41	30	—	119
Health Visitors	9	7	17	14	—	47
Almoners and Social Workers	1	2	1	3	1	8
Home Teachers for the Blind	1	1	2	2	—	6
Home Help Service	2	2	2	2	—	8
Occupational Therapy Service	—	1	2	1	1	5
Welfare Officers	4	1	3	3	—	11
L.C.C. Housing	—	—	—	2	—	2
Housing Authorities	7	5	12	7	—	31
Voluntary Services	2	2	5	7	12	28
Total	72	64	121	119	22	398

comparability terms were strictly defined: each worker was provided with a booklet containing definitions and instructions for completing the forms. Completed forms were returned to the survey office at the end of the recording in a business reply envelope. When they had been checked further visits were paid, if necessary, to remedy omissions or clarify answers. Further visits were paid to 174 of the 359 workers completing schedules and many others were telephoned.

Permission was always obtained from the head of the service before approaching a worker but participation was voluntary.

In the analysis of characteristics of clients of different services, differences have been regarded as significant if there was less than one chance in 20 (5 per cent) that they occurred by chance.

The information recorded on clients

1. Name and address (Recorded on detachable slips and used only for matching purposes).

2. *For client and all members of his household*
   (*a*) sex, (*b*) age, (*c*) marital status (legal and *de facto*), (*d*) age of completing full-time education *or* present schooling, (*e*) present employment status, (*f*) occupation, (*g*) industry, (*h*) chronic illness or disability.

3. *Household characteristics*
   (*a*) Town or village of normal residence.
   (*b*) Length of residence at present address.
   (*c*) Any member on a Council re-housing list.
   (*d*) Number of rooms occupied.
   (*e*) Type of dwelling.
   (*f*) Type of tenure.
   (*g*) Amenities within dwelling.
   (*h*) Housing standards.
   (*i*) Sources of household income.
   (*j*) Approximate weekly household income.

4. *Characteristics of social problems* (a brief description and:
   (*a*) Does any member of the household have or cause a problem which could be classified under one or more of these 21 headings? (see Table 1 in Chapter I for list).
   (*b*) If yes, do you consider it serious or not serious, temporary or long-term?
   (*c*) If yes, is it due to physical illness or disability, low intelligence, mental disorder, personality difficulties, moral weakness, accident or misfortune, other circumstances beyond the control of the individual?
   (*d*) Are *you* (social worker) currently trying to assist, directly or indirectly?

5. *Client-worker relationship and interview*

    (*a*) Date of client's first referral to service.
    (*b*) Referring source.
    (*c*) Reason for first referral.
    (*d*) Regularity of visits.
    (*e*) Number of visits in last 12 months.
    (*f*) Date and place of contact.
    (*g*) Reasons for contact (listed).
    (*h*) Services given at and following contact (listed). See Table 2, Chapter I.
    (*i*) Approximate time spent at contact, and dealing with case in week following it.

6. *Contacts with other services*

    (*a*) names of other agencies contacting or contacted.
    (*b*) reason for contact.
    (*c*) names of other agencies known to be visiting.

7. *The future*

    (*a*) How soon, if at all, are problems with which you are dealing likely to be resolved?

Methods and Questions used in the Survey of Social Welfare Staff

At the interview when staff were asked to record details of their clients, they were also asked to give some information about themselves and their views on their work and their answers were recorded by the research workers on standard question forms. Only one worker was not interviewed since her employer did not wish her to be questioned. Two workers attached to a national voluntary organisation who recorded details of five Bucks cases handled during the year were also not interviewed personally. Two workers did not want to disclose their age and a number did not indicate whether or not they were regular church attenders. One person after the interview in which she freely gave information asked the research team to return the form on which her answers had been recorded. It was returned and destroyed. Since the total social welfare staff of the county were included, no statistical tests of significance were done.

The information recorded on social welfare staff

1. Name, post held, area covered, salary, grading.
2. Age, sex, marital status, number and age of children, occupation of spouse if working.
3. Place of birth. Father's occupation at time of birth. Number of siblings. Last school attended and school leaving qualifications.
4. Further education, including academic courses, vocational training, in-service and refresher courses. Dates of courses and duration.
5. Views on the adequacy of training for the social work aspects of present work and on the need for further study or training.
6. Occupational history—i.e. post held, employer's business, area worked in and length of service—from leaving school to holding present post.
7. Participation in voluntary social welfare work—type of work, organisation and area—length of service.
8. Religious affiliation and church attendance.
9. Attitudes to work. What would you list as the major rewards and satisfactions of your work? What do you feel are its major drawbacks? On the whole, are you glad or sorry you came into it? If you could start again, what work would you choose to do?
10. Since you came into this kind of work has there been any significant change in the type of person you deal with, the type of problem they present, or the way in which you deal with them?

11. Would you say that the personnel of other services, who may also be concerned with your cases, are on the whole co-operative or unco-operative? Can you give me an illustration of what you have in mind?
12. Name of interviewer and date of interview.

Methods and Questions used in the Survey of General Practitioners in Social Welfare

A sample of 70 G.P.'s was drawn at random from the Bucks Local Executive Council's list. Four doctors refused to participate and interviews were not arranged with four who were found to have no Bucks patients, and one who had retired. Two doctors died and one left the county before the interview. The four refusals were not replaced; but reserves were chosen at random from the Executive Council's list to replace the other eight. In all, 66 of 70 available general practitioners were interviewed, the refusal rate being 5·7 per cent. Forty-four per cent of the G.P.'s listed and 42 per cent of those drawn in the sample practised from addresses outside the county.

Table 37

NUMBERS AND PERCENTAGE DISTRIBUTION BY AREA OF DOCTORS ON EXECUTIVE COUNCIL LIST AND IN THE SAMPLE

| Area of County | Number of General Practitioners | | | Percentage Distribution | |
	On Local Exec. Council List	Sample drawn	Declined to take part	Local Exec. Council List	Sample Interviewed
North	45	11	—	13	16
Central	58	16	3	17	19
South-West	118	19	—	34	29
South	125	24	1	36	36
All areas	346	70	4	100	100

Interviews were arranged to ensure an even geographical and seasonal spread. None took place during the first quarter of 1961 to avoid inconvenience to doctors in a period of pressure. It is likely that during this quarter doctors would have had heavier visiting and more attendances at surgeries and would have seen a higher proportion of elderly people.

Each doctor was asked to set aside the personal cards of patients seen on the day prior to the interview. The interviewer recorded on a standard form the age, sex, marital status, chronic illness of each of these patients, their family composition, housing, occupation of chief economic supporter, and whether or not the doctor considered the patient or a member of the family had or caused a social problem. If problems were mentioned, information was recorded on the type of problem, the action taken by the doctor, and referrals to and consultations with other agencies. At the same interview general practitioners were asked to discuss the social problems they met in the course of their practice and the use they had made of the statutory and voluntary welfare services. These issues were not asked or recorded systematically, although care was taken to ensure that all the topics were covered by using a check list. Tests of significance were not used in the analysis.

APPENDIX D

Methods and Questions used in the Survey of Voluntary Organisations

A list of voluntary societies thought to have social welfare interests was compiled by consulting the Directory of Voluntary Societies published by the National Council of Social Services, the Clerk of the Bucks County Council and the county's health and welfare department staff. Youth organisations were excluded even though many place great emphasis on training for service to the community.

We wrote to secretaries of all the national organisations and asked for information about their work in Bucks. All those with locally organised branches or groups and all purely local societies were asked to provide information about their activities during 1961, together with any published report describing their work. Some societies—e.g. the Bucks Federation of Women's Institutes—suggested that their objects were not primarily social welfare ones but the recreation or education of their own members, and they did not provide information.

With limited time and resources, it was not possible to interview more than a few representatives of voluntary organisations. Nearly all the information analysed was obtained in a postal enquiry, standard forms being used for the purpose. In one instance, the chairman of an organisation refused to answer the written questions but provided most of the required information in a personal interview.

The information recorded on voluntary workers' activities

1. Name of organisation and branch.
2. Secretary's name and address.
3. *Financial assistance.* Has your organisation given Bucks' residents financial assistance in 1961? If yes, about how many were helped and what sums of money were involved? Was any help in the form of loans? Did you refer people in need of financial assistance to any other body, statutory or voluntary? If so, which one(s)? How many of the assisted were in need due to illness or disability, bereavement, old age, desertion, mismanagement, other?
4. *Material help other than money.* Did your organisation give gifts or loans other than money? What were they of? How many recipients of different kinds of gift were there? Did you refer people to other bodies for material gifts or loans? If so, to which bodies?
5. *Nursing care and domestic help.* Did voluntary workers give such help? If yes, to about how many people and for what reasons? How many people did this voluntary work?
6. *Home and sick visiting.* Did you organise regular home or hospital

visiting? If yes, what kind of people were visited and how many took part in the work? Did you refer people for this kind of help to other bodies, and if so which?

7. *Transport, outings, holidays and convalescence.* Did your organisation arrange car transport for disabled, free day outings for elderly and handicapped, holidays away from home, convalescent care? If yes, how many were helped and how many provided the help? Did you refer for these purposes to other bodies and if so which?

8. *Advice or guidance.* Did your organisation give advice or guidance on any of the following matters and if so to how many: employment, legal rights and duties, housing, marital problems, child care and discipline, problems of young people, mental health, physical disability, adoption, illegitimacy, retirement or care of the elderly? About how many members took part in this work? Were they specially qualified for it? Did you refer people to other bodies for advice or guidance and if so to which ones?

9. What changes, if any, have occurred in the type of personal problem dealt with in recent years?

10. Has the growth of statutory social welfare services influenced your work in the last ten years?

11. Does your organisation have any difficulty in finding people to undertake voluntary work? If yes, what are the reasons and how do you attempt to overcome the difficulties?

12. What limits, if any, are imposed on your activities by (a) lack of funds, (b) lack of personnel, or (c) other shortages?

Table 38

THE AGE AND MARITAL STATUS OF MEN AND WOMEN SOCIAL WELFARE STAFF

Status	Age groups					
	Under 35		*35–44*		*45 and over*	
	Men	Women	Men	Woman	Men	Women
	%	%	%	%	%	%
Single	45	75	10	74	6	72
Married	55	25	90	26	94	28
Total	100	100	100	100	100	100
Number*	20	73	30	81	52	132

* Age of 1 person unknown

Table 39

THE NUMBER OF CHILDREN OF THE MARRIED MEN AND WOMEN SOCIAL WELFARE STAFF

Number of children	Men %	Women %
None	19	50
1–2	62	41
3 or more	19	9
Total	100	100
Number of married	87	78

Table 40

OCCUPATION AND TYPE OF EMPLOYMENT HELD BY SOCIAL WORKERS
FOR LONGEST PERIOD IN THE FIVE YEARS PRECEDING ENTRY TO
PRESENT OCCUPATION* †

(a) Occupation held prior to present one	All workers	Category of worker:			
		All men	All women	Occupations with pre-entry qualification	Occupations with no pre-entry qualification
	%	%	%	%	%
Administrative & clerical	49	60	40	36	58
Personal, professional services	22	13	32	43	9
Armed forces, police	11	16	6	10	12
Manual	8	11	7	6	12
Domestic	10	—	15	5	9
(b) Type of employment unit					
Public sector, charitable, non-profit making	62	61	63	70	57
Private sector	32	29	25	27	35
Family	6	—	12	3	8
All workers— Number=100%	157	76	81	63	94

* Excluding those who entered under 25 years.
† Excluding district nurse-midwives and health visitors.

M

Table 41

RELIGIOUS AFFILIATIONS OF SOCIAL WELFARE STAFF AND FREQUENCY
OF ATTENDANCE AT PLACES OF WORSHIP

| | | | | Category of worker: | | |
Religious affiliation	All	Men	Women	District nurses health visitors	With pre-entry qualifi- cation	No pre-entry qualifi- cation
	%	%	%	%	%	%
Anglican	67	73	63	58	74	71
Catholic	8	5	10	11	5	5
Non-conformist	20	17	22	25	16	20
Agnostic or atheist	3	5	2	2	4	4
Other and unrecorded	2	—	3	4	1	—
Frequency of attend-ance at place of worship						
Regularly	44	32	49	53	60	29
Irregularly, seldom	46	50	44	40	26	60
Never	8	16	5	3	14	10
Unrecorded	2	2	2	4	—	1
Total Number = 100%	389	102	287	164	89	136

Table 42

SPARE TIME VOLUNTARY SOCIAL WELFARE WORK UNDERTAKEN BY
SOCIAL WELFARE STAFF

| Type of voluntary work | All | Men | Women | Category of worker: | | |
				District nurses, health visitors	With pre-entry qualifi-cation	With no pre-entry qualifi-cation
	%	%	%	%	%	%
Youth and child leadership	18	21	17	10	35	17
Sunday School teaching	3	3	3	2	—	4
Organisation, secretarial	18	32	11	8	18	23
Visiting, personal services, domestic or communal	13	9	14	6	18	14
V.A.D., other nursing and first aid	3	—	5	7	1	2
Teaching, examining	11	5	14	19	6	4
Any kind of voluntary social service	63	70	59	51	76	63
No voluntary social service	37	30	41	49	24	37
Total Number = 100%	389	102	287	164	89	136

Table 43

PERCENTAGE OF SOCIAL WELFARE STAFF WHO REGRETTED ABSOLUTELY
OR PARTLY HAVING ENTERED PRESENT JOBS, AND PERCENTAGE WHO
WOULD CHOOSE OTHER WORK IF GIVEN THE OPPORTUNITY TO CHANGE

| Opinion | All | Men | Women | Category of worker: | | |
				District nurses, health visitors	Pre-entry qualifi-cation	No pre-entry qualifi-cation
	%	%	%	%	%	%
Regret partly or absolutely having entered present occupation	16	27	11	14	6	22
Given opportunity would choose other work	33	46	29	24	33	49
Total Number = 100%	389	102	287	164	89	136

M*

Table 44

THE PROPORTION OF STAFF OF DIFFERENT SERVICES SPONTANEOUSLY COMMENTING ON REWARDING AND DISSATISFYING ASPECTS OF THEIR WORK

Aspects of the work	All	Men	Women	District nurse-midwives	Category of worker: Health visitors	Pre-entry qualifica-tion	No pre-entry qualifica-tion
	%	%	%	%	%	%	%
(1) Desire to help people							
Rewarding to help people in need	80	86	79	88	72	78	89
Dissatisfying: clients' ingratitude or hostility	16	27	14	15	9	9	27
Dissatisfying: inability to see results, number of failures	9	13	8	3	15	12	12
(2) Working freedom							
Rewarding to have freedom to arrange work	57	54	59	70	26	56	58
Dissatisfying: too much red tape, control from head-quarters, poor leadership	22	31	19	10	22	28	26

(3) Working conditions							
Dissatisfying: heavy working schedule, too rushed to maintain standards	21	23	21	12	28	33	21
Dissatisfying: absence of facilities to help clients	34	40	32	18	41	39	33
Dissatisfying: hours of work, time 'on call', lack of leisure	26	12	31	59	2	20	15
(4) Financial							
Rewarding: financially or in job security	9	11	8	11	4	3	10
Dissatisfying: low financial rewards	17	25	14	16	13	16	19
(5) Prestige and status							
Rewarding: value of job recognised	15	18	14	14	13	19	15
Rewarding: esteem, appreciation, friendliness of colleagues	8	5	9	8	7	12	7
Dissatisfying: lack of support or appreciation from headquarters or from other professional groups, value of work unrecognised	23	25	23	17	48	27	20
Number of staff = 100%	389	102	287	118	46	89	136

Table 45

THE PROPORTION OF CLIENTS AGED 60 AND OVER AMONG THOSE
SEEN BY THE STAFF OF DIFFERENT BRANCHES OF THE SERVICES

Name of service workers	Number of workers recording	Per cent of clients aged 60 and over	Name of service workers	Number of workers recording	Per cent of clients aged 60 and over
Home help organisers	8	75	District nurse-midwife-health		
Home teachers of the			visitors	16	38
blind	6	73	Hospital almoners	17	31
National Assistance			Hospital P.S.W.	2	28
Board officers	20	70	Deaf missioner	1	17
County almoners	8	55	D.R.O.'s	8	11
Voluntary casework			Slouth Industrial		
agencies	5	54	Health Service	1	12
M.P.N.I. welfare			Health visitors	46	5
service workers	3	52	Policewomen	11	1
District nurse-			Education depart-		
midwife	91	50	ment	24	0
Welfare officers	11	42	Child care officers	14	0
Occupational thera-			Probation officers	15	0
pists	5	41	Moral welfare		
Housing authority			workers	9	0
welfare workers	22	40	N.S.P.C.C.	5	0

Table 46

PERCENTAGE OF MAIN CLIENTS SEEN DURING THE TYPICAL VISITING
WEEK WITH DISABILITIES

Type of illness or disability	Per cent of clients	Type of illness or disability	Per cent of clients
Rheumatic	8	Digestive	3
Heart or circulatory	8	Skins	2
Neurological/strokes	8	Diabetes	2
Respiratory	5	Neoplasms	2
Sensory (blind/deaf)	5	Other	1
Mental illness	4		
Senility/confusion	4	At least one disability	43
Mental subnormality	2	No recorded disability	57

Table 47

HOUSING CONDITIONS OF ALL HOUSEHOLDS IN BUCKS AND OF SOCIAL
WELFARE CLIENTS

Housing situation	Percentage distribution: All private households*	Households of social welfare clients†
Tenure		
Owner-occupied	48	34
Rented from local authority	26	36
Rented from private person or company	18	18
Held by virtue of employment or as part of business	8	5
Unknown	—	7
All tenures	100	100
Type of building		
Permanent building occupied	99·3	97·9
Caravan or houseboat	0·7	2·1
All buildings	100·0	100·0
Densities: persons per room:		
less than one	77	64
one	14	17
less than two more than one ⎱		16
more than two ⎰	9	3
All densities	100	100
Amenities: absent or shared:		
Cold water	2	5
Hot water	18	20
Fixed bath	16	19
Water closet	7	10
Persons per household‡		
1	10	14
2	29	22
3–5	54	51
6	4	6
7	2	3
8 or more	1	4

† Excluding clients permanently living in hospital, residential hostels or
homes.
* Census 1961.   ‡ Households with all members present on Census night.

Table 48

THE SOCIAL STATUS OF SOCIAL WELFARE CLIENTS' HOUSEHOLDS COMPARED WITH THAT OF ALL RETIRED AND OCCUPIED MALES IN BUCKS AGED 16 AND OVER IN 1961

Description of social status	R.G. Social Class	Bucks Males 16 and over*	Chief male economic supporters of social welfare clients' households
		%	%
Professional, scientific, managerial, administrative	I and II	18	16
Skilled manual, supervisory, self-employed manual, clerical, distributive	III	53	44
Semi- and unskilled agricultural and personal service	IV and V	29	37
Armed forces	—	—	3
All status	All	100	100

N.B.—The social status of *female* chief economic supporters (20 per cent of the total) was not analysed.

Table 49

CHANNELS THROUGH WHICH CLIENTS CAME TO THE ATTENTION OF
THE SOCIAL WELFARE SERVICES

Channel	Percentage of all clients
Personal, including client, relative, neighbour, friend	24
Health service workers	
General practitioner	30
Hospital	9
Local authority	19
Staff of other services	
Law, police, probation	6
Education, schools	4
Housing	1
Social security (N.A.B., M.P.N.I.)	1
Employment (M.o.L. and industry)	1
Voluntary societies	2
Unknown or other	3
All channels (number=4,488)	100

Table 50

INTERVAL BETWEEN CLIENTS' FIRST REFERRAL AND VISIT DURING
RECORDING WEEK

Interval	Percentage of clients
Less than 1 month	20
1 month < 3 months	10
3 months < 6 months	12
6 months < 1 year	10
1 year < 5 years	34
5 years < 15 years	11
15 years or more	1
Unrecorded	2
Total (number=4,488)	100

Table 51

ACTIVITIES PERFORMED AT OR SHORTLY AFTER THE CLIENT-WORKER CONTACT

Nature of activity	Percentage of all interviews (Number = 4,488)
Service to client	
Nursing, advice on treatment of illness, health education, etc.	45
Financial or material assistance or advice	14
Advice on employment, occupations, education	13
Help with emotional problems, reconciliation, relationships	8
Institutional care for adults, permanently or temporarily, convalescence, holidays	5
Provision of domestic help	5
Care for children, other than with natural parents, fostering, adoption, etc.	3
Assistance with legal position and problems	2
Advice on housing or provision of housing	2
Other activities	
Check on circumstances for agency and report back	32
Relatives of client interviewed and/or assisted	17
None	
No activity or service recorded	9

Table 52

INSTANCES IN WHICH WORKERS REPORTING ON SAME HOUSEHOLDS
KNEW OF THE OTHER'S CONCERN OR WERE IN CONTACT

Agency of reporting worker	Number of instances	Percentage of instances:			
		No knowledge of other worker reporting	Knowledge but no contact with other worker reporting	Contact with other worker	Total
Health services					
District nurse-midwives	117	53	37	10	100
Health visitors	75	40	35	25	100
Almoners (hospital and county)	66	58	11	31	100
All other health workers	94	38	37	25	100
Services for children and law and order	124	51	19	30	100
All other services					
N.A.B., M.o.L., M.P.N.I., housing, voluntary case-work agencies	82	73	19	8	100
All instances	558	52	27	21	100

Index